JOHANN SEBASTIAN BACH

COMPLETE ORGAN WORKS

A Critico-Practical Edition in Eight Volumes

Provided with a Preface containing General Observations on the Manner of performing the Preludes and Fugues

and

Suggestions for the Interpretation of the Compositions contained in Each Volume

by

CHARLES–MARIE WIDOR

Professor in the Conservatoire at Paris and Organist at the Church of St. Sulpice

and

Dr. ALBERT SCHWEITZER

Privatdozent at Strassburg University and Organist of the Société J. S. Bach of Paris

VOLUME I

Preludes and Fugues of the Youthful Period

Ed. 841

G. SCHIRMER, Inc.

DISTRIBUTED BY
HAL•LEONARD
CORPORATION
7777 W. BLUEMOUND RD. P.O. BOX 13819 MILWAUKEE, WI 53213

Contents of Volume I

The Plan of the Critico-Practical Edition

The organ compositions of J. S. Bach have been handed down to us in part as engraved works, in part as autographs, and in part as copies.

The engraved works comprise the Prelude and Fugue in E♭ and the great *Choralvorspiele* (Chorale-Preludes) which appeared together about the year 1739 as Part III of the "Clavierübung"; six *Choralvorspiele* in trio-form, which were published by Schübler in Zella between 1747 and 1749; and the canonic variations on the Christmas song "Vom Himmel hoch, da komm' ich her," published by Balthasar Schmid in Nuremberg about 1747.

As autographs—most of them now in the possession of the Berlin Library—have been preserved a series of Preludes and Fugues, the Sonatas, the Passacaglia, the *Choralvorspiele* in the "Orgelbüchlein," and the eighteen Chorales which Bach revised and copied out toward the close of his life, in Leipzig.

For the rest, we must rely on copies made by friends or pupils, either in their original handwriting or in more recent copies from the latter. For these our chief sources are J. P. Kellner, J. Ph. Kirnberger, J. L. Krebs, and J. Chr. Kittel. The copies made by Schwenke of Hamburg are also of great value to us.

Laudable services in the collecting, sifting and cataloguing the autographs and copies were rendered by J. N. Forkel (Bach's first biographer), F. Mendelssohn-Bartholdy, G. Pölchau, S. W. Dehn, Fr. Hauser, A. Dörffel, F. G. Griepenkerl, W. Rust, Ph. Spitta, and A. Kopfermann.

In 1844 Peters' Bureau de musique in Leipzig began, under Griepenkerl's direction, the publication of its critical edition of Bach's organ works in eight volumes. In view of the status of investigation at that time, this was a grand achievement. A few years later, in 1850, the great Bachgesellschaft founded by Schumann was organized to prepare a critically correct complete edition of the Master's works. For the organ works, the main share of the labor was performed by the indefatigable Rust.

The edition of the Bachgesellschaft has provided a trustworthy musical text of Bach's organ works—a task of peculiar difficulty in cases where only copies, from whose collation the best reading had to be established, were available.

For practical use, this edition will not be adopted. It is too inconvenient in size and shape, and the arrangement of the pieces is unfortunate. Moreover, the price is too high.

An edition in which both the critical and the practical requirements should be realized, is a need recognized by all organ-players. The present edition is an attempt to satisfy this demand.

THE PRACTICAL FEATURES

It is based on the text of the great Bach edition, which it presents without additions of any kind. The player has the piece, in its traditional form, before his eyes. It is not meant that he should receive it laden with the details of an interpretation which, by being incorporated with the musical text itself, advances a claim to be authentic and universally approved. "Editions for Practical Use," having the musical text overladen with fingering and pedalling, marks for dynamics and phrasing, directions for registration and alternation of the manuals, do not promote art in a desirable way. They either engender habitual unthoughtfulness, or they irritate the player by continually holding before his gaze a conception not in harmony with his own. In any case they tend to prevent him from entering his own experiments and experiences in his music-book. The era of these "practical" editions, which undertake the player's guardianship, is past.

On the other hand, the organist will certainly desire to become acquainted with the traditions, with the experiments and experiences of others, for the purpose of stimulation and suggestion.

Whoever traces the development in the reproduction of Bach's organ works will arrive at the conviction that the way is preparing for a certain general agreement. Schools and interpreters who took their departure from wholly divergent conceptions are drawing nearer to each other. Eccentricities and mere tricks of virtuosity, wherewith vogue for the Master's works was formerly sought, at a time when the art of organ-playing was under the spell of the pianistic and orchestral virtuoso, are more and more forsaken. We have grown weary of "conceptions" wherein the player flaunts his personality by obscuring Bach.

Everywhere resounds the call: "Back to simplicity!" It becomes increasingly clear that Art is on the right path only when its goal is to evolve solely that which is natural—inherent—in the works of Bach, and fittingly interpret it.

The Editors advocate the "simple" interpretation, and in this edition urge its claims to acceptance. They have left the musical text untouched, so as not to violate the principles of a true critico-practical edition, and have recorded their conception in prefatory general disquisitions on tempo, phrasing, registration, and alternation of manuals. These latter are followed by special observations on the execution of the several pieces included in each volume. The player has full liberty to choose what pleases him, and to mark his music accordingly.

With the *Choralvorspiele* are printed the words of the hymns to which they belong. It is astonishing that this elementary artistic requirement remained unheeded in all previous editions, considering that so many *Choralvorspiele* can be rendered fully intelligible, as regards their deep inner meaning, only through the poetry which inspired the music.

ORDER OF ARRANGEMENT

Concerning the order of the pieces the rule has been observed that all arrangements originating with Bach were to be followed unreservedly and in detail. The Preludes and Fugues were not arranged by him in collections; but he did thus arrange a number of Chorales. He grouped the pieces in the "Orgelbüchlein," the Chorales on the songs in the Catechism (in Part III of the "Clavierübung"), and the Eighteen Chorales. These collections are reprinted as such.

In other cases the natural artistic principle has been followed, of keeping masterworks and youthful compositions apart. This presents few difficulties.

It is impossible to give precise chronological data for all the various compositions. Furthermore, a chronological arrangement could not be recommended for practical use, when ability to find a given piece quickly is a desideratum. Therefore, in the several volumes of Preludes and Fugues the pieces are arranged according to the keys; this order was chosen by Bach himself in the Well-tempered Clavichord, and so received artistic sanction.

The *Choralvorspiele* in the several groups have been arranged alphabetically according to first lines of poems, wherever this course does not conflict with original collections by Bach; these latter are provided with alphabetical indexes to facilitate the finding of any desired chorale.

In this way critical and practical requirements have been brought into harmony.

CHARLES-MARIE WIDOR
Professor in the Conservatoire at Paris
Organist at the Church of St.-Sulpice.

DR. ALBERT SCHWEITZER
Privatdozent at Strassburg University
Organist for the Bach Concerts at Strassburg.

ARRANGEMENT OF THE CRITICO-PRACTICAL EDITION

VOLUME I.   Preludes and Fugues of the Youthful Period.
VOLUME II.   Preludes and Fugues of the First Master-Period.
VOLS. III-IV. Preludes and Fugues of the Mature Master-Period.
VOLUME V.   Organ Concertos and Organ Sonatas.
VOLUME VI.   Chorale-Preludes (youthful works); Chorale-Fughettas; Short Chorale-Fantasias; Partitas (Chorale-Variations); Harmonizations of Chorales.
VOLUME VII.   Chorale-Preludes in the "Orgelbüchlein"; Chorale-Preludes and the longer Chorale-Fantasias; the Six Chorales in Trio-form.
VOLUME VIII. Songs in the Catechism (Part III of the "Clavierübung"); the "Eighteen Chorales."

The Interpretation of the Preludes and Fugues

General Observations

I. THE TEMPO

THE TEMPI OF THE EIGHTEENTH CENTURY

We know nothing positive concerning the tempi in which Bach played his preludes and fugues on the organ. Voices of tradition assert, that he performed his clavichord pieces in very lively time. We should beware of drawing, from these assertions, too sweeping conclusions with regard to his organ-playing. He cannot have played faster than the organs of the period permitted.

Instruments from the middle of the eighteenth century, which are still in existence (the Silbermann organs in Saxony and Alsatia may be specially mentioned), afford opportunity for experimenting with tempi and establishing approximate limits. Any one who has played on such manuals and familiarized himself with the heavy action and deep keyfall, knows that under most favorable conditions they permit only a modern *moderato*.

Moreover, in Bach's conception of *andante* and *adagio* these movements were not so slow as a modern musician would take them. Whoever has penetrated into the spirit of the musical art of the eighteenth century is aware that the various tempi were then not felt to lie so far apart as in the period beginning with Beethoven. The circle was narrower. Our extremes were lacking. Their *vivace* corresponded to a lively *moderato*, their *adagio* to a not too leisurely *andante*.

As everybody knows, the sign for *alla breve* in Bach does not signify a doubling of the tempo.

THE INFLUENCE OF SPACE

The influence of space in the auditorium on the regulation of the tempo is recognized. In practice, however, it is too often not taken into calculation. One does not sufficiently consider what a decided retardation is caused by the nave, with its sonorous but sluggish acoustics, or remember, that the actual tempo is less important than the actual impression which, under the given conditions, it makes on the hearers.

No organist should neglect to go downstairs occasionally to note the effect of fugues and preludes executed by another player at some previously fixed metronomic rate. He will be surprised at the relative effect of the tempo, and thereafter abstain from choosing a tempo simply because it sounds right on the organ-bench. This testing from the body of the church is indispensable in settling the tempo.

FROM THE HEARER'S STANDPOINT

Besides the acoustic effect, another matter must be taken into account. The player is familiar with the prelude or the fugue. He has the music before him. The grasping of the piece as a whole or in detail gives him no trouble. On the hearer's part, the conceptive process is much more complicated. His receptive and conceptive faculties are strained to the utmost, if he desires to obtain a fairly clear impression of the movement of the parts. From the exertion required of him to follow the successions of tones and harmonies as parts of a finished polyphonic structure, their movement seems more rapid to him than it really is. The danger of inability to cope with the task which he unconsciously undertakes, begins with a tempo which may easily appear slow to the player, whose conceptive process is carried on as a matter of habit and with the aid of the printed music. An inconsiderable increase in tempo may suffice to render a comprehension of the piece impossible even to a musically trained auditor; he then hears only the sweep of intertwining harmonies, but can no longer follow the individual parts in their simultaneous progression.

Opportunity frequently offers to observe that listening organists criticize the tempo of a piece as too slow, whereas musically well-educated non-professionals of fine discrimination do not share this impression. The former know the piece by heart; the latter do not.

Hence, the organist should always make it a rule to take the tempo somewhat slower than he thinks it ought to be. The hearer, attempting to follow and grasp the whole, will find it quite fast enough.

First and last, aim at clearness and plasticity. No detail should be slurred over, no point should be lost. When the listener is enabled to hear all the notes, he will feel that the tempo is correct.

From the foregoing it is clear that the value of metronome-marks is subject to qualifications. When they are given it should be distinctly understood that they are to be followed or criticized with due reserve.

WHAT DECIDES THE TEMPO?

The tempo of a given piece is decided by the length of the smallest notes which occur in it, whether these be eighth-notes, sixteenths, or thirty-seconds. The figures in which these notes are combined must come out clearly and effectively, and ought never to sound hurried. From this viewpoint the tempo of the theme is fixed.

The manner of notation does not in the least indicate the movement in which a composition is to be performed. This is decided by the fundamental movement assumed for the figures in eighth-notes, or sixteenths, or thirty-seconds. Now, this movement is very nearly the same in all the preludes and fugues. The runs in thirty-second-notes which dominate one piece are conceived in the same movement as the sixteenths which rule in another, and these, again, like the eighth-notes in yet another piece. Bach's preludes and fugues for the organ lie close together as regards tempo, and appear like variations based on one common fundamental movement.

In an organ composition by the Cantor of St. Thomas's the hearer imagines something of a religious nature, something commensurate with the æsthetic effect of the nave, and uniting in itself animation of movement, tranquillity, and sublimity. The anticipations with which he awaits the performance are artistically justified. It is for the player to fulfil these anticipations, and not to impair—far less destroy—the impression of sublime animation that lies in Bach's organ music, by undue speed or hurry.

Do not try to bring out the animation in the works of our Old Master by trivial tricks of "temperament," such as men are apt to hit upon in this Era of Unrest. The temperament that Bach presupposes is something simpler and greater. Rightly to conceive the movement of the preludes and fugues, one must hear them within, and comprehend them as the animated expression of sublimity. There is need of self-collection and withdrawal into this higher sphere, before one can hope to interpret it through the tones and movements wherein Bach has symbolized it. The fact that so many organists mistake the tempo, and cannot banish haste and unrestfulness from their playing, is owing less to a lack of artistic insight than to their failure in attaining that profound inner composure without which they remain strangers to the realm of sublimity to which the preludes and fugues belong.

UNITY AND ELASTICITY OF TEMPO

After choosing the tempo, its conservation is a matter of high importance. Bach's organ works do not bear modern accelerations and retardations. Any alteration of the fundamental movement must be kept within definite bounds.

This does not mean that one ought to play the preludes and fugues monotonously; quite the contrary. They demand a shading of the tempo carried out into the least details. Such shading is indispensable to the development of the musical train of thought; but it must not become obtrusive, or exhibit any straining after effect.

Retardation or acceleration must be so restrained, that the hearer shall not for a moment lose his mental hold on the fundamental tempo.

A retardation is in order where one wishes to throw decisive entrances or

important modulations into relief. Complications in the part-leading necessitate, of course, a certain *allargando*. In the approach to a climax, too, a retardation is appropriate; here it has the effect of an actual *crescendo*. Hastening, in such passages, has not a good effect. It robs them of their grandeur.

Contrariwise, a slight acceleration is always proper in the episodes dividing the principal sections, when the passage is in only two or three parts.

These hints can convey only a very imperfect notion of the refined art of tempo-shading in the performance of Bach's organ works. Words can express but little in this case. Everything depends upon the player's listening to and observing himself; not leaving anything to the inspiration of the moment, but preparing the whole piece beforehand, and thus knowing exactly how much of its construction he can render intelligible to the hearer by means of discreet accelerations and retardations.

Some preludes and fugues are developed out of the conflict of two musical ideas. Here two tempi are interwoven. But the gradation must be so fine as merely to set one off against the other, allowing the transition from one to the other to be made naturally and unconstrainedly.

II. THE PHRASING

THE HISTORICAL VIEWPOINT

It is generally assumed that the *legato* style of organ-playing was an achievement of Bach and his school. Just how far this assumption is correct historically, remains to be ascertained. Probably Händel, and other organists of his time, also practised the *legato* style. But it would appear that Bach and his disciples elevated the continuous *legato* to a principle, through their development of the fingering to its modern perfection.

It should also be remarked, that it is difficult to play otherwise than *legato* on an organ with an eighteenth-century action, and that one cannot quite comprehend the contention, that Bach's direct predecessors, and also other organists of his own time, were in the habit of "lifting" the notes. This idea may arise from a misunderstanding. From the sixteenth century to the close of the seventeenth the action was so imperfect and so heavy, that a continuous *legato* was out of the question; besides, the primitive mode of fingering, in which the thumb was hardly used at all, permitted of no real *legato*. At Bach's time, however, both action and fingering had made such great progress, that no important difficulty then stood in the way of introducing the *legato* style. Its advantages were sufficiently obvious.

It is certain, in any case, that his works require the *legato* style. A performer who plays figures in sixteenth-notes and eighth-notes *staccato*, for the sake of variety, sins against the spirit of the Master. The fact that Bach no-where prescribes the *legato*, is evidence that he considered it a matter of course.

PHRASING, ON THE ORGAN, MUST TAKE THE PLACE OF ACCENT

This *legato*, however, is not a lifeless concatenation of tones, but only the external integument beneath which moves the animated phrasing. Within the general *legato*, the tones group themselves naturally into phrases and sec-tions, and these again combine one with the other in broader divisions. Play-ing Bach on the organ means to articulate and declaim musically in a large auditorium.

It would seem hardly needful to add, that musical divisions which are naturally of considerable breadth ought to be contrasted by the aid of a "break" (phrasing-pause) between them, effected at the expense of the last note; yet in reality this maxim is not seldom slighted. Our purpose is to call attention to the more delicate articulation within a theme or a figure.

On the organ the accentuation of individual notes is impossible. One tone follows the other in a uniform series. Any tone may be held on the same level of power for as long or short a time as one pleases. Herein resides the æsthetic nature of the sacred instrument. Its effects are attained only along broad lines and with sustained tones; not by means of tones which dominate the others through stronger accentuation. Thus it produces the impression of the sublime, the infinite; of the things which lie beyond the sphere of subjectivity.

But as, in point of fact, no theme or figure is conceived without accents, the æsthetic uniqueness of the organ is purchased by contrasting disadvantages. The smooth flow of tones is marred by a certain imperfection; the effect of the figures easily becomes heavy, inert, because their formal relations cannot be made clear by accentuation. The effects obtained on all other instruments by accent and phrasing combined, must be brought out on the organ by the latter alone. Lucid interpretation becomes an "art." It is achieved only by phrasing in such a way as to produce the illusion of "accenting."

The organ-playing of Bach and his son Friedemann is said to have exercised an indescribable charm on the listener. Assuredly, this was not brought about by mere virtuosity. The secret probably lay, in no small degree, in their ability to relax the rigidity of the organ-tone by the aid of phrasing, thereby lending the sound of the instrument the glamour of plasticity and expressive power. Every player should keep this ideal in view.

BACH'S PHRASING FOR VIOLIN AND ORGAN

It is not hard to discover what Bach understood by "phrasing." Any one desirous to know, has only to consult the works in which he indicated it

down to the least details. Most noteworthy among these are the Brandenburg Concertos and a number of sacred and secular cantatas. From these scores more may be learned than could be specified in treatises.

True, in these pieces the phrasing of the bow-instruments is the principal matter. But as these latter present the nearest approach to perfection, in the binding and graduation of tones, that is musically imaginable, they reveal the ideal aim of Bach's phrasing in general. The phrasing taken for granted in the organ works, is analogous to that of the orchestral pieces.

In Bach we have to do, not with orchestral style or organ-style, but with *obbligato parts* whose execution he in one case entrusts to the orchestra, in the other to the organ, and for the phrasing of which he often demands wellnigh the impossible of the various instruments. Observe what he requires in this particular of the wood-wind! He writes for them as if they were able to phrase like bow-instruments. And similarly with the organ. He takes the nature of the instrument in so far into account, as usually to let the several parts progress in decidedly simpler lines than when he composes for orchestra; in this respect the piano works also differ from those intended for bow-instruments. None the less, he conceives these simpler lines executed in a manner analogous to the phrasing of the violin-bow. Most of the themes look as though they had been imagined for bow-instruments. A fugue for solo violin is transcribed for organ! He arranges violin concertos of an Italian master as organ concertos! This shows that for Bach the organ-style was merely a modification of that which holds good for the string-orchestra.

To play an organ fugue perfectly means to execute it as if it were per-formed by bow-instruments controlling the tone of organ-pipes.

HOW TO PLAY REPEATED NOTES

The simplest rules for the phrasing which we have to extort from the organ, are not difficult of formulation.

Repeated notes are sustained only one-half their time-value; the other half becomes a rest. The following theme

is to be played as if it were written like this:

A strict insistence on this rule may strike the player as pedantic. But the hearer does not receive the impression that the repeated equal notes are separated in exaggerated style; he notices only that he can now apprehend something which otherwise eluded him.

Just as one is obliged, when speaking in public, and more especially in a vaulted auditorium, to articulate more forcibly than in ordinary conversation, so that the words may sound distinctly and naturally, are we obliged to articulate the repetition of the same note on the organ.

Only in the case of quite long notes should the rest occupy less than half the time-value. Even with half-notes taken at the usual tempo of the fugues and preludes, we should still adhere to the rule.

Where a succession of separated notes or chords is to be played, a differentiation of the pauses may be tried, in order to obtain rhythmic and dynamic effects. But in general, even in such cases, it will be found advantageous to adhere to the strict rule and, above all, to strive after the clearness and plasticity which the rule insures.

To indicate the articulation, it will be found practical to use the ordinary breathing-mark (').

All the above applies only to cases in which the same tone is repeated in the same part. Where some other part takes the note in question we have, not a repetition, but a taking-over. The note is then not lifted, for that would give the listener a wrong impression of the part-leading, as if a repetition had taken place in the same part. The note must be bound by keeping the key down.

Do not play this way: but thus:

It will not sound to the listener as if a key were held down, but as if one part had taken over the tone from the other.

These two rules are self-evident. They find their justification in choral singing. Nevertheless, their observance is far too inexact. Their precise observance is technically not so easy as would appear at first glance. Their demands on the reflective faculties and the fingers are frequently not inconsiderable.

Before beginning to practise a piece, the player will find it a good plan to go over it with pencil in hand, carefully providing notes repeated in the same part with breathing-marks, and writing in slurs where any note is taken over by another part. By so doing he will greatly promote the clearness and correctness of his interpretation.

Where a part progresses from one tone to another, always play *legato*. The notes must not, however, follow each other like a string of pearls, but must develop into longer or shorter periods, contrasted with each other by breathing-spaces of greater or less length. This "phrasing within the *legato*" can scarcely

be indicated by signs. As in elocution, we have to do with a most delicate gradation of values. The actual relations may be suggested by means of breathing-marks and short slurs gathered into a group by longer slurs passing over them.

GROUPING AND SUB-PHRASING WITHIN THE LEGATO

For the study of one of Bach's organ-works, therefore, a minute investigation into the structural development of the parts is required. To discover their natural phrase-grouping, the organist will have to sing them to himself. How great has been the loss to art in general that so many musicians do not begin by singing, as was formerly the rule, and then, with the natural feeling for phrasing and style which they have gained through vocal work, take up the study of instrumental playing! Bach was a choir-boy! This shows in every measure of his organ-figuration!

It makes no small demand on the conceptive powers of a player to fix his attention on the various shades of phrasing of four or five *obbligato* parts progressing together, and so performing a task which in a quartet or quintet is distributed among as many individual players. No less concentration is needed so to control the fingers that the mental concept shall be in some measure realized —to make each of these interwoven figures pulsate with warm, individual vitality within the common *legato*. But this detail-work cannot be approached in too serious a spirit; and he who earnestly applies himself to it, will surely find that it bears in itself a reward for player and hearer alike.

The structure of Bach's periods, as with every creative artist, has an individuality. His consists in frequently thinking in *auftakt*-forms. In his works a succession of sixteenth-notes, or eighth-notes, or quarter-notes, is not always to be phrased as if the groups of notes simply carried out some scheme of accentuation immediately preceding; it happens quite as often that they contrast with the latter and press forward to a different rhythm in which they merge in unity. In his conception of the phrasing the line

very often does not present the ordinary grouping indicated by the measure-accent and the notation, but divides into *auftakt*-periods, through which—and this is a most important point—secondary accents are produced, which antagonize the measure-accent and bring out the notes on the weak beats.

Consequently, this line is not always to be played so:

but is often phrased as follows:

And as these short *auftakt*-periods blend into larger ones, the breathing-pauses and accents are graduated and receive their appropriate values. Thus the following grouping is formed:

The phrasing directly indicated by Bach for passages on the piano and organ by their apportionment between the hands, shows us in what animated phrasing he conceived his figures, and how wide a departure is made from his intentions when his works are droned off in the monotonous *legato* of scales and finger exercises.

Through the antagonism between the measure-accent and the accentuation called for by the phrasing, the tone-line becomes instinct with life, variety, buoyancy, vigor. The hearer apprehends and is fascinated. He no longer hears a "run"; the motives blend before him to plastic form.

This means that the charm of Bach's running passages and figurations is destroyed by too great rapidity and spurious brilliancy. The listener should be able to hear every tone. But far too frequently he gets an impression as of something hurled through the air, twisting in tangled confusion, and finally falling at his feet.

THE LIFTED NOTES

The lifted notes, which interrupt the *legato*, are not to be played in a modern *staccato*, but rather as if they were contrasted on the violin by up-bow and down-bow. The elastic, short, springing lift of the note was unknown to Bach. It could be executed neither on his bow-instruments nor on his keyboards; the old bows were not sufficiently tense, and the keys of organ and clavichord did not "repeat" readily enough. When the Master writes dots over the notes, (which occurs very seldom in the organ pieces), he does not intend a *staccato*, but a somewhat sluggish lifting of the notes, corresponding to our *tenuto*. The tone is held for the greater part of its time-value, and the key is allowed to rise only a trifle earlier, so that a break in the succession is audible.

Placing the themes of the fugues and preludes side by side, it becomes apparent, that they were conceived in a style analogous to those for bow-instruments. Therefore, such notes are to be lifted as would require similar treatment

in the stroke of the bow; we play *legato*, where a *legato* is in place on the violin.

This rule contains the general principle for the phrasing. But it must not be observed pedantically. One should always bear in mind that in transferring violin-phrasing to the keyboard many modifications and limitations become necessary.

All depends on the regulation of the interval of time between the rise of one key and the fall of the following key. In lifting notes the most various gradations are possible. The interval may be made so wide, that the tones are separated by a noticeable space of time; or it may be so brief, that the notes seem nearly *legato*.

TENUTO AND LEGATO

But the borderland between lifting and *legato* is narrower, beyond all comparison, on the organ than on the violin. The differentiation between the time-intervals of successively depressed keys can express hardly a tithe of what the elasticity of the bow can embrace. The distinction between lifting and binding is far less fluent than on the violin. Therefore, many passages to be played on the violin in a *legato* not absolutely strict, can be executed on the organ only in strict *legato*. Thus the *legato* gains ground; the player is unable to bring out all the shadings between *tenuto* and *legato* which his mental conception of the theme demands, and so has to make up his mind to bind smoothly in many cases where he does not really desire the strictest *legato*.

On the piano the limitations in phrasing inherent in the keyboard are not so manifest, because Érard's ingenious invention of the double escapement, which forms the basis of all modern actions, permits of a wide series of gradations between *tenuto* and *legato*, and enables the player to execute much which is actually beyond the capacity of keyboard instruments as such. The hammer has become elastic. The organ remains, and will always remain, a simple keyboard instrument. Here it is a mere matter of opening and closing a valve by the aid of a key; this fact is unalterable.

IDEAL AND REALIZABLE PHRASING

Thus we are obliged to distinguish between an imagined ideal phrasing, and the phrasing which can be realized. The latter is always a simplification of the former. The never-ending controversy over the interpretation of themes usually arises from the circumstance, that a clear comprehension of the above-explained distinction has not been reached, and discussion proceeds without settling beforehand whether the ideal phrasing or its realizable approximation is under consideration.

In the theme of the Fugue in *F* minor, the first three notes are certainly not conceived as bound in the same way as those following. They call for a *tenuto* bordering on *legato*, though plainly distinguishable from it. The ideal phrasing would read thus:

On the organ, however, the distinction can hardly be brought out. By deliberately separating the first three notes one from the other, we should be guilty of a decidedly unhappy exaggeration; by binding them in correct style, they lose the peculiar effect of ponderous pressure which, from the structure of the theme, should be theirs. This problem has to be met in almost every fugue-theme.

We shall not be able to avoid playing the notes, whose ideal phrasing-values should be indicated by *tenuto*-dashes under a slur, in an actual *legato*. But let it be borne in mind, that not everything thus similarly bound is necessarily on the same level according to the true phrasing of the theme. Above the Player, the Organist must still imagine an ideal phrasing, even though he cannot do away with the incongruity between idea and reality. Whoever prefers to indicate the phrasing by means of graphic expedients—*tenuto*-dashes, slurs, breathing-marks—should seek to intimate the Ideal, leaving the player free to realize whatsoever he can of it. All phrasing-marks ought, therefore, to be considered merely as symbols, for whose interpretation on the organ a simplified meaning is presupposed.

Remember, at the same time, that by dint of purposeful practice one can wrest more from the organ than would seem possible at the first glance. Carefully trained fingers learn to operate with finely differentiated values as regards the release of a key and the pressure on the next. They learn to make the most of the infinitesimal intervals between the tones, which, although not destroying the effect of a *legato*, make the hearer aware of something different from the ordinary binding. In order to render his striving after this refinement effective, the player must never lose sight of the ideal phrasing. This points the way toward an intimate perfection of the organ-technique.

THE PHRASING AND THE KEYBOARD

From all this it is self-evident, that the key-action is a matter of the highest importance. One can bring out a great deal, with respect to phrasing, on an organ with a good action, that would be impossible on an ordinary keyboard.

For judging of the action, three factors are to be considered: Readiness in speaking, heaviness or lightness of touch, and springiness of the keys.

If the organ is badly voiced, and the tone blares or rumbles instead of speaking naturally and smoothly, proper phrasing is rendered simply impossible.

With respect to the connection between key and pallet, the best is a good tracker-action. With such an action, the smoothest *legato*, and at the same time the clearest separation of the tones, can be brought out. The interlocking system of levers lends a certain elasticity to the action, and establishes, as it were, a living contact between finger, key and pipe. The nearest approach to this is the ordinary pneumatic lever (invented by Barker).

With the electric action the articulation is good. But the tones stand out in such sharp relief, that it is very difficult to obtain a *legato* thoroughly satisfactory to a trained ear.

The pneumatic action is prone to a certain sluggishness. Hence, the articulation easily becomes indistinct, and the *legato* is in danger of degenerating into a blurring of the successive tones. Fate has so ordered it, that this kind of action is practical, cheap, and dependable, so that one may expect to find it in the majority of organs.

Fortunately, a cleverly devised system of key-springs, and the weighting of the keys, or the installation of a mechanism for regulating their movement, can greatly counteract the defects of the electric and pneumatic actions. See to it that both dip and rise of the keys are even, and that the springs regulating the touch work evenly and with sufficient resistance to make the fingers exert a clinging pressure, enabling them to control the key-movement with precision. The hand must be able to come into living contact with the keyboard, so that it may feel the exact position of the key at every instant. Only when the key comes to the aid of the finger, is it possible for the player to lift and bind in a suitable manner.

The Regulations for Organ-building proposed at the third session of the International Music Association (Vienna, 1909), have established in detail the requirements of an artistically satisfactory keyboard.

WHAT NOTES OUGHT TO BE LIFTED?

Concerning the notes which should be lifted in playing, organists are probably in substantial agreement. Everything which departs from the natural movement of the line, and appears characteristic in rhythm or interval-progression, should as a rule be played *non legato*, to give it proper relief.

The beginning of the theme of the Fugue in *A* minor ought, therefore, to be phrased as follows:

Under the limitations to which the rule may be subjected, is to be mentioned the common experience of singers and players on wind-instruments, that ascending octave-intervals taken *legato* have a better effect than when lifted. Taking this suggestion into consideration, we should phrase the theme of the great Fugue in *G* minor in the manner following:

Observe, that in the above an indication of the ideal phrasing is aimed at. In actual execution the eighth-notes marked with the *tenuto*-dash, but included within the slur, can hardly be played otherwise than in *legato;* so that, in point of fact, only the eighth-notes on the third beat in the second measure can be lifted.

In the second category of the notes to be executed in *non legato* are to be named those which, in any way whatever, are opposed to the measure-rhythm, and bear the accents of the theme or the figure. The classic example of this class is found in the theme of the Fugue in *A* major:

Bear continually in mind that on the organ anything affected, harsh, restless or obtrusive in the phrasing, is of ill effect. The phrasing of organ pieces should be so natural and delicately shaded, that the hearer does not notice it *as phrasing*, but has only the feeling that the tones are united into a living whole, and pulsating with sensient rhythm.

The phrasing of the piece is often forgotten over the phrasing of the theme. The figuration of the individual parts rolls on in a heavily monotonous *legato*. It gives the impression of a statue of which only the head is sculptured, leaving the body a rough block of stone.

In general, it will be observed, in Bach, how the phrasing of the parts, as such, grows motive-wise out of the phrasing of the theme. Be guided by this influence, and search out its full development. Then the polyphonic weft will cease to produce the impression of a compact mass, and will become, as if spontaneously, buoyant and translucent.

Much is often spoiled by the player's failure to follow the phrasing of the hands in that of the feet, so that the pedal-figures, through their heaviness and lack of animation, cover and drag down those of the other parts. How often are alto and tenor swallowed up by the density of a bass unenlightened by a phrasing through which the inner parts might be followed.

HOW TO PLAY CHORD-PROGRESSIONS

Special care is likewise demanded in the execution of successive chords. Very frequently the chords are "lifted" so as to have the effect of detached "solid" chords. This may be appropriate in certain cases, but by no means in all. Do not forget, that in Bach these chord-successions usually result from the movement of *obbligato* parts. The chords ought not, therefore, to be lifted bodily, but played according to the rules governing polyphonic playing. Notes repeated in the same part are lifted; play all the rest in strict *legato*. Frequently three or four parts repeat the same tone, and only one or two progress by an interval. The lifted notes, sustained for but half their time-value, preponderate. The hearer will receive the impression, that the full chords are separated one from the other; he will not notice the fact that one or two of the parts are bound. He will only wonder why it happens that he can follow the progress of the harmonic movement more readily and clearly than usual.

Where the bound notes preponderate over the lifted notes, it seems to him as if the entire chords were running on in a peculiar and strikingly agreeable rhythmical *legato*. This result is due to the lifted notes, which give the chord-successions their precision and set the *legato* parts in proper relief.

Thus the much-discussed question, whether Bach's chord-successions ought to be played *legato* or by lifting the chords, decides itself. In the majority of cases, the bare alternative is not applicable. It is not the chords *as chords* that are played smoothly, or separated; the *legato* or *non legato* results from the phrasing of the individual parts. Hence, according to the given conditions in each case, we have chords entirely lifted, or chords entirely *legato*, or chords in which some of the parts are lifted while others are bound.

This procedure endows the successions of chords with a natural variety and shading otherwise unrealizable. Furthermore, it renders more intelligible the movement of the individual parts, which is naturally not so clear when, as is usually the case, the entire chord is lifted; for, by this lifting, both the repeated notes and those which progress by intervals (these latter being characteristic points in the harmonic progression) are equally abbreviated.

Experience teaches us, that this manner of playing successive chords is also frequently applicable where Bach does not write strictly *obbligato* parts.

The above is elucidated by the following examples:

Prelude (Toccata) in *D* minor, meas. 8–11.

Fugue in *D* minor, meas. 52-53.

Prelude in *D* major, meas. 52-57.

PHRASING, FINGERING, AND THE TECHNICS OF PLAYING

The observance of this phrasing makes considerable demands on the player's technique. But they are not of such a nature, that the average organist is unable to cope with them, providing that he really tries. What one requires here, is a thorough training of the fingers. They must become so independent, that the simultaneous *legato*, lifting, and "spacing" (of the pauses indicated by the breathing-marks) present no difficulties. And this is brought about simply by reflection, practice, introspection—and a good fingering.

The organist has little use for fingerings marked by others. Even when they are good, their only result is to accustom him to easy-going and thoughtless methods.

The general principles for a correct employment of the fingers need no explanation. Any player who ventures on Bach, must be assumed to know them. But no one, not even the pupil, can be spared the trouble of thinking out and experimenting with a fingering, for each piece, which permits of a smooth *legato* and clear phrasing. A thorough-going, reliable technique can be acquired only by one who, wielding pencil and india rubber, writes in, erases, corrects his fingerings, and so through personal experience arrives at a clear understanding of underlying principles.

The same is true of the pedalling. We mention, as a matter of history, that the pedal-boards of the eighteenth century were very short and narrow. It was impossible to use the heel on them. Consequently, Bach always played with the toes, alternating or crossing them; now and then, where the notes lay close together, he may have employed the slide from one key to another. Modern pedal-boards allow a more convenient and faultless pedalling.

But the most beautiful *legato* and phrasing avail him nothing, when the player's technique is lacking in precision, so that the keys are not simultaneously depressed and released with the most painful exactitude. Most organists have no idea of the sins they commit in this line. It ought to be a matter of course that, among all professional artists, he who plays the largest and most complicated of instruments should exercise the keenest observation and sedulously watch his own attitude. Just the contrary is the case. Very many organists literally do not hear themselves play, and never notice that they sway their body back and forth and to and fro. They do not feel the necessity for controlling the fingers by the ear, neither do they heed the careless habits of their hands. When the latter have to participate in any way in the depression and release of the keys, precision invariably suffers. It is possible only when their fingers do the work alone and the excessive movements—the raising or turning of the wrist, the shifting of the weight of the hand to a finger sustaining a tone, the stretching and contracting of the finger-joints—are avoided.

All sorts of aimless motions go on unconsciously, allowing the player no clear conception of what his fingers are about. Only when self-observation is well developed, when the fingers are controlled by the ear, and concentration never relaxes for an instant, can a plastic and impressive interpretation be achieved. And in these particulars Bach demands the highest degree of perfection.

III. THE ORNAMENTS

In Bach's organ works the ornaments play a less conspicuous part than in the clavier compositions. But the player should be thoroughly familiar with the peculiar manner in which the prescribed trills and other embellishments are to be performed, if he does not care to find himself at variance with the Master's intentions.

On the third page of the "Clavierbüchlein," written for his son Friedemann, Bach gives the following "explication" of the signs by writing out their execution in full:

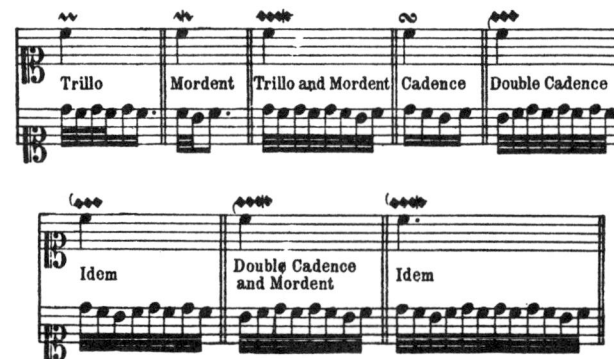

Accent (rising)   Accent (falling)   Accent and Mordent   Accent and Trillo

Observance of these directions will insure correct performance. The Trill, however, requires some further explanations. Bach indicates it indiscriminately by the signs *t*, *tr*, 〰, 〰, without particularly designating the way it should be played, or its length. In general, it should fill out the entire time-value of the principal note, or at least the greater part of it. Begin, as a rule, with the higher auxiliary, and do not permit yourself to be put out by the (for a modern ear) harshness of the resultant harmonies or the increased difficulty of execution.

For rather long trills it is an excellent plan to pause an instant at first on the principal note, and then begin trilling with the higher auxiliary; more particularly when a movement or theme commences with a trill, or when the higher auxiliary has been struck immediately before.

It is not correct to pause on the principal note in case that note has been struck immediately before.

The Bach trill should be played slowly, especially on the organ. The least haste is of ill effect. When played against a figuration in eighth-notes, its own movement should be in sixteenths; against sixteenth-notes it should be executed in thirty-seconds. In every case it must be nicely adjusted to the measure-rhythm.

Trills in the pedal were intended for the clear, incisive tone of the old pedal-bass. On an organ with rather dull 16-foot pedal-registers it will be best to omit some pedal-trills here and there.

These remarks apply to long trills extending over several beats, an entire measure, or even several measures. Shorter trills, filling out only a quarter-note or half-note, may naturally be treated with greater freedom, especially when they are not obliged to accommodate themselves to an opposing contrapuntal figuration in eighths or sixteenths, but are executed above sustained harmony. The effect is excellent when they are started slowly and finished in an accelerated movement.

Among the works for organ there are several which, according to modern taste, are overladen with ornaments. Such pieces are, in part, youthful compositions, and in part numbers written rather for the pedal-cembalo (harpsichord with pedal). The omission of some of these ornaments can hardly be regarded as a crime.

IV. REGISTRATION. ALTERNATION OF MANUALS

FUNDAMENTAL PRINCIPLES

The foremost rule is, that clarity of execution must not be interfered with by the registration. Anything which makes the tone dull, heavy and rumbling, is to be condemned. Never gain power at the expense of clearness, but always remember that the hearer, when he can plainly follow four or five parts progressing side by side, will assuredly receive a grateful impression of fullness.

For a second rule keep to this: That everything undertaken in the way of registration and change of manuals must grow out of the nature and plan of the piece. Every variation in tone must be dictated by some "happening" in the piece itself, and be proportioned to the importance of the happening. At any cardinal point in the development of the prelude or fugue, a decisive change of tone is appropriate; in less important transitions a mere modification of power or color is all that is called for. A player whose main idea in registration is to obtain variety and surprising effects, destroys the plan of the piece, and renders its artistic comprehension by the hearer impossible.

Therefore, do not seek mere effect in your registration, or let it go haphazard, but first of all study out the design and development of the prelude or fugue, and strive to comprehend its structural logic. Which is the principal theme, which the subordinate? What stands in the foreground, and what in the middle distance or in the background? Is any given section the crown of something preceding it, or the preparation for something that follows?

All this must be duly considered, and thoroughly "tried out," to make the registration and the changing of manuals result in setting the piece in the right perspective and color. The organist should resemble the painter, who, before taking up his brush, with a crayon sketches the outlines on his canvas.

This preliminary work may require weeks, or months; one puts it aside to let one's ideas crystallize, and then takes it up again. It sometimes seems as if no progress were being made, as if the matter were growing more confused. But at the end of the work it usually happens that one hits on something clear and simple, and wonders at the devious paths taken to attain it.

The point cannot be urged too frequently, that a prelude or fugue is not to be considered as an isolated case, but that different ones should be compared with each other in order to discover the general principles inherent in their structure. Many an intricate case may be explained in the light of a simpler one.

Those rare pieces are invaluable, in which are found directions derived from Bach himself for the alternation of the manuals. Foremost among these is to be mentioned the Prelude (Toccata) in *D* minor.

The study of the Brandenburg Concertos is also of importance. The relations between principal and secondary themes, *tutti* and *soli*, are made clear through the instrumentation. From this we can judge how Bach employed the great-manual and the subsidiary manuals in his organ works.

ADVANTAGES AND DISADVANTAGES OF THE MODERN ORGAN

It would be scarcely correct to say, that the development and improvement of the organ must influence the interpretation of Bach's organ works; that it should prompt us—or even require us—to play them in a manner fundamentally different from that in which the Master himself played them. His conception of their interpretation will always be the decisive one. In this conception he was, of course, guided by that which was or was not possible on his organ. But do not fancy that you are acting in Bach's spirit if you employ his preludes and fugues to show off to an astounded audience all the descriptions and degrees of effect whereof a modern organ is capable, and of which he did not dream while penning the compositions.

The improvements of the organ should serve only as a means for fulfilling the intentions which formed part and parcel of the pieces at their inception, in the highest possible degree of perfection;—more completely than could be accomplished on the instruments of the Master's period.

Do not forget, that the nature of the organ has in no wise been modified by modern improvements. Finer foundation stops and mixtures than those of Silbermann are not made; at most we succeed in making the Gambas and Salicionals prompter of speech and rounder of tone. The old reed-pipes did not speak so readily as ours, which detracted from their usefulness as solo stops. But, on the other hand, they possessed a lighter, broader tone which blended ravishingly with that of the foundation stops and mixtures. The "full organ" of the old instruments was finer than that of ours, being clearer, warmer, and more pellucid, and wholly without burdensome or oppressive effect. This ideal has been restored to its place of honor by the Regulations for Organ-building proposed at the Vienna Congress. Organ-builders and organ-players of discernment had already perceived that the dull, shrill tone which results from too narrow a scale and too high wind-pressure, and which robs the foundation stops, mixtures and reeds of their fine penetrative effect, is not suitable for setting forth the polyphony of Bach's works.

The advantages of the modern organ are of threefold sort. The player can couple the manuals together without exertion; the swell-box permits of dynamic modulations of tone which modify the inflexibility of the organ-tone; numerous ingenious inventions allow the organist to change the tone-color as rapidly and frequently as he will.

It should be noted, that in the organs of the eighteenth century no couplers of pedals to manuals existed. The intercoupling of the manuals was effected by pushing one manual into another, their actions thus interlocking so that when one was played on the other went with it. Coupling and uncoupling during a movement were impracticable. To push the manuals together, the organist had to use both hands, and lay hold of handles projecting from either end of the manual. The organist's helper could not do this for him while he was playing, for while one action was in movement it would not interlock with another. Thus the modern organist is much better off than the Master; he can shift the couplers at pleasure while he is playing.

In the old organs there was not even a coupler between swell- and choir-manuals, because the great-manual lay in the middle. This arrangement of the manuals was not the product of untrammeled design, but of necessity. The keyboard of the second manual had to be the lowest, because the wind-chest belonging to it was behind the organist, so that the connecting mechanism had to be carried under his bench. If the choir-manual (Manual II, or "Rückpositiv") had been placed above the great-manual, its mechanism would have crossed that of the latter.

From this arrangement there also resulted difficulties in changing manuals. In passing from the second to the third, one was obliged to reach across the first. Hence it came, that in the fugues and preludes little use was made of the swell-manual, but ordinarily the great- and choir-manuals were used in alternation.

Modern acquisitions are, therefore, of great value. But it is only in well-arranged organs that they are really effective. The subsidiary manuals must not be too weak, as contrasted with the great-manual; more especially, all varieties of registers should be represented on them—the foundation stops of 8-, 4- and 2-foot tone, besides mixtures and reeds; some of these last, if possible, of 4-foot tone.

There must be no wide gulf between any pair of manuals; otherwise the contrast obtained by alternation of manuals is too sharp. On the other hand, the difference between them must be clearly marked, else the effect of alternation will lose its charm.

Each manual embodies, in its tone, an individuality. They should be differentiated from one another not only (and not so greatly) by strength, but rather by timbre. The great-manual should possess a full, broad, mellow tone. The choir should have something of the clear, breezy, keen sound of the old *Rückpositiv* which projected out into the church behind the organ-bench. The intonation of the swell should be marked by a certain richness and intensity. When three such manuals are coupled together, the wealth of tone resulting from the combination of their individual effects is astounding.

We must not fail to mention, that most of Bach's compositions are calculated for the alternation of but two manuals. For the prelude and the fugue the organist employed, as a rule, only the great-manual and the choir-organ, the latter, as aforesaid, projecting out into the church. The swell-manual was usually so weak—besides being provided in many cases with only partial registers—that it was chiefly used for accompanying solo voices. Note the fact, that in his Prelude (Toccata) in *D* minor Bach mentions only *Hauptwerk* (great) and *Positiv* (choir). Hence, all the Master's works can be interpreted in accordance with his intentions on a good two-manual organ. Where there are three manuals the organist will, naturally, profit by his advantages; especially as our swell-manuals are not so inferior to the others as was the case in the instruments of the eighteenth century. Do not fancy, however, that all three manuals ought to be brought into action for every prelude and every fugue.

CRESCENDO AND DECRESCENDO

A matter of importance is the kind and number of registers on the swell-organ. The opportunity of swelling and diminishing the tone must be properly exploited. The *crescendo* and *decrescendo* to be produced by opening and closing the swell-box, should not be limited to this manual alone, but should render it possible to influence, through intercoupling of the manuals, the dynamic effects of the entire instrument. It is only when employed in this dual capacity that the swell-box performs its full duty. By its aid a continuity in *crescendo* and *decrescendo* may be effectuated, which were otherwise wholly impracticable, and which is of high importance in the interpretation of Bach.

Supposing one is playing a fugue or prelude with all manuals coupled and all foundation stops drawn, and that the piece requires an augmentation up to full organ. The swell-box is closed. Now, on the swell one can add the mixtures, and finally the reeds, without noticeably altering the general tone-effect of the three combined manuals. On opening the swell, the effect of the added mixtures and reeds is brought out. We obtain an ideally controllable *crescendo*, apportioned at pleasure over a series of measures, and leading up to a full organ *en miniature*—for in the added stops all the various kinds of tone are represented. We can now go on adding the mixtures and reeds of the choir and great manuals without causing an undesirably violent "outburst" of tone. The new registers act, to be sure, as a reinforcement, but do not transform the character of the tone-mass to such an extent as they would have done, had not the mixtures and reeds on the swell already been sounding.

Should the prelude or fugue require a diminution from full organ to the tone-color of the foundation stops, the mixtures and reeds on the great-manual are first retired, followed by those on the choir. Then the swell-box is closed gradually, so that what mixtures and reeds still remain to affect the timbre slowly melt away as in the distance, and when these stops are retired, after the swell-box is closed, the effect is scarcely perceptible.

In the foregoing, only a formula is set forth. But it may suggest how the modern improvements of the organ can be made to serve the cause of Bach-playing. For, in the preludes and fugues of the Cantor of St. Thomas's, we

have to do with that "Art of Transition" to which Wagner so enthusiastically refers in his writings.

The swell-box must be employed only to bring out gradually and evenly any *crescendo* or *decrescendo* called for in Bach's works and extending through several successive measures. A *crescendo subito* obtained by the aid of the swell-pedal, is always of ill-effect. The *diminuendo subito* may be employed in exceptional cases (in *piano* passages, and combined with a well-graduated *rallentando*) to throw into strong relief some important and striking modulation.

The organist should be warned against an exaggerated use of the swell-box in the preludes and fugues. It has a wholly unrestful effect. Too little of it is better than too much. Rather let the swell-pedal severely alone, than employ it with bad judgment, and make the organ sound like an accordion. The swell is correctly used only when the listener remains quite unaware of its employment.

When your swell-manual has a good set of stops, and the swell-box is well constructed, it will be unnecessary to have a swell-box for the choir-organ also; and it would appear entirely superfluous to have such a box for every manual on your organ. The art of Bach-playing would reap no advantage from it, for the effects obtained by a swell of such proportions are too extreme to be used in performing the preludes and fugues. Furthermore, take care not to have too much wood in and in front of the organ, for it injures the tone of the foundation stops.

In two-manual organs, the registers of the second manual should be in the swell-box.

Many organists delight in producing a *diminuendo*, from full organ to *piano*, by retiring stops either with the hand or by the aid of the *crescendo*-pedal. This is a clumsy, inartistic effect, wherever it may be used. To a sensitive ear this splitting-up and shredding of a chord—for that is what it amounts to, even with the best *crescendo*-mechanism—will always be a torture. This artificial dying-away of the chord formed no part of Bach's intention. He meant that it should be sustained, both in the orchestra and on the organ, in like strength and tone-color. If a conductor were to take it into his head to stop, one after the other, the brass-wind, the flutes, the oboes, and a section of the strings, on some chord of one of the Brandenburg Concertos, finally sustaining it with a bare quartet, he would cause an unexampled commotion. Should the same thing, only on a larger scale, be allowed on the organ just because the *crescendo*-pedal makes it so easy of execution?

"PRO ORGANO PLENO"

The direction "pro organo pleno" has given rise to most manifold misconceptions. It has been thought to mean that the piece in question ought to be played with full organ from beginning to end. That is not the case. In itself the direction is meaningless, and merely indicates that the composition is written for a "whole organ" ("*ganze*" *Orgel*), that is, an instrument with two manuals and a complete pedal, and not for a simple "Regal" (also called "Positiv") having but one manual with one or two stops, or for a one-manual organ with an incomplete pedal of only one octave, such as was considered good enough for village churches down to the middle of the nineteenth century. Even to the present day the local dialect in various parts of Germany clings to the distinction between "whole" and "half" organs (*ganze und halbe Orgeln*). Hence, the direction "pro organo pleno" has a purely historical significance. It means no more for organ music than the corresponding "For the Pianoforte" does for piano compositions. When a composer for piano affixes this heading to his work, he is merely following a tradition of the time in which our piano appeared as something new among other incomplete types, and achieved a place for itself. As every "Klavier" nowadays is a piano, every organ, too, is an "organum plenum."

THE EMPLOYMENT OF REED-STOPS

Should we, or should we not, employ reed-stops for the preludes and fugues? On this head we find two opposed opinions. Some say, No: These are the zealots of Clarity, who fear that the trumpets, trombones and clarinos might mar the lucidity of Bach's polyphony. The others advocate the employment of reed-stops, because they would not dispense with the strength and color which these stops supply to the full organ.

From an historical viewpoint, the zealots of clarity are wrong. It is traditional, that Bach showed a great partiality for reed-stops, and raised no objection whatever when he found sixteen of them in the organ at St. Catherine's in Hamburg. It follows, that he used them. It must be stated, on the other hand, that reed-stops do not always have a good effect in Bach-playing. Doubtless they are frequently misused.

In order to set this question in the proper light, we must consider, that there is an important difference between the reed-stops of the Master's period, and ours. The modern reeds, on a heavy wind-pressure, have a somewhat blaring tone; they are penetrating and dominating. Moreover, since they do not speak as readily as the foundation stops and mixtures, the full-organ effect inclines to become heavy, and the elastic *legato* will not come out. The tones do not follow smoothly one after the other, but sound as if torn apart—an effect which, in the figurations of a prelude or fugue, often amounts to an actual perversion.

In the "full organ" of the old instruments the reed-stops do not produce the same unpleasing effect, although their workmanship is imperfect, and they often buzz or rattle. They blend well with the foundation stops and mixtures, and have a tendency to clarify and brighten the tone-color.

The same question is raised with regard to the orchestra. There is always an element of risk in the production of a cantata with trumpets. This is not simply owing to the fact that present-day trumpeters are unprepared to meet the technical requirements of Bach-playing, and that the construction of our instruments does not permit of bringing out these high figurations with the needful agility. Even if these difficulties were once overcome, the interpretation would nevertheless suffer from the tone of the instruments now used. They sound out too harshly from the orchestra. The right balance between them and the wood-wind and strings is unattainable, because their tone is so much bigger than that of those for which the Master wrote.

Thus the reed-stops on our organs, and the trumpets in our orchestras, although in many respects an improvement over those which Bach had at his disposal, are not so well suited for performing his works as could be desired. But this does not mean, that we must do without them. The scores in which combinations of oboes and trumpets occur show what a partiality Bach had for metallic effect in his tone-blending, and permit us to form an opinion concerning his employment of the organ-registers. The imperfect speech of the reeds did not prevent their use. In the first place, they were not so sluggish as is generally supposed by those who judge merely by the condition of poorly preserved old organs. Besides, anyone can perceive that such reed-stops, when drawn together with foundation stops and mixtures, speak far more promptly than when played alone. The flue-pipes producing the same tones help the reeds to speak—carry them along, as it were.

These considerations bring us to the conclusion, that reed-stops *are* to be employed for the preludes and fugues, but not without caution and calculation. Excessively strong and blaring stops are to be excluded. They do more harm than good. The tone should be reinforced by reeds only in so far as the foundation stops and mixtures can naturally absorb and cover them. Repletion supervenes at the moment when the tone loses flexibility in runs and figurations. Where mixtures and foundation stops are good, only a few reeds are required to give the proper effect of a "full organ" to the polyphony.

The only satisfactory solution of the problem would be to make room on our organs for the old, mild-toned reeds side by side with the intense modern ones.

We should also mention, that it almost invariably has a bad effect to draw reed-stops while playing on choir or swell. In this case their hurtful influence on the *legato* becomes most pronounced, because the needful counterbalance of broad foundation stops and full-toned mixtures is not available. On the other hand, the reeds of the subsidiary manuals coupled with the foundation stops and mixtures of the great-manual produce an excellent effect.

Every organist will have to settle with his own conscience what he shall do, in soli for pedal, with his 16-foot Posaune.

FOUNDATION STOPS AND MIXTURES

It should be observed, that the modern organist possibly makes a somewhat exaggerated use of his couplers of pedal to manuals. In Bach's polyphony not the *loudness* of the bass, but its *distinctness*, comes in question. Among the other parts, it ought to be distinguishable. Consequently, by coupling, one often attains just the opposite of what is aimed at. Although the pedal without coupling is weaker, it still possesses an individual timbre which renders it easily distinguishable; with couplers drawn, it becomes louder, but loses its peculiar timbre among the low tones of the manual foundation stops, and also grows less distinct, and thus not so clearly prominent as before. Therefore, be cautious in your employment of the great-to-pedal coupler (this being the one most frequently drawn), and do not forget the 4-foot Principal in your specification, even for a small organ, as it is of great importance for the distinctness of the bass in the preludes and fugues; on the old organs it is hardly ever missing.

The Preludes will, in general, be played louder throughout than the Fugues; for in the latter absolute clarity and transparency of tone must be preserved at all hazards.

In both, the blending of foundation stops and mixtures is to be considered as the fundamental timbre; provided, that the former are clear and the latter not too shrill. These two qualifications are not always present in organs built nowadays; and then the interpretation of Bach's organ music suffers more than one is usually willing to admit to oneself. According to the Master's conception, his works should be played with a rich, full tone, and run on for long distances in an even *forte*—in such a *forte* as the blended foundation stops and mixtures produce. But one often finds an organ which does not command this *forte*, whose continuous effect is agreeable and not wearisome. In such an organ the foundation stops are too "thick" and the mixtures are voiced too loud. Thus the player is obliged to seek variety in order to interrupt the level *forte*, and in so doing enters on the downward path of artificialism—for which the imperfection of his instrument is to blame. A further bad feature in this case is, that for his *forte* effects he often has to omit the unpleasant mixtures altogether, and make shift with the foundation stops alone. This tone-color is lacking in character, clearness and brilliancy, all of which are expected by Bach in the leading sections of his preludes and fugues. So the general impression is weak. To improve it, the player quite naturally grasps at some cheap effects.

We know nothing positive concerning the manner in which Bach employed the 16-foot registers on the manuals. However, it can hardly be right to keep them drawn throughout entire preludes and fugues. The Master probably used them for chord-effects. In such places the fullness and depth of tone produced by the addition of the 16-foot stops is powerfully effective. But the moment we have to do with passage-playing, or the purely contrapuntal progression of the parts, these stops are out of place. And so, for the fugues, they require but scant consideration.

The foundation timbre for preludes and fugues is derived from the 8- and 4-foot foundation stops. Their function may be compared with that of the string-group in the orchestra. The 2-foot registers should serve rather to brighten the tone than to strengthen it. The finer their voicing, the oftener can they be employed.

Registration, in the preludes and fugues, consists in associating the mixtures with the foundation stops, and adding the reeds to these where it seems appropriate; alternating backward and forward between these tone-blendings as the logic of the piece demands for setting forth the several sections in due contrast.

BRILLIANT REGISTRATION

One may be inclined to regard this mode of procedure as too severely plain, and to advocate a registration more ingeniously devised to exhibit the fine points and the possibilities in tone-combination of the given instrument. One might, with a certain show of reason, cite Forkel, Bach's first biographer (his worklet was published in 1802), who tells of the astonishment which mastered the organists and organ-builders when they saw Bach draw his stops. "They thought it impossible," he writes, "that such a combination of registers should sound well, and were greatly surprised, when it came to the test, that the finest effects were thus obtained; only there was something strange, out of the ordinary, in the tone of the organ, which they could not produce with their style of registration."

But this is no charter for investing the preludes and fugues with every possible or impossible effect of registration. The passage quoted above applies to the registration used in playing trios and *Choralvorspiele*. In these one was permitted to show his ingenuity, and to create surprise by unexpected tone-combinations. Solo stops, or carefully calculated blendings, were employed.

But even if this passage—which, like all that Forkel wrote on organs and organ-playing, fails in precision—were intended to apply to the preludes and fugues likewise, it would not justify a registration aiming at a wealth of variety, at striking and showy effects, with frequent change of the registers. It speaks of an adjustment of tone-color before beginning to play, not of alterations undertaken while playing. Whoever has sat in front of an old organ, with its long stop-knobs, knows that the organist could at best make but slight changes in the registration during his performance. In a *Choralvorspiel* or trio no changes at all were made, as a rule. That was quite a matter of course. Who, while playing in an orchestra trio, would have taken it into his head to exchange his instrument for some other!

In the preludes and fugues the organist had only to consider the addition or retirement of groups of stops, and not the employment of solo stops. Examine the scores of the Brandenburg Concertos and of the cantatas. In these, too, Bach operates with groups. He lets the wood-wind, or the trumpets, enter or cease all together. The individualization of the modern art of instrumentation is foreign to him. Who cares to hear these concertos played otherwise than they were conceived?

On the organ his procedure is the same. The foundation stops correspond to the strings; the mixtures and reeds to the wood-wind and the brass. It is a primitive instrumentation and registration. At a certain period, when Art was proud of having escaped from primitive conditions, of her progress toward perfection in the blending and the individualizing of tones, the question might have been raised whether the works of Bach should be interpreted in the light of this progress, in order to make amends, in their performance, for that which was impracticable for the Master. They who thought thus, did not know the Bible, and had forgotten the sentence, "No man putteth a piece of new cloth unto an old garment." The Primitive, as it is found in Bach, is not something obsolete and surpassed, but a self-sufficient form of art bearing the stamp of a completeness which, in its kind, is the equal of any other. The progressive refinement in the application of tone-values does not lead us away from Bach, but rather—the longer its life is drawn out—back to him. Our yearning goes out again toward this grand simplicity; we smile to think that any one could imagine overlaying it with modern arts and artifices. This seems to us as preposterous as if it were proposed to allow an impressionist to renew the frescos on the ceiling of the Sixtine Chapel.

The sweeping grandeur of the preludes and fugues permits of no attempt at introducing effects with solo stops, and at seeking variety within the group of affiliated foundation stops on the same manual.

But this does not signify, by any means, that the various preludes and fugues are all to be played with one and the same registration. Each has its own peculiar fundamental tone-color. It is for the organist to discover the nuance suited to the character of each. For the one, the 2-foot registers are appropriate at the beginning and all the way through; for another, even the 4-foot registers must be sparingly drawn; a third should be played with a preponderance of the flute-tone, and in yet another, the character of the conception requires the diapasons; some need the sharpness of the mixtures from the start; while in some it will be well at the beginning, and all through, to blend with the tone a dash of the metallic sound of the reed-stops.

The player's delicacy of perception shows in his choice of nuance for this fundamental tone-color which is continued throughout the piece, which he now reinforces, and now subdues. In the preludes, the distinctions to be considered are slighter than in the fugues. The meditation of the individual coloring for a fugue-theme is a perplexity and a delight which the player should ever taste anew.

This, of course, refers only to blendings in the registration, not to solo stops.

THE GREAT-MANUAL, AND THE OTHERS

Preludes and fugues should invariably start on the great-manual with a suitable fullness of tone, precisely as the introductions to the cantatas and the Brandenburg Concertos begin with a *tutti* in the orchestra. It will be recognized more and more, as time goes on, that it is an abomination to the Lord when a fugue-theme is first whispered out upon the swell, and only gradually gains courage to speak out on the great. Such a theme has, by nature, something strong in it, and must announce itself with decision at the very outset. The works for orchestra show—even were it not established by tradition and the nature of the fugue itself—that the initial entrance of the theme ranks as a *tutti* passage. Take up the Bach fugue-themes one by one, and you will discover none—whether for organ, or pianoforte, or orchestra—conceived *piano*. Probably another century will have elapsed before pianists yield to this truth in their interpretation of the Well-tempered Clavichord. It would not be amiss for organists to permit themselves to be converted sooner.

An apparent qualification must be mentioned. Through the greater number of registers allotted to the subsidiary manuals, the difference in volume between the several manuals of the modern organs, as compared with the old ones, has been sensibly decreased. In particular instances the organist may, therefore, think best to take advantage of the opportunity afforded by this greater fullness of choir or swell, or by coupling them, to obtain that volume of tone for giving out the theme which Bach could get only on the great-organ. There are occasions on which this way of giving out the theme might be found desirable. Such occasions, however, are probably rare; for it is difficult to imagine any reason that could influence the player to renounce the generous fullness of tone peculiar to the foundation stops of the great-organ, and to announce the theme in a coloration not in accordance with its majestic spirit. Do not forget that Bach's themes elevate all emotions, whether of joy or of grief, into the sublime, and that this must find expression in the timbre wherewith they are presented.

Were it not for dread of laying oneself open to the reproach of being a narrow-minded zealot, one might venture the opinion, that notwithstanding the equalization of manuals on the modern organ, the themes ought, without exception, to be given out on the great-manual.

BRINGING OUT THE THEME

It is a much-debated point, how far the player may go in his endeavor to bring out the theme, so that the hearer may be able to recognize and follow it through the interweaving of the parts. The answer is, in reality, not hard to find: He must not overpass the limit beyond which the development and total impression of the piece itself would suffer.

Organists often sin against this maxim. Some actually sacrifice the fugue to the theme. They rather plume themselves on an interpretation through which a listener of even less than average musical intelligence must always notice the theme, whether he will or no. Amid the cheap applause thus won they do not consider that those among their audience who knew the fugue were writhing in torture, because all that they could hear was the theme with something round about it—not the fugue itself, but scraps of it passing on before them. They had to listen, while parts, which were tranquilly pursuing their course on the great-organ, suddenly bolted to some other manual and hid their diminished heads, only to allow the theme in alto or tenor to stand out in bald relief.

No such mode of procedure was contemplated by Bach. He no more thought of it than did any other musician of the eighteenth century. At that period it was assumed, as a matter of course, that the majority of an audience were possessed of those elements of musical intelligence which would enable them to follow *obbligato* parts. It was not thought necessary to proffer them aids; it was expected that the logic of the musical construction would guide the hearer to keep track of the theme. Whoever was incapable of doing so, was left to his fate, and had to shift for himself as best he might. We should not neglect to observe that on the old organs, with their transparent tone, the several parts stood out more distinctly than on most modern instruments. Any one who has played Bach fugues on a Silbermann organ, or heard them so played, has been surprised at the way in which alto and tenor came out, and how plainly the theme could be followed through them. Only on such organs can one realize how it was that Bach and his contemporaries could disregard each and every special device for bringing out the theme, and could let the polyphony make its impression as a whole.

We must return, in principle, to the same viewpoint. Let Art take precedence of a mistaken indulgence toward the weaker brethren; let us again strive, by our playing, to educate our hearers to an understanding of polyphony, and encourage organ-builders once more to construct instruments on which Bach's preludes and fugues may be brought out as finely and transparently as on those of the eighteenth century.

It must be pronounced inadmissible to treat the first development of a fugue, in which the parts enter one after the other, as if the other contrapuntal parts were a mere accompaniment to the theme, and perform them on a weaker manual. A person who cannot follow the theme through its repetitions with each of the newly entering parts, will hardly be helped to a better understanding of the art-work by having said theme persistently underscored. Therefore, keep

on steadily with all the parts on the great-manual. An exception may possibly be made in the case of a few fugues whose commencement is not worked out in the strict style. But even in these the organist will learn, through experience, that truth lies, after all, in simplicity.

Similarly, in the principal sections in the course and at the close of the piece, the parts should proceed, as a rule, side by side on the same level. Attempts to bring out the part carrying the theme on any particular manual will generally fail, for the simple reason that it is impossible to play all the other parts correctly with one hand. In a few cases, where there is a conjuncture of favorable conditions, one may try to obtain an effect by letting the entering theme stand out boldly. This may be taken into consideration in case a passage, which has already been heard on the great-manual, is repeated on choir and swell coupled together, so as to leave the great-manual free for an approaching emphatic giving-out of the theme. But when the other parts are already in play on the great-manual, they must not be forcibly transferred to some other manual unless following the inner musical logic of the piece—not merely to make the theme more prominent. Such a procedure is to be condemned without exception.

With respect to the episodes played on the subsidiary manuals, the matter is different. True, even here Bach took no trouble to bring out the theme. But, as the episodes contain fewer parts progressing simultaneously, and variety is permissible, it will be easier to arrange to give the theme a manual by itself— but, of course, only when good taste, and the technical execution of the parts, permit.

One will sometimes overcome difficulties arising from the part-progression by coupling the pedal to one of the manuals, after retiring the pedal stops, and then employing it for playing the lowest of the manual-parts; this leaving one hand free to bring out the theme on some particular manual. By such innocent devices one may obtain wonderful effects. In any event, however, they afford the organist great satisfaction at his own cleverness, and let him fancy that old Bach is looking over his shoulder with a smile of approbation.

DYNAMIC DEVELOPMENT OF THE FUGUE

Is it true that every fugue ought to pursue its evolution in a grand *crescendo?* It is certain that most of them inwardly bear the idea of a victorious thematic climax, and that, to us moderns, a successive increasing of the tone-power appears appropriate. But this may easily give rise to exhibitions of bad taste, or exaggerations.

It is a mistake to begin the fugue, in order to work up a more effective *crescendo*, with a thin *piano* instead of a wholesome *forte*, and so to lead the hearer far on through a desert twilight of tone, that the later fullness of brilliancy may have a more overwhelming effect.

Neither is it fitting to bring out a sudden swell to "full organ" in the last few measures or—still worse—on the very closing chord. As a rule, the tone-level in which the fugue ends should be already reached with the final decisive entrance of the theme in the pedal. The hearer should be in the position of a wayfarer on a mountain-path, who, arrived at the height, yet sees before him a level stretch wherefrom, as he goes onward, he can look down on hill and valley. Thus should he, who is following a fugue, be able to rejoice in the breadth of tone whereto it has attained, and be sustained a while on this height. Whatever intensification, toward the close, may reside in the music, can no longer be expressed by any *crescendo;* now all effect must come solely from the conception itself and its immanent musical logic. One who does not inwardly feel the final climax, even though not one additional register be drawn, will not grasp it if it be coarsely worked up by increasing loudness of tone.

During the dynamic development in the course of the piece, take care that the natural construction of the work does not suffer. In both fugue and prelude the principal sections and the episodes should be clearly contrasted. We proceed in these as in an orchestral concerto, in which the "*tutti*" and the "*concertino*" alternate. The effectiveness of the *forte* is continually renewed by the intervening *piano* passages.

Hence, a continuous *crescendo* can in no case be applicable. If the distinction between principal section and episode be obliterated, the fugue will be destroyed. The more distinctly the interruption of the *forte* and its resumption are brought home to the hearer, the more clearly will the fugue, as Bach conceived it, stand out before him. It will not do, for the sake of continuity in the *crescendo*, to range an episode in the same line with a principal section; for then the beautifully rounded outlines of the fugal framework would be spoiled.

The dynamic development can, therefore, be accomplished only by bringing out more and more strongly the successive principal *tutti* passages in contrast with the episodes on the subsidiary manuals; either by immediately increasing the tone-power of each successive section, or by the gradual reinforcement of a *crescendo* throughout its course.

As the fugue ought to begin on the great-manual with at least a combination of 8- and 4-foot foundation stops, a reinforcement of tone is obtainable only by the addition of mixtures and reeds in the course of the following principal sections. Thus the *crescendo* progresses from a *forte* to "full organ." In certain fugues the mixtures, or even reeds, will be drawn with the foundation stops at the beginning, and thus participate in the original *forte*, so that the *crescendo*-line becomes still shorter.

In its externals, therefore, the working-up of a *crescendo*-effect has its limitations. It would seem as if we were trying to do much more in this line than Bach intended. Probably he himself did not strive overmuch to increase this effect by drawing more stops, but let his *forte* registration at the beginning

of the piece stand till the end with no considerable changes, relying upon the intrinsic development of the thematic material to make the impression, upon the hearer, of an intensification in the effect. And when we follow this plan, the effect produced by this simplicity is astounding.

LIMITATIONS IN DYNAMIC SHADING

Bear in mind, in general, that it is not necessary to bring out every *crescendo* and every *decrescendo* found in the music by increasing or diminishing the tone. This would produce merely an unrestful changeableness, wearying the listener and effacing the outlines of the piece. The same thing occurs when the dynamic shifts are exaggerated by changes of registration.

The dynamics of Bach's organ works are only partially calculated for external realization. Much is to be apprehended only mentally. The attempt to throw everything into relief by changes of registration, or by using the swell-pedal, does more harm than good. When the hearer does not receive the impression of a certain stability in the tone-power and timbre belonging to a definitely bounded section, he cannot thoroughly understand and enjoy either prelude or fugue.

Hold fast to the rule, therefore, that in the dynamics of Bach's organ works large things and small are not to be set on a common level. There are *crescendi* and *diminuendi* which may be brought out far better by means of a delicate shading of the tempo, than by registration or the use of the swell-pedal. In this regard the player's artistry may act, during the closing intensification, in a directly suggestive fashion on the hearer's sensibility to tonal effects.

PRINCIPAL SECTION AND EPISODE

It is usually not difficult to distinguish between the principal sections and the episodes. Wherever the pedal coöperates, one has to do, as a rule, with a principal section; when it ceases for a considerable time, and when, besides, there are fewer parts in action, we have an episode. This is equally true of both preludes and fugues.

Difficulties appear when comparatively short passages for manual alone occur between similar passages with pedal; is the principal section interrupted here, or not?—should we go over to a subsidiary manual, or in any other way lessen the tone-power?—or is the passage for manual alone to be conceived as a *crescendo* leading up to the coming pedal-passage, and played accordingly?

The question cannot always be decided. Sometimes one answer seems as reasonable as another. The shortness of the manual-passage does not invariably prove that it is not to be played as an episode on a subsidiary manual.

Besides the thematic structure, the technical plan of the piece often throws light on the matter. When the transition to a subsidiary manual, and the subsequent return to the great-manual, can be naturally and readily accomplished, it is not at all improbable that we have to do with an episode. But where the change of manual can be made only with difficulty, and entails a tearing asunder of the parts, it may be assumed that Bach did not intend a change of manual at that point, but remained on the same manual.

In the works of the master-period, such equivocal passages are rather seldom met with, the structure of these works being clearly and sharply defined. Their principal and secondary sections are as plainly contrasted as in the Brandenburg Concertos. The works of his youthful and transitional periods, however, are less strict in form, so that one does not always feel quite sure how Bach intended them to be performed.

The number of episodes varies in the different fugues. Some show only a single contrasting section; the first development is followed by an intermezzo, and this latter leads into a *tutti* with which the fugue closes. Others contain two episodes, which are separated by a principal section, so that there are three *tutti* periods to take account of. In others (for instance, the great fugue in *E* minor) we find several episodes.

In passages where pedal is employed, Bach kept his hands on the great-manual throughout. It was hardly possible for him to use the pedal together with the subsidiary manuals for the preludes and fugues, because their combined foundation registers did not blend perfectly with those of the bass, as regards either power or timbre. A change in the pedal registration, and a weakening of the tone, was not to be thought of, for the pedal carried the theme. It was a different matter with the trios and *Choralvorspiele*, because in them the pedal-tone was accommodated to that of the subsidiary manuals from the start.

Nevertheless, various cases can be enumerated in which Bach probably employed the pedal with a subsidiary manual, though sometimes only transiently. They may be recognized by the fact, that their bass carries no strictly defined part. It marks a fundamental bass tone, and then immediately releases it; or it accompanies the manual-parts through a few eighth-notes or sixteenths.

Cases are quite frequent in which the pedal is used throughout, while the hands are occupied alternately on the great-manual and choir-manual. The Prelude (Toccata) in *D* minor, for which we possess Bach's directions for the employment of the manuals, affords a most interesting example of this sort, by means of which we can identify passages to be similarly performed in other works.

But in all cases where the pedal carries through a continuous part, especially when the theme appears in its course, it is intended to be played together with the great-manual.

It goes without saying that we, on our organs, may sometimes employ the coupled subsidiary manuals where Bach, on account of the pedal, had to go over to the great-manual. But we shall make no excessive use of even this liberty; because the round fullness of tone required for the genuine *tutti* passages is usually obtainable only on the great-manual.

In numerous preludes the pedal goes along wellnigh uninterruptedly from beginning to end. This signifies, that Bach played them on the great-manual throughout, and it will be best for us to follow his example. Just these pieces are made to suffer direfully through modern refinement, with its *crescendi* and *decrescendi* and changes of manual anywhere and everywhere, as if it were quite unimaginable that a piece should be played through in one unchanging timbre and tone-power. A recognition of this truth would mean positive salvation for many of Bach's finest creations.

With others, which, on account of the pedal, are likewise to be played altogether on the great-manual, some variety may advantageously be sought by adding or retiring mixtures and reeds.

CHANGES OF MANUAL

His method of changing the manuals is a touchstone for the insight and taste of the organist. After the place where the change is to be made from great to choir (or swell) is chosen, and also the place of return, the question arises, What will be the best way to transfer the several parts from one manual to another? In the works of the master-period, the way in which Bach intended this to be carried out is generally clearly exposed by the thematic structure. Either we find a sort of cæsura, which makes it possible to lift both hands together for the change of manual, or the parts leave off in such a manner that the player can first shift one or two of them to the new manual, the others following.

In other passages—and these are found more particularly in the works of the earlier periods—the matter is decidedly complicated. Comparison, consideration, and experimentation, often discover a wholly unexpected expedient. But sometimes no satisfactory solution can be found, and one is obliged to get over the difficulty as best one may, with the sole consolation that the Master himself was to blame. He did not think to lead and coördinate the parts in such a way as to form natural "lifting-places" for the hands; and thus put himself and all his successors in the position of having to tear apart things which belong together.

When we meet with these difficulties in a work that otherwise bears the stamp of maturity, let us regard them as an invitation to reconsider the opinion that a change of manual is demanded at the place in question. It will not infrequently prove to be mistaken. The player will decide not to make the change here, but at some preceding or following place where conditions are more favorable.

MANNER OF CHANGING MANUALS

Every organist knows by experience, that whatever is undertaken in the lower part of the keyboard passes off much less conspicuously than it would if occurring in soprano or alto. One may go over, with the left hand, from choir or swell to the heavily registrated great-organ, without making any very special impression on the listener. Conversely, one may leave the left hand on the great-manual, and go over to the choir with the right, without the change being so marked as one would naturally expect. The sustained tone-color of the lower parts covers the change going on in the higher registers. The experienced organist will be able to cope with many difficulties with the aid of this "covered" change.

Frequently, when a period closes on sustained chords, with which (in one part or another) the figures of the new section already enter, the chord-formation appears to forbid these entering parts from starting immediately on another manual, as would naturally be done otherwise. In such a case one is not obliged to sustain the chord during its entire printed time-value, but may allow it to sound long enough to satisfy the requirements of musical logic, and then begin the new figure in freedom on the other manual.

On the other hand, one or two held-over notes provide an excellent spring-board for vaulting from one manual to another. Take them on both manuals together, and let go of those on the first manual on an accented beat of the measure. The effect is often positively surprising.

Obvious considerations require, in passing from the great-manual to another, and more particularly when some lower part enters on the latter, that the player should somewhat retard the tempo just after the change, considerably prolonging the first note or notes. Just as the eye, at a change from a strong to a weak light, needs a certain time to adjust its vision, the ear must accommodate itself to the reduction in tone-power, before it can hear. Should we simply play along *in tempo*, it will lose the beginning of the new figure; whereas it will not feel a tastefully executed prolongation as a delay, but only receive a grateful impression of ability to grasp, at its inception, the part thus softly played.

In fact, this differentiation in the tempo on changing manuals plays an important part throughout. Without it, even the most carefully executed transition has a harsh and unpleasing effect. In this field the player finds opportunity to display great nicety of calculation and a fine appreciation of rhythmic flexibility. The hearer must not become conscious of the player's manipulation of the tempo. He should merely obtain the impression that the transitions from one timbre to another are effected quietly and smoothly, without any disturbance whatever of the rhythm.

Beginners, and organists who observe carelessly, usually commit the blunder of slowing down the tempo at the moment when the change of manual takes place. By so doing they attract the hearer's attention to what they are about,

and attain the precise opposite of that which they proposed. The *rallentando* must come earlier, and lead into a tempo in which the change of manual can be executed without a hitch. The organist should follow the example of the engine-driver, who does not put on the brakes when he reaches the curve, but when he sights it.

It is frequently puzzling to decide when one ought to return to the great-manual from one of the others. In general the rule holds good, that when the pedal enters both hands should already be on the great. But sometimes the passage appears to demand that the transition should occur together with the entrance of the pedal; in other cases the hands must even remain on the subsidiary manual after the pedal-part comes in, not going over to the great-manual (together or separately) till later in the measure where the pedal entered, or even after it.

No rule can be given for deciding the cases as they occur. The organist must make up his mind what is best to do in each given case, not forgetting that the manner in which the hands are transferred to the great-manual has an important bearing on the effect of the entering pedal-part. This latter often sounds best when the hands have been on the great-manual for some time before; in other cases the effect is better when the change of manual is made either just before the pedal-entrance, or simultaneously with it, or after it. All one can do is to experiment, consider, and compare.

But always bear in mind that a part must not go from a subsidiary manual to the great at a point which is thematically insignificant. This is precisely as inartistic as if an orator were suddenly to raise his voice at an unimportant point in a sentence. In his earlier works Bach not seldom puts his interpreter in a position where he has to act in opposition to his better judgment in this matter: this is hardly ever the case in the later preludes and fugues. Where it appears that a return to the great-manual, near the entrance of the pedal-part, is practicable only by doing violence to the self-evident rule, try it somewhat earlier or later. Your trouble will rarely go unrewarded. Oftentimes the best place for a change of manual will be considerably previous to the entrance of the pedal. Do not let this disconcert you. If such a transfer can be made naturally and smoothly, with proper regard for the musical logic and the part-leading, it was surely intended by Bach that the return to the great-manual should be effected thus early.

The relative positions of the manual keyboards must, of course, be such as to facilitate the change of manuals to the utmost. For this reason Bach insisted on having the successive keyboards as near together as practicable. Besides, he demanded keys which were shorter than ours. On many modern organs the height from one keyboard to the next is so great, that the simplest change entails difficulties. The standard keyboard adopted in the Regulations for Organ-building is a compromise between Bach's requirements and the ulterior advantages of our larger modern keyboard. Did we not have to take into consideration the keyboard measurements of the modern grand pianoforte, we should hark back to the old narrow gauge of the organ keyboard, because it naturally admits of the easiest connection. From Bach's style of notation we can perceive that he assumed the player to be capable of stretching a ninth or a tenth without risk. With our modern measurements this is not so readily accomplished as on the old keyboards. Possibly a mistake is made in requiring that the organ keyboard shall not differ too noticeably from that of the modern piano. Those who have occasion to play on old organs will observe how readily the fingers accustom themselves to the narrower keys, without becoming unfitted for the piano.

TRANSITIONS AND CONTRASTS

On the old organs the different degrees of tone-power are thrown into sudden contrast by changes of manual. Modern instruments allow more delicate transitions. We are enabled to pass from the principal section to the episodes through a finely graduated *diminuendo*, and back again through a similarly graded *crescendo* into the new *tutti*. We are in a position to define the lines given in the composition with greater precision than the Master could. Our aids to registration permit us to transform the great-organ into a subsidiary organ, by retiring stops, so that it becomes an intermediary between the *tutti* and the choir (or swell). And we can often remain on the great-manual, when thus toned down, for some time, where Bach would have had to pass to another manual. Conversely, we can return to the great-manual sooner than he could, and increase to the tone-color later required for the principal section by bringing on new registers. On three-manual organs, by passing from choir to swell and then slowly closing the swell-box, we can obtain a long drawn out *diminuendo;* and increase gradually, by reversing the operation, up to the change to the great-manual.

The modern organist will make generous use of this possibility of shading the transitions from principal section to episode, and vice versa; and, in so doing, will act in entire accord with Bach's intentions. Still, he should remember that this procedure is not appropriate in each and every case. The artistic effect very often lies in precisely the simple, direct juxtaposition of the two tone-colors, so that any refinement of the transition destroys the effect. There are cases in which the relieving of the tone-power of the episode by that of the principal section should be accomplished with a certain suddenness, surprising and carrying away the hearer, in order to achieve the effect proposed by Bach. Contrariwise, in other preludes and fugues, the Master's thought receives its perfect interpretation through the medium of an almost uninterrupted *crescendo* from episode into principal section. Rules cannot be given for deciding when

one or the other procedure is appropriate; it is a matter for the artistic sensibility. Not infrequently there will be room for disagreement as to the best effect. And so we find ourselves squarely confronting the question, just how far the interpretation of Bach may be modernized. It is probable that those who incline to the side of "too little," rather than "too much," will most nearly approach the truth. Overrefinement in the transitions brings in its train the risk that the hearer may lose track of the clear thematic construction. Furthermore, in the abrupt contrasting of loud with soft and of soft with loud there lies an inexhaustible charm—a charm banished from modern art. And the hearers may claim, as their privilege, that Bach's works should not be divested of this charm.

On going from a modern organ to one of Silbermann's a player feels, at first, only a lack of all the auxiliary devices which appeared indispensable for a delicately graduated interpretation of Bach's works. But in a short time there is a change. One begins to delight in the obligatory simplicity, and is surprised to see how little the refinement of the transitions is missed, and how characteristic, yet natural, withal, are the effects now obtained simply because one has control of but a few gradations of tone-power which cannot be shaded off one into the other. There are works, whose full beauty is manifested only under such conditions.

In any case, even when the most modern of organs is at command, see to it that the hearer is enabled clearly to follow each successive stage in the development of the piece. If Bach is really to be understood, our audiences must regain an appreciation for the formal construction of his works; and it is for the player to expound this form by the manner of his interpretation. A serious attempt in this direction will show him that his audience is both receptive and teachable, and will likewise reveal to him how grateful modern hearers are for grand simplicity in art.

The passages which form the introduction to, or even interrupt the course of, some of the preludes, should usually be played on the great-manual. Those who have chosen another manual have missed the grandiose pathos which these figurations are intended to express.

Let particular attention be given to the echo-effects. It is very easy to make a mistake in the contrasting of the periods involved. Only those in which really analogous sentences occur, are to be performed on different manuals in alternation. The moment the analogy is not quite clear, it is better to keep to the same manual. The search after variety regardless of cost, brings forth no good fruit.—The above applies to the one-part figurations. In the polyphonic sections of the preludes one will often be able to operate with brief contrasted passages of similar effect to an echo, though not in strict echo-style. In this regard the directions given for the Prelude (Toccata) in *D* minor are highly instructive.

ADDING AND RETIRING REGISTERS

Much depends upon the manner in which the stops are drawn and retired. The "covered" bringing-on of mixtures and reeds on the swell-manual with closed swell-box, so that these stops only gradually assert themselves as the box opens, and then relieve the entrance of the mixtures and reeds on choir and great of all abruptness, is a help in many difficult situations. Again, some "lift" provided by the phrasing often affords a chance to draw a stop, or several stops, without producing that slapdash reinforcement of tone so justly dreaded by the organist. But the cases when stops have to be added without interrupting the playing occur oftener than the player could wish. In these the rule applies, that stops should be drawn on a strong beat at the very instant when pressure begins on the key, so that the change of sound enters simultaneously with the new tone on the strong beat. The reason for this rule is obvious: When the reinforcement falls on the strong beat, it acts like an accent, and the contrast is far less violent than it would be were the entrance differently timed.

Conversely, it is usually (though not by any means always) advantageous to retire stops on the less accented beats. The retirement will then be felt, not as a sudden change (which it is, in reality), but more like a *diminuendo* embracing the entire measure. The hearer will hardly be aware when the change of stops takes place, because his attention is not so specially attracted by the weaker beat. This comes from the fact that the Rhythm is not created by the regular succession of periods consisting of equal time-units, but arises out of the will and energy of the player, to which it owes its life, its light and shade, and which force the hearer to accept it in the form set forth by the player.

In four-four time the diminution is very often best effected on the third beat.

If the rhythm of the given section runs athwart the natural measure-rhythm, the registers should be drawn on the syncopated beats, and retired on the others.

It produces an excellent effect when the registers are drawn or retired on tones which are sustained in one or two parts. The reinforcement on the strong beat then makes an agreeable impression, and the sudden diminishment in tone-power on the weak beat will, so to speak, not be noticed.

The above purely formal considerations do not decide as to the place at which the change in registration shall be effected. They are merely auxiliary to those other factors which are derived from the particular circumstances governing each given case. The change in registration must always coincide with a turning-point in the development of the musical thought, such as the entrance of the theme or of some important modulation, and should be "toned down" as far as may be by a clever gradation of the tempo.

Do not continually toss the hearer from one variety of tone or power to another. Instability is never good.

Do not forget, more especially, that registration forms an excellent medium for distinguishing the various keys through which the piece is carried. As long as you remain in one key, do not meddle unnecessarily with the registration—unless weightier reasons determine a different course. Should the key change, the transition may be made noticeable by a shift in the tone-color, even where the logic of the musical construction would not otherwise call for it.

Analogous sections in either prelude or fugue should be played with similar registration. This renders it much easier for the hearer to follow the plan of the piece; besides, this is the sole artistic mode of procedure. What would be said of an architect who chose a certain color for a wing, or some intermediate structure, or an ornament, and another color for the part symmetrically balancing it! If this be inartistic, why should a player deliberately set about making it impossible for his hearers to recognize, by means of their timbre and tone-power, those sections of a prelude or fugue which balance each other in the construction of the piece? Is it not a sufficient demand on their conceptive powers, that in music the analogous sections are not viewed together side by side, as in architecture, but must be compared according to their successive appearance by an effort of memory? The various ways in which a player should help his audience in this respect, are of great importance, more especially in the preludes.

HELPS AND HELPERS IN REGISTRATION

Probably no differences of opinion now exist concerning the technical appliances required for carrying out the registration of Bach's works. In the preludes and fugues the player hardly ever has a hand free; consequently, the couplers and combination pedals should be arranged as foot-pedals, or both as foot-pedals and knobs (tablets, pistons) connected one with the other. As it is the drawing or retiring of groups of stops that comes in question, and not an entire transformation of the tone-color, the combination pedals, composition keys, etc., are to be so arranged that drawing certain stops or groups shall not, as a rule, interfere with those already in action. The international Regulations for Organ-building recommend, as most practical, a "free adjustable combination action," permitting the organist to set in advance, on any manual, those stops which he wishes to bring on at a given moment. Each manual, and also the pedal, has its own piston or pedal for bringing on this free combination; and, if desired, another piston or pedal can be added, which brings on the prepared combinations on all the manuals simultaneously.

As it is usually the mixtures and reeds which have to be drawn while playing the preludes and fugues, the combination pedals which control these stops might be made to do, at a pinch. But there seems to be no reason why appliances for preparing registers should not be extended to embrace all the stops. If (according to the international Regulations for Organ-building) another pedal or piston be added, acting so as to retire the former registration when the prepared registration enters (instead of simply adding the latter to the former),—even when brought on by the same pedal or piston, and thus acquiring freedom of combination in the generally accepted sense, we should have a console arrangement which, while extremely simple, would be equally serviceable for Bach and modern organ-music.

It should be noted, that the Regulations recommend that the pedals controlling the couplers should be placed on the left side, and those for the free combinations on the right. This is proposed, not merely for the sake of a convenient uniformity, but also because the combination pedals for the stops are those most often used, and the player has his right foot free far more frequently than his left.

Concerning the availability of the *crescendo*-pedal—which, "on being depressed, gives a gradual *crescendo* from the softest stop to the full organ"—in the interpretation of Bach's preludes and fugues, there is much difference of opinion. The extreme view, which forbids its use altogether, is quite intelligible in consideration of the misuse which has been made of this appliance. As it is, the *crescendo*-pedal is a somewhat inartistic device. It brings on the stops in a prearranged succession, and can never be so governed as to bring out the reinforcing stops on the strong beat. Hence, the ordinary employment of this device flatly contradicts all æsthetic considerations touching the correct way to draw and retire the registers. It can, therefore, be used only when a considerable number of stops are already drawn, so that the entrance of those which the *crescendo*-pedal brings on is covered. But any player who uses it except for a final intensification, swelling from *piano* to *fortissimo* and diminishing by the same means, only proves that he is mentally too slothful to think out a proper registration and (as Nietzsche puts it) left his ears in the drawer when he went to the organ.

With delicate registration the player will often find it desirable in certain places not to bring on or retire the stops in groups, but during two or more successive measures to draw them one by one on the strong beats, or to retire them similarly on the weak beats. For this process there are no mechanical aids, nor can any such be invented. Here the most complicated console leaves one in the lurch. So the player will be obliged, willy-nilly, to call upon a "helper." The effects obtained by such refinements are often of exquisite beauty.

Bach himself most assuredly took on helpers when his registration went more into detail than usual. The still preserved registration of the *Choral-fantasie* on "Ein' feste Burg" could not have been carried into effect without a helper. Similarly, for the great Prelude in *D* major, and a number of compositions of the later period, the registers must have been drawn by assistants; for in these works are found episodes played with pedal throughout. In such cases it would seem as if Bach attempted to employ the great-manual like a subsidiary manual. This presupposes that assistants pushed in the stops of the great-manual and pedal, and then drew them again at the instant when the principal section entered. It must not be forgotten that Bach, when he happened to preside at the organ during service, which was probably not seldom the case, could call upon the regular organist, or one of his own sons, or some chorister who knew the instrument, so that he was never at a loss for an assistant. What a pity it is that none of those who so often saw him play, left behind any notes concerning the style of his playing and his handling of the registration!

Experience proves that one can accomplish on an old organ, with the aid of two expert assistants, everything in the way of registration which is required for executing the preludes and fugues. It is probable, however, that the Master oftentimes contented himself with the registration set for each manual at the start. There are pieces whose grandest effect resides in the greatest simplicity. The modern organist will have two registrations ready for a whole series of preludes and fugues. One will be comparatively simple, and so calculated that he can carry it through alone with the aids which his organ affords. The other will be a refinement of the first, and will require for its manipulation the help of an assistant.

In any event, however, be the registration simple or complicated, the player must take care that the flow of the piece shall in no wise suffer on account of any changes he may make in timbre or tone-power. This is a fact which has still to find general recognition. How often is some chord sustained overlong, or the entrance of another delayed, or the tempo of a measure unduly slowed down, only because the player has to adjust his registration just then! Such interruptions are unavoidable on organs whose stop-control is operated by hand only, as the organist must raise his hand from the keys to grasp the stop, and cannot get along without this "artistic" pause. At best he may be able to deceive himself into believing that the delay has been so cleverly calculated and glossed over as to escape his hearers' notice.

Where the stop-control is operated by the feet, the organist has no excuse for interruption of this kind except his own carelessness. Of course, the foot-practice required for properly operating the register-pedals demands great patience. The movements at the points where changes occur must be gone over and over again, until the distance and time are accurately gauged to the hundredth part of a second, and the pedal put down without disturbing the harmonic and rhythmic flow.

These difficulties, too, are such that every serious organist will conquer them by dint of purposeful application. The feeling of freedom which comes over the player who has arrived at the point when the registration of his piece can be managed without assistance and with no impairment of the playing, is a rich reward even for great toil.

We may observe, *sotto voce*, that it is scarcely an unpardonable sin if, in order to free the right foot at the proper moment for managing the register-pedals or the swell-pedal, one more or less "arranges" the pedal-part at that point (in case of necessity), transposing a prolonged note an octave higher or lower for the time being, or introducing other similar facilitations. Even a person to whom the piece is familiar will hardly ever notice such little subterfuges.

It is remarkable that the preludes and fugues are so written—although Bach never thought of managing the registration by the aid of the feet—that no serious difficulties, so to speak, are met with in controlling the stops.

EXTRINSIC AND INTRINSIC

For rightly interpreting Bach's works something else is needed, which is too frequently lost sight of. The impression of grandeur and sublimity must not be impaired by any externalities unpleasing to the eye. It has become the fashion to set up organs in such a way that the player is visible to the audience. This is an æsthetic aberration without parallel. Contrasted with the organ, the form of man is far too insignificant. And though the organist play never so quietly, he nevertheless moves to and fro before the hearers' vision, in sorry contrast with the majesty of the music. Anything more unedifying can scarcely be imagined than to "see" a Bach fugue played.

Why should an undisturbed enjoyment of the grand old Master's music be reserved for the blind alone? In olden times the organist was always hidden behind the *Rückpositiv*. And in the modern organ, too, some arrangement should be made for keeping him invisible.

This question has not merely a material, but also a symbolical, importance. The fact that he is to remain in concealment should remind the organist that through the organ the spirit of Bach speaks to the assembly, and that his own part is too seek retirement and complete absorption in his work. The vanity of the virtuoso, the thrusting forward of one's self, the striving to exhibit one's own "conception" and to be somebody alongside of Bach, must fall from him like a garment outworn. Not until he is humbled before himself and his artistic ego has been chastened, will he be capable of comprehending that grandeur which he, as a mediator between Bach and the folk of our times, is permitted to make manifest.

The preludes and fugues of the Master of St. Thomas's reveal the realm of the Sublime. This signifies, that he who presides at the instrument must approach his task with a sanctified emotion, with something of a prophet's humility and consecration of spirit. If he has not penetrated to this arcanum, though his performance have the polish of perfection, that which lies in and beyond the tones will not be kindled to life. To himself, and to the others, his playing of Bach will be only a deception.

As to all things that spring from the Truth, the words of Scripture apply to the preludes and fugues of the Master: "The spirit giveth life."

ALBERT SCHWEITZER.

Suggestions for Performing the Preludes and Fugues of the Youthful Period

Preliminary Observations

The remarks on the interpretation of the several preludes and fugues will be strictly limited to a statement of formulas.

The directions are calculated, in most cases, for a two-manual organ. For the preludes and fugues Bach generally employed only his great-manual and his *Rückpositiv* (choir), his third manual not being sufficiently full-toned to be used on a level with the other two. On the earlier organs an alternation between choir and swell could not well be considered, because the great-manual lay between them. It is certain that all the Master's works can be performed on a well-arranged and finely-voiced two-manual instrument in a correct and wholly appropriate manner.

For a number of preludes and fugues, however, our "suggestions" are intended to be carried out on a three-manual organ. But the directions may be transferred without difficulty to one having only two rows of keys.

In a two-manual organ, Man. II should be in the swell-box; in a three-manual organ, Man. III.

All manuals are supposed to be provided with good foundation stops, compound stops ("mixtures"), and reeds. The swell-organ should be abundantly furnished with stops of all classes. The effect obtained by opening and closing the shutters should be such as to make itself felt when the swell-manual is coupled to the great and the hands are playing on the latter.

In its relation to the instrument as a whole, the swell-organ should impart flexibility and a capacity for modulating the tone-effects.

The Fifth, Twelfth, etc., are reckoned among the foundation stops; Thirds and Sevenths, and their octaves, are to be used with the compound stops.

For the arrangement of the combination or composition pedals, pistons, etc., and of the couplers, the suggestions of the international Regulations for Organ-building have been adopted as drafted by the committee headed by Dr. Albert Schweitzer and Abbé Dr. Xaver Mathias. The couplers and auxiliaries above-mentioned should be workable either by hand or by foot, as occasion serves.

The player is not expected to use the ordinary *crescendo*-pedals, which bring on the stops in a succession fixed beforehand.

The suggestions can be carried out, in general, only with the aid of an assistant for drawing or retiring the stops at the proper place. This is the method adopted by Bach himself when he wished to shade his registration with special care.

Should the player prefer to make the changes in registration himself, with the help of modern appliances, he may simplify our suggestions accordingly by drawing or retiring his stops in groups where the editors propose to bring them on or retire them successively.

The decisive factor is not the arrangements for facilitating registration—for in Bach-playing these may frequently be replaced to advantage by an assistant—but the tone produced. Your instrument must have at command fine, clear-voiced stops, neither too dull nor too blaring. The foundation stops, mixtures, and reeds, when combined, must produce a *forte* through which the polyphony can be clearly traced, and which does not weary the ear.

For such an ideal instrument, which any good organ-builder can construct if allowed the means and the time, the Editors' suggestions are calculated. They afford merely general indications as to place and direction in which an alteration of timbre or a change of manual is to be effected. It remains for the organist to fit these formulas to the instrument on which he has to play.

For instance, when choir and swell are not provided with good mixtures, the effect which the Editors propose to obtain on the ideal organ by drawing or retiring these registers will have to be realized by the use of foundation stops, more especially those of four-foot or two-foot tone, by coupling and uncoupling the manuals, or in some other suitable manner.

When some of the foundation stops are too dull or too harsh in tone, they should not be employed in every case where the Editors suppose all the foundation stops (eight, four and two-foot) to be drawn. On the other hand, you may draw one or another of these stops as a substitute (but only in case of need) for a missing mixture stop.

Unfortunately, a good interpretation of Bach's organ works depends not alone on the artistic quality of the player, but also on that of the instrument. Organists of all nationalities should, therefore, see to it that in cathedrals, village churches and concert-halls only simple, substantial, finely-voiced and full-toned instruments are set up, to the end that coming generations may find it easier to play Bach well than our own, in which far too many organists are condemned, by the defects of organs built according to wrong principles, to an incomplete interpretation of the Master's works.

The better the instrument, the fewer will be the needful readjustments of the Editors' indications.

Respecting the reinforcement and reduction of the pedal by drawing and retiring stops and couplers, the Notes contain hints only in exceptional cases;

it being assumed that the pedal will follow the manuals with a suitable volume of tone [suitable bass!].

Suggestions for the intercoupling and uncoupling of the manuals are also seldom made. In this matter the player will be governed by the special arrangements of his instrument and the relations subsisting between the several manuals with regard to volume and quality of tone.

Of course, directions for using the swell are also given only in passages of special prominence.

The Editors have been particularly careful to indicate, as precisely as possible, the way in which a change of manual is to be effected, wherever it occurs, as a great deal depends upon this.

Wherever a phrasing is proposed, the "ideal" phrasing is intended, which shows the player how the phrase is to be understood and conceived. It will depend on his own artistic sense, the quality of the voicing of his organ and its keyboard facilities, how closely he can approximate the ideal phrasing in the audible interpretation.

The "breathing-mark" (') indicates a noticeable "lift" (break). Inserted between notes which are repeated in the same part, it signifies that they are to be sustained for only half their time-value.

Short slurs included under one long one ⌢⌢⌢ show the units which combine to form a period or figure. They should be set off by brief, hardly perceptible breaks.

Tenuto-dashes under a slur ⌢ – – – call for a sort of free *legato* in which the notes are not smoothly connected, but slightly separated. In reality, such tones will frequently have to be played in an ordinary *legato*, as the organ does not control the more delicate nuances between *tenuto* and *legato*.

Notes marked with the simple *tenuto*-dashes, without a slur, are to be separated. They should be sustained for the greater part of their time-value, the key being allowed to rise just before the next key is depressed, so that an extremely brief break results.

During the progress of their work it has become increasingly evident to the Editors that the Notes have on the whole a tendency toward sketchiness. In many cases they had to content themselves with mere hints, instead of going into details; other points, which should have been reasoned out, had to be stated as simple assertions; and some more or less plausible alternative readings could not be mentioned at all.

Any one who realizes the difficulties encountered in concisely explaining the musical processes involved in the interpretation of preludes and fugues, will be indulgent toward the present attempt—the first ever made in this direction; in forming his opinions he will strive to penetrate the artistic thought of the Editors, and to associate himself with them in spirit as they, during their arduous common labors, were associated and felt themselves at one with each other and

with other known and unknown colleagues, near or far. Such association is always found where men meet in a common striving after perfection, and hear a voice saying: "Put off thy shoes from off thy feet, for the place whereon thou standest is holy ground;" and feel that in being permitted to touch the sacred instrument and set forth the works of Johann Sebastian Bach, a blessing has entered into their lives.

CRITICAL PRELIMINARY OBSERVATIONS TO VOLUME I

All the compositions contained in this volume have been handed down to us only in copies. For Fugue No. 3, in *C* minor, the autograph was still extant toward the middle of the nineteenth century. Griepenkerl used it for the edition of Bach's organ works which he prepared for the firm of Peters in Leipzig. After this, it disappeared. The editors of the great Bachgesellschaft edition had to content themselves with copies.

Most of these compositions probably belong to the period covering Bach's sojourn in Arnstadt (1704-1707) and Mühlhausen (1707-1708). Several of them may possibly be referred to the time when he lived as a student in Lüneburg (1700-1703) or—temporarily—as a violinist in Weimar (1703-1704). Some of these works may have been written even later, during the first years of his organistship at Weimar (1708-1717).

I. Fantasie in C Major. (Page 2-3.)

As the pedal-part continues uninterruptedly throughout, Bach intended that the piece should be played on the great organ without change of manual.

As to registration, opinions may differ. Shall we play it with foundation stops alone, or add the mixtures and reeds?

In any event, the section between measures 21 and 29 will be played more softly than the rest. In case mixtures and a few reeds were drawn at the start, retire them on the second beat of measure 21, and then gradually bring them on from the second beat of measure 29 to the end of measure 34.

II. Prelude and Fugue in C Minor. (Page 4-9.)

PRELUDE

The Prelude is to be played from beginning to end with loud stops—foundation stops and mixtures, at least. For the pedal solo Bach assuredly employed reeds; from measure 20 onward they might well be drawn on the manuals also.

On the third beat in measure 9 retire the reeds in the pedal; and do not draw the pedal couplers in what follows, so that the bass notes may not obscure the middle parts. Begin reinforcing the pedal suitably with measure 20, but not before.

FUGUE

The theme of the Fugue is one of the most admirable that the Master ever conceived. Who can say why it is that this simply and gracefully moulded tone-line should be tinged with such an unfathomable melancholy?

Begin it on the great-manual with foundation stops. In measure 13 transfer both hands to the choir. On the first beat of measure 17 let the right hand go over to the swell, the left following on the second beat.

In the course of the succeeding measures the swell-box closes slowly, so that its movement shall end in the middle of measure 21. Here it again begins to open, and should stand wide open at the middle of measure 24. Now the left hand enters with the theme on the choir-manual, the mixtures of which have meantime been drawn.

Beginning with measure 28, play the theme with the left hand on the great, which has been uncoupled from the others. The tenor should be executed on the pedal, provided that this latter reaches to *F*, after the pedal stops are retired and the choir-to-pedal coupler drawn. From the fourth eighth-note of measure 28 the right hand also plays on the choir, and in the middle of measure 29 takes the *g* which is usually not found in the pedal. From measure 30 on the left hand plays the tenor (of course on the choir), while the right hand executes the alto on the great-manual. In the middle of measure 31 the left hand may likewise go over to the great.

In the meantime one should have drawn the 8-foot and 4-foot stops on the pedal, and strengthened the latter, if need be, by coupling with the manuals. Then the pedal takes up the fragment of the theme in measures 33 to 35.

On the first sixteenth of the third quarter in measure 36, couple the swell (on which the mixtures have been drawn while the box was closed) to the great; open the swell-box in the course of the next two measures; on the third beat of measure 39 couple the choir (its mixtures having been drawn) to the great, and add to the pedal the 16-foot foundation stops.

On the first beat of measure 46 the mixtures of the great-organ also enter.

In order to bring out by added brilliancy of tone the victorious expression to which the theme soars in the figurations at the close of the fugue, the reeds also may be drawn from measure 50 on.

III. Fugue in C Minor. (Page 10-17.)

In this case we have to do with a series of three conjoined fugues. The first extends to measure 37; it is followed by a second, extending to measure 70, whose theme grows out of motives of the first; in the third the first and second themes appear simultaneously. In many respects this work has the appearance of a sketch for the Triple Fugue in *E♭* major.

The three parts must be contrasted by different registration; and the central fugue should be played most softly. The work is most effectively brought out by playing the first fugue on the great-organ with all the 8- and 4-foot foundation stops; the second (assuming the organ to be modern) on choir and swell coupled together, with the 2-foot registers and the mixtures drawn; the third on the great, with the added effect of the choir and swell mixtures, and the further addition, in the development, of the great-organ mixtures and the reeds.

For a registration going deeper into detail, the following scheme might be suggested. With manuals coupled together, begin with the foundation stops and mixtures, and possibly the lighter reeds of choir and swell. From measure 14 to 18 employ foundation stops only. For the passage extending from the end of measure 18 to the middle of measure 23, draw the mixtures and, perhaps, one soft reed on either choir or swell; performing the succeeding passage (to the beginning of measure 29) again with the foundation stops alone. For the *conclusio*, entering with measure 29, bring on the mixtures of all manuals, including the great, and as many reeds as may seem requisite for fullness.

It is probable that Bach, as he used the pedal, also played the second fugue on the great-manual, drawing only foundation stops, possibly excluding the 4-foot registers. The modern organ permits us to employ the choir-organ (with swell coupled), in which case a suitable diminution of the pedal-tone is taken for granted. Individual taste will decide, whether mixtures shall be added. One might, conceivably, draw only foundation stops at first (with swell closed), open the swell from measure 46 to 48, add the mixtures for the second half of measure 52, at the same time going over to the swell-manual, so as to bring out the alto on the choir from the second half of measure 57 onward, also carrying the soprano over to the choir with measure 60. With measure 63 the tenor might enter on the great-manual; from measure 65 onward the alto, yielding to technical necessity, would likewise descend to the same manual; thus closing the fugue, from the entrance of the pedal, with both hands on the great.

When the second fugue has been performed with this intensification, one should commence the third with foundation stops alone, so as to hold the effect of mixtures and reeds in reserve. Points for the stepwise addition of mixtures and reeds might be chosen as follows: Entrance of theme in soprano in measure 76; "lift" between the first and second eighth in measure 82; entrance of theme in alto in measure 88; possibly the "lift" after the first quarter of measure 91. The height of the intensification must have been attained at the entrance of the pedal in measure 96. In the middle of measure 107 un-couple the pedal, leaving only foundation stops drawn. Do not bring on the original volume of tone until the closing measures.

IV. Allabreve in D Major. (Page 18-21.)

This piece is difficult to registrate. As Bach uses the pedal throughout, he certainly played it on the great-manual alone. The conception being majestic, he probably began with mixtures and reeds and continued them to the end.

Were one to attempt, in the passages where the pedal rests, to go over to choir or swell, he would have to reckon with the greatest difficulties both in the change itself and the return to the great-manual (which would have to be effected before the entrance of the pedal); this fact would seem to render more than questionable the advisability of acting contrary to Bach's intentions. The player must also renounce the idea of "bringing out" the theme.

The only thing that one can attempt is, to bring about a gradation in the tone-volume by which the chief episodes of the piece can be contrasted. But such changes will always have a more or less forced effect. They have no logical justification; others might be substituted for them with equal propriety.

Exempli causa, we suggest the following: Begin with the manuals coupled together, both mixtures and reeds being drawn. From measure 63 on, gradually retire the mixtures and reeds of the several manuals, so that with the entrance of the pedal-part in measure 72 only the foundation stops are still out. On the second quarter in measure 90, the swell-box being closed, draw the mixtures and (if you like) the reeds of the swell-organ, and open the box slowly up to the entrance of the pedal. After lifting the chord in measure 113, add the

mixtures and reeds of the choir, at the same time (if you think best) suddenly closing the swell-box, which would enable you to bring on a fresh *crescendo* to the entrance of the pedal-part.

In measure 167 add the mixtures and reeds of the great-organ, and close with the same volume of tone that you began with.

However, in a spacious auditorium having a superior organ which does not jar or rumble, it is advisable to play the work through without any change in the tone-color, as Bach probably played it. Its majestic character will thus be shown forth at its best.

Do not forget that smoothness and flexibility of tempo and clearness in the phrasing are indispensable to the effect of this grandly conceived polyphonic tone-weft.

V. Toccata in Four Divisions, in E Major. (Page 22-33.)

Begin the first division on the great-manual, with foundation stops, mixtures, and even reeds, drawn. On the last beat of measure 18, the last beat of measure 19, the third beat of measure 20, and the first beat of measure 27, the mixtures and reeds may be successively retired either altogether or in great part; adding them again gradually to the foundation stops from measure 35 onward.

Phrased according to rule, the theme of the fugal second division would read thus:

Still, another reading is supposable in which, for the first period of eighth-notes, the down-slurs are omitted, the up-slurs being retained; so that the beginning would appear thus:

Start with the combined foundation stops, to which the mixtures on swell and choir are added. In case the section from measures 19 to 27 be regarded, on account of the fewer number of parts and in spite of the employment of the pedal, as a transitional passage to the episode, go over to the choir-manual with the beginning of measure 19 and play the theme from measure 20 onward on the great, during which the pedal is suitably reduced. On the other hand, the entire section may be played on the great-organ, with its mixtures added. This way has the more sweeping effect.

In either case the organist, from measure 27 onward, will have his left hand on the choir and his right on the swell, in order that in measure 32 (on the sustained note) he can go to the swell with his left hand also.

With the second 16th in beat 3 of measure 36, transfer both hands to the choir; from the fourth eighth-note of measure 40 they will be on the great-organ, which should be augmented from measure 45 on, by reason of the entrance of the theme in the soprano. But it is likewise intelligible when the passage from the middle of measure 44 to measure 56 is played more softly than the preceding, at first with both hands on the choir-manual, bringing out the theme in measure 48 as a solo on the great, and then (say about measure 50, from which point the distribution of the parts on two manuals is no longer practicable) again returning to the great with the left hand.

From measure 56 on the matter again becomes quite simple. The left hand remains on the great; the right goes over to the choir either on the second sixteenth-note or at the end of the measure. If mixtures and reeds were already drawn on the great, retire them imperceptibly where the theme descends. On the last quarter of measure 60 the left hand also goes over to the choir, and stays there till the beginning of measure 67, where it takes up the alto and tenor on the great-manual; the right will follow least noticeably on the last eighth-note of the measure.

There is a temptation to go over to the choir in measure 75 with soprano and alto, so that the theme may stand out more prominently. But this would interrupt the closing intensification. It is better to keep both hands on the great-organ, reinforcing it on the second eighth of measure 75, and again on the second eighth of measure 79, and thus arriving, when the pedal-part strikes in, at the volume of tone in which one wishes to close.

The third division, a short intermezzo, is to be played straight through on the great, with foundation stops and mixtures.

The Fugato which serves as *finale* to the Toccata, proves to be rather formless, and this renders it more than difficult to settle on a logically correct registration. The registration sketched below is, of course, only a mere suggestion, without claim to being a satisfactory solution.

Begin on the great-manual, with choir and swell (on which the mixtures, too, are drawn) coupled. In measure 24 retire the mixtures, lifting the chord soon enough to gain time, and pass to the choir-manual with the left hand. The right follows on the second eighth-note in measure 27. On the second eighth in measure 31 it goes over to the swell, followed in turn by the left hand on the third quarter in measure 32, or on the second eighth in measure 33. The swell-box closes slowly. Meanwhile the pedal has been uncoupled; the 16-foot pedal-stops are retired, so that the pedal-entrance in measure 39 is effected with only the 8-foot stops drawn, possibly brightened by Flute 4' or Octave 4'.

With measure 44 both hands are transferred to the choir, and the 16-foot registers are added to the pedal. On the second eighth in measure 49 the right hand goes over to the great, following the left, which carried the tenor to the same manual on the first beat of the measure. From measure 55 onward the mixtures of choir and swell are brought on; from measure 71 the mixtures of the great-organ, and also the reeds, are introduced, employing, for each successive reinforcement, the phrasing-pauses between the first and second sixteenths of the measure.

VI. Fantasie in G Major. (Page 34-41.)

Begin the Fantasie on the great-organ with a blend of tone in which the mixtures of choir and swell are present from the outset.

More stops may be added on the second eighth-note in measure 9. On the second eighth-note in measure 16 the right hand goes over to the choir; the left hand follows on the second sixteenth of the second count, or not until the second eighth in the next measure.

On the second eighth in measure 23, alto and soprano are transferred to the swell, the left hand following in measure 24; the swell-box closes from measures 28 to 31.

In measure 32 the left hand passes to great, the right to choir. The contrast with the preceding is rather strong, but the effect is good. In measure 34 the tenor will, of course, also be played on the great. On the second eighth before the last in measure 35 the right hand goes over to the great-manual.

In the course of the following measures one might feel tempted to return to the subsidiary manuals once more. But a more careful examination will bring the conviction, that this passage involves a dynamic increase up to the entrance of the pedal-part in measure 46, and affords a good opportunity to add stops, some of which might well be reeds.

Whether one should return to a subsidiary manual at measure 52, appears dubious. If one does it, one cannot go back to the great-organ before measure 64. But this whole section is in such a triumphant vein, that the player will probably execute it on the great.

Should one desire to close with "full organ," it must enter on the third quarter of measure 65.

Execute the Adagio with soft stops. For the Allegro Bach probably employed foundation stops, mixtures and reeds throughout.

VII. Prelude in G Major. (Page 42-45.)

In this piece no structural plan is discoverable whereon an even halfway logical registration might be founded. Consequently, all we can do is to introduce a certain variety in the *forte*. This variety, being of an arbitrary character, cannot be reduced to a formula.

VIII. Fantasie in G Major. (Page 46-55.)

Do not be seduced by the *"Très vitement"* into playing the wonderful passages in the Introduction too fast.

Changes of manual must take into account the natural echo-effects in the music itself. From measures 1 to 18 change with each measure, playing the odd measures on the great-organ, the even measures on choir or swell, and striking the first note of each even measure on both great and subsidiary manual together. Consequently, the left hand will begin the figure on the subsidiary manual, excepting only in measures 2, 6 and 18, in which the first note does not need to be struck on the great-manual too, because the period really comes to an end with the preceding measure. In measure 19 change between the even and odd quarters. From measure 20 onward keep on one manual, there being no further identical passages for contrasting effect.

Up to this point, only the foundation stops and mixtures of the uncoupled manuals have been used. Beginning with measure 21, the low-ranging passages afford opportunity for employing the couplers and adding the reeds (at first on the swell), in order to rise in the last two measures to that majestic fullness of tone with which the *Grave* division should enter.

It is not at all probable that Bach essayed any alterations whatever in the tone-color of this grand five-part chorus. A change of manual is quite impracticable. Still, we may be permitted to employ some shadings of the full tone, such as the modern organ has at command. But mixtures and reeds must participate in the timbre throughout.

Having played as far as measure 48 with the foundation stops, reeds and mixtures of all three manuals, we take advantage of the phrasing-pause afforded, before the third quarter of this measure, by the entrance of the principal motive in soprano to retire the mixtures and reeds of the great organ. Before the second quarter in measure 57, retire the reeds and mixtures of the choir, to which end a good opportunity is found in the "lifts" between the repetitions of the same note in soprano and second alto, aided by the modulation.

From measure 60 on the swell-box closes slowly, after which the reeds and mixtures of the swell tinge the general tone-color but slightly. On the third quarter of measure 71, again draw the reeds and mixtures of the choir, begin opening the swell-box gradually, and during the course of measures 85 to 90 also add successively the reeds and mixtures of the great-organ, retiring these latter together after lifting the first chord in measure 90.

Being now in *A* minor, as in measure 48, we play with like registration, which has the further advantage of giving due prominence to the majestic pedal-part.

On the first beat of measure 96, likewise retire the reeds and mixtures of the choir. The swell-box closes slowly from measures 97 to 103, and remains closed up to measure 114. On the third quarter of this measure, again draw the mixtures and reeds of the choir. During the following measures, open the swell-box; on the third quarter of measure 120 draw the great-organ mixtures, and on the third quarter of measure 135 and the same of measure 138 add the reeds, thus arriving at the volume of tone with which we started.

The division marked "*Lentement*" is played on the great with foundation stops alone. From the middle onward, where the pedal sustains *D*, add very gradually the mixtures and then the reeds, in order to close with full organ.

There are organists who hold to the opinion that the "*Grave*" should be played with foundation stops only. But, with this registration, the majesty of the imposing chorus is hardly brought out to the full.

The beautiful part-leading of this piece might tend to raise a doubt as to whether it is really one of Bach's youthful works. On the other hand, the design and construction of the composition, like those of the Allabreve in *D* major (No. IV), seem somewhat unfinished. That clarity of thematic design, in which (from a certain point onward) Bach's later works so peculiarly excel, is wanting.

IX.   Fugue in G Major.   (Page 56-61.)

This admirable youthful work, which, despite awkwardness in the modulation, is a perennial delight to the modern ear by reason of its fresh and sweeping inspiration, is based on a distinct plan. It embraces three grand *tutti* passages (measures 1 to 40, 45 to 59, 68 to 95), between which are inserted two episodes (measures 41 to 44, 60 to 68), these latter to be played on choir and swell.

Begin with the foundation stops of all three manuals coupled together, to which it will be found advantageous to add the mixtures of the swell from the outset. Whether it is best to go over to the choir-manual from the second half of measure 14 to the first half of measure 17, cannot be decided. One fact militates against it; the pedal-part has not yet entered, and the measures in question appear like an intensification leading up to its entrance. During these measures reinforcing registers may be drawn, and should be brought on in the phrasing-pauses between the third and fourth eighths in measures 14, 15, 16 and 17.

For a further augmentation the entrance of the theme in soprano at the end of measure 24 is well suited. Here it might be a good plan to transfer the left hand to the choir-manual, so that the theme may stand out boldly.

At the entrance of the pedal in measure 28, the left hand will naturally return to the great. At the repetition of the theme in soprano at the close of measure 32, it is permissible to add any suitable stop. It is evident that measures 35 to 37 are not to be played on a subsidiary manual, for it would be impossible to return gracefully to the great-manual at the end of measure 37.

On the last eighth but one in measure 40 lift all the parts together, and come in on the swell-manual with the fourth quarter (foundation stops and mixtures drawn), returning on the last eighth of measure 44 to the great, whose combination has remained standing. Increase in such a way that when the theme enters at the close of measure 53 you will have arrived at full organ, or nearly so.

On the last eighth but one in measure 59 all the parts are again lifted together, and come in with the fourth quarter on the choir, retaining its mixtures, while meantime the reeds and mixtures of the great-organ are to be retired.

With the second sixteenth in measure 66, return to the great, whose mixtures and reeds are gradually added from measure 74 onward, so that for the return of the theme at the end of measure 78 we arrive at the combination with which we propose to finish the piece.

Some players go over to the choir for measures 79 and 80. This would seem to be hardly advisable, for then the (in its way) grandiose final intensification, beginning with measure 74, would be interrupted.

X.   Fugue in G Major.   (Page 62-67.)

This fugue was not written for organ, but for the double-keyboard Pedal-Cembalo, an instrument then in great vogue; *f* signifies "first keyboard," *p* signifies "second keyboard." These directions should likewise be observed when performing the piece on the organ.

It is best to play it for the most part with foundation stops and mixtures. For the augmentation from measure 57 onward, reeds might also be drawn. But be careful throughout to keep the tone light and clear, otherwise this Fugue for Cembalo may have a decidedly unwieldy effect on the organ.

XI.   Prelude and Fugue in G Major.   (Page 68-75.)

PRELUDE

The stately character of the Prelude requires that it should be played through with foundation stops and mixtures, to which the reeds may also be added. Should variety be desired, we would propose that, after lifting the chord in measure 31, the reeds and mixtures be retired, and the following measures played in the timbre of the foundation stops. From measure 37 onward, gradually bring on the mixtures and reeds again; then retire them after lifting the chord in measure 40, employ foundation stops alone till measure 46, and from that point increase until the close. Where pedal tones are sustained, throw off the pedal couplers, otherwise the middle parts will not "come out."

The short *Grave* is played with full organ.

FUGUE

Players who consider the direction *"Alla breve e staccato"* in the Fugue authentic and binding, will follow it, and play the piece without *legato* from beginning to end. It is likely that they will not be overpleased with the result, and may hearken unto reason, which counsels them to "bind" and "lift" in this fugue as in all the rest, and to leave the correctness of the aforesaid direction undecided. Remember, that it is no autograph which we possess, but a copy. It is not improbable that the *"e staccato"* was not Bach's idea, but a notion of the copyist's.

On beginning, the foundation stops and mixtures (including those of the great organ) are drawn. The first section (up to measure 39) sounds best when the registration remains undisturbed, allowing the fanciful logic of the music to speak for itself.

On the second eighth-note in measure 39 carry both hands over to the choir, not retiring its mixtures. In measure 46 the tenor remains on the choir, while the alto goes over to the swell, whose mixtures are also retained. In measure 53 the left hand joins the right on the swell. The swell-box closes slowly up to measure 56, the tempo being, at the same time, imperceptibly retarded.

In measure 56 the theme enters on the choir-organ; the left hand remains on the swell until, in measure 60, it follows the right. The swell-box opens.

The return to the great-manual is a matter of some difficulty. Shall it not be ventured until the second quarter of measure 66?—this appears most natural and has the least ill effect. Or will it be better to go over to the great with the tenor already in measure 61, letting the other two parts follow in measure 64? A satisfactory answer is not readily found.

In any event, from measure 66 onward we shall play on the great, with the foundation stops and mixtures of all the manuals.

After the first chord in measure 71, retire the mixtures of great and choir, and even those of the swell, and play the succeeding measures on the great with foundation stops. In measure 83 the right hand goes over to the choir, the left remaining on the great; in measure 89 the right hand goes to the swell, the left to the choir. Say from the second eighth-note in measure 90, both hands will be on the swell. The swell-box closes gradually to measure 100, so that the theme seems to vanish in the distance.

With measure 100, the theme enters in the right hand on the choir. From measure 104 the alto also will be performed on the choir, to which the left hand should probably not go over till measure 106.

It is advisable to transfer both hands to the great-manual as early as the second eighth-note in measure 110, then augmenting up to the entrance of the pedal by adding the mixtures of swell and choir and opening the swell-box. In what follows, bring on the mixtures of the great, and also the reeds, so that

with measure 136 you have arrived at the tone-volume in which the piece is to close.

As the two episodes for the subsidiary manuals are rather long, they may be more richly invested by playing them on the great, softened down to the semblance of a subsidiary manual. But, with a three-manual organ, there is no necessity for doing this.

On a two-manual organ the player will perform what we have apportioned to the choir on the reduced great-organ.

XII. Prelude and Fugue in G Minor. (Page 76-85.)

PRELUDE

Begin the Prelude on the great-organ with foundation stops, mixtures and reeds. For the runs from measure 14 on, retire the reeds.

From measures 19 to 30 alternate by playing, in each measure, the odd beats loud and the even beats softly. It has a fine effect to carry out a gradual *diminuendo* at the same time, alternating at first between great and choir, and then between choir and swell. While doing so, throw off successively the mixtures and 2-foot registers of great and choir, but retain those of the swell, so that the closing of the swell-box (which should begin about measure 27) shall have due effect, and the tone retain its clarity. Measure 31 is played wholly on the swell.

With measure 32 the left hand goes to the great-manual, the right to the choir; the swell-box begins to open; the mixtures of the choir are brought on; on the second thirty-second-note in the third beat of measure 33 the right hand goes over to the great-organ, whose mixtures will then be drawn successively. From measure 37 onward, reeds may also be brought on.

See to it that the phrasing of this magnificent piece is absolutely precise.

FUGUE

The Fugue starts on the great, with foundation stops. On the last beat of measure 19 you may draw the mixtures of the swell; on the second beat of measure 22 (just after raising the first sixteenth-note) the mixtures of the choir may enter.

From measure 25 on one ought, properly, to go directly over to the choir; however, as the episode is long, remain for the time being on the great, meanwhile retiring the mixtures of the choir on the first note in measure 25. Retire the swell mixtures on the first beat of measure 28, where it loses its accent by reason of the suspension. After the second beat of measure 30, transfer the right hand to the choir. With the last quarter of measure 32 the left hand, which till then was on the great, goes directly to the swell, so that the theme is played on the choir as a solo. After the second beat of measure 37, the right hand also goes to the swell. The swell-box, which before this began to close slowly, finishes this movement during the next two measures. Thus a *diminuendo* covering thirteen measures is brought to its conclusion.

In measure 39 the left hand goes to the choir, and plays on this manual the theme and the first sixteenth-note of each beat; the other sixteenths are taken by the right hand, likewise the middle part in the following measures; this part ought really to be performed entirely on the swell, but has to be divided between the hands on account of technical difficulties. Such a procedure is incorrect; but the theme stands out well, and the hearer will hardly note the distribution of the middle part as a disturbing element.

With the second sixteenth-note in measure 43 the right hand may go over to the choir. This change is not a particularly happy one at this point.

The return to the great-manual can be carried out in the following manner: The left hand goes over to the great on the second beat of measure 44, and plays two parts upon it from measure 46 onward, while the right hand effects the change on the third beat of measure 47. Or, let both hands remain on the choir till measure 47, and then make the change on the second sixteenth-note of the second beat of that measure.

During the phrasing-pause between the first and second sixteenths of the third beat of measure 52, introduce the mixtures and reeds of the swell (box closed), and then open the swell-box slowly in the course of the next two measures; add the choir mixtures on the first beat of measure 55, at the instant when alto, tenor and bass are lifted and the first tone of the theme sounds alone; and draw the mixtures of the great-organ on the second sixteenth-note of measure 60.

During the ascending runs in measure 64, opportunity will be found to bring on the reeds.

The player who transfers to the choir for measures 56 to 64 will be in evil case, as this section is evidently conceived, not as an episode, but as an intensification leading into the final entrance of the pedal.

XIII. Fantasie and Fugue in A Minor. (Page 86-97.)

FANTASIE

The Fantasie begins on the great-organ with foundation stops 8', 4' and 2'. Look out that the sustained pedal does not cover the other parts. It will make itself heard, even if kept rather weak.

The Introduction of the Fantasie consists of several sections built up one over the other. With each successive section the registration increases in fullness. Between the first and second thirty-second-notes of the third beat of measure 4, draw the swell mixtures; draw those of the choir at the corresponding point in measure 7, and those of the great at the same point in measure 9. On the second beat of measure 11, draw the reeds of the swell (box closed); then open the swell-box during the *rallentando* on the two following chords, and add, on the first eighth-note of the Presto, the reeds of choir and great, unless you prefer to draw them before on the chords of the preceding measures.

The one-part run in the Presto is conceived in a resonant, vibrating timbre, which may be obtained by throwing off the greater part of the foundation stops on the first eighth-note of the first measure and continuing with reeds and mixtures and a few foundation stops.

From the middle of measure 24 commence gradually drawing the foundation stops again. This shading of the tone-color has a very fine effect. The pedal is sustained softly; it might not be a bad idea to draw only the 8-foot foundation stops at first, adding the 16-foot registers in measure 48.

In measures 28 and 29, 31 and 32, 34 and 35, 37 and 38, 40 and 41, the first half should be played on the great-manual and the second half on the choir; the intermediate measures being, of course, played on the great.—But one might also take alternate measures, performing measures 28, 31, 34, 37 and 40 on the great, and measures 29, 32, 35, 38 and 41 on the choir.

The effect is not at all bad if the two-measure groups are successively played softer and softer, the last being executed with foundation stops only. If you prefer to play them all equally loud, it will be best to retire the reeds.

In case foundation stops alone are sounding in measure 41, during measures 42 to 48 continually add stops up to full organ. In measures 42 and 43 Bach probably did not intend any further echo-effects, although identical motives appear on similar counts.

At the moment when the closing chord of the Fantasie, upon which the fugue-theme enters, is lifted, throw off the reeds of all the manuals, and the mixtures of great and choir. The first note of the fugue, which is held down as the chord is lifted, should be sustained for an instant in the new tone-color.

It is just as difficult to execute this manœuvre cleanly and precisely, as in the similar case in the celebrated Passacaglia in *C* minor, where the fugue likewise enters on the closing chord. As a general thing Bach does not weld prelude and fugue together in this manner; furthermore, it is unlogical, because the prelude closes with a volume and color of tone decidedly different from that in which the fugue begins. But on the cembalo no objection could be made to this procedure, which, on the organ, is bound up with so many difficulties.

Now, both the Passacaglia and the present Fantasie were, in reality, originally intended for the cembalo with pedal. This is clearly indicated by the sparing employment of the pedal in the Fantasie, as well as in the fugue in *A* minor. The style of the two pieces likewise points irresistibly to the same conclusion. Where can an organ-fugue be found that is so loosely constructed as this one?

Thus the welding of prelude and fugue is explained. This solution gives us freedom. For performance on the organ, we are not obliged to begin the fugue on the last measure of the prelude. Draw your own conclusion from the difference in the instruments; close the prelude, make a pause, change the registration, and commence the fugue. By so doing we shall doubtless follow Bach's intention.

As the fugue was written for cembalo, one can hardly succeed in devising a registration for the organ along broad lines and, at the same time, based on sound musical logic. On the other hand, the changing of manuals is a simple matter.

FUGUE

Begin on the great-organ, having drawn its foundation stops together with the mixtures of the swell. With the second sixteenth-note in measure 8 transfer both hands to the choir, and in measure 11 let the theme enter on the great. From the last quarter-note in measure 14 onward, play with both hands on the swell, and close the swell-box during the course of the four following measures. By suddenly going over to the great-manual on the first beat in measure 19 we obtain an effect which is good as far as it goes. The theme is carried by the 8- and 4-foot registers of the pedal, coupled to great.

After the first eighth-note of the second half of measure 23, transfer both

hands to the choir; let the theme enter (measure 27) in the right hand on the great-manual, the left hand remaining on the choir.

From the second half of measure 30 up to the end of measure 33, play the soprano on the swell, the alto on the choir. In measure 34 change so as to play the first and third counts on the choir, and the second and fourth on the swell. Stay on the choir for measure 35; in measures 36 and 37 play the first half of each measure on the choir, the second half on the swell. For the sustained alto, too, stretch across from one manual to the other. In measure 38 the odd counts are played on the choir and the even counts on the swell.

From measures 31 to 38 the swell-box gradually closes. In measure 39 the left hand goes over to the great, and the right hand to the choir; in the second half of measure 42 the right hand also goes over to the great, while the theme is played by the pedal (as from measure 19 on) with 8- and 4-foot registers.

It would seem best to remain on the great-manual from measure 46 onward, adding the mixtures of the choir and possibly even some of those of the great. The succeeding measures are conceived as an augmentation leading up to the real entry of the theme in the pedal in measure 69.

For the return of the theme in measures 52 to 55 the 8- and 4-foot registers of the pedal may again be employed.

In the course of measure 55 close the swell-box, which will have no perceptible effect, as the mixtures of the great are already drawn. This will render it practicable to bring on the reeds of the swell on the suspensions in the following measures without rendering the enhancement noticeable. It will not be apparent until the swell-box opens in the course of measures 60 to 61, with their accompanying *rallentando*.

On the first count of measure 64, add the reeds of choir and great. In measure 69 the pedal enters with a suitable volume of tone, in which, of course, the 16-foot registers are combined. For the sustained tone from measure 74 onward uncouple and reduce the pedal, so that its volume shall be the same as at the beginning of the Fantasie.

One ought, in point of fact, to begin measure 74 with foundation stops alone, this being the commencement of the *finale* woven out of reminiscences from the Fantasie. As this procedure is hardly practicable from a technical standpoint, one should retire the mixtures and reeds in the course of the following measures, so that finally one has only the foundation stops of all the manuals and the mixtures of the swell. This *diminuendo* should come to an end with measure 76.

With the above combination, continue on the great-organ through measures 77 to 83. On the first beat of the Adagio, with the swell-box closed, draw the mixtures and reeds of the swell, and begin opening the box, so that the newly added registers may attain to full effect in measure 85; then, on the first and third beats of the next two measures, bring on the mixtures and reeds of choir and great. From measure 83 onward the player will, of course, have augmented the pedal by coupling the manuals; after the first quarter in measure 87, the pedal-couplers will be retired.

While playing this measure and the next one, retire successively most of the foundation stops, in order to obtain once more the brilliant, vibrating tone of the mixtures and reeds in which the corresponding division of the Fantasie was performed.

During the pause in measure 94 the mixtures and reeds are retired, and the foundation stops again come into action. At the pause in measure 98 a few mixtures will be added to them.

Let every organist experiment for himself how to bring on an augmentation for the close, which is so little suited to the organ.

This piece, originally designed for the pedal-cembalo, does not produce, in all its divisions, an effect of even excellence on the organ. Nevertheless, the organist will always turn with pleasure to this grandly conceived and boldly wrought composition, and will learn, from the manual-changes so unmistakably indicated in the music, a great deal which will be of value to him in interpreting those of the Master's works originally conceived for the organ.

The registration which we have suggested leaves room for argument. Any one who takes the trouble to try it through will discover that it possesses the advantage over many another scheme, that, with all the variety which it provides, it follows a plan consistent with the structure of the piece.

XIV. Prelude and Fugue in A Minor. (Page 98-103.)

PRELUDE

The first eleven measures of the Prelude are played on the great-organ with foundation stops and mixtures. Throw off the mixtures after lifting the chord in measure 12. When the theme enters in measure 21, draw the mixtures of choir and swell; in measures 29 and 30, add those of the great. Thereupon begin closing the swell-box, so that at the beginning of measure 32 the swell reeds may be brought on quietly; then, by again opening the swell, an effective *crescendo* may be commenced, which will be carried to a climax by adding the reeds of choir and great.

FUGUE

For the registration of the loosely constructed Fugue we should have two different combinations in readiness for alternation in bringing out the theme. It will be best to play on the great-organ uncoupled, with foundation stops 8' and 4'; while choir and swell, with foundation stops 8', 4' and 2', and mixtures, should be coupled together.

Begin on the great. Go over to the choir in measure 8. At the end of measure 12 the left hand takes up the theme on the great-manual, the right following in measure 14. Meantime the swell-box is closing, so that on the second quarter of measure 17 the swell can be coupled to the great, without making the entrance of the theme unpleasantly loud by reason of this augmentation. In the succeeding measures open the swell-box slowly so as to bring out the mixtures of the swell beside the foundation stops of the great.

On the third beat of measure 22, also couple choir to great. Still remain on the great after measure 25; but on the second beat of this measure uncouple the choir, and after letting the swell-box close, likewise uncouple the swell-manual on the fourth beat of measure 27.

On the last beat of measure 29 transfer both hands to the choir. In measure 31 let the soprano enter on the swell, the left hand following on the second beat of measure 32. At the same instant the right hand goes over to the choir. The swell-box opens.

On the second beat of measure 34, both hands are on the choir-manual; on the last beat of the same measure the right hand goes over to the great, and the left follows at the beginning of the next measure.

For the commencement of measure 37 couple swell to great. Couple great to choir on beginning measure 41. While the swell-box is closed, bring on the reeds of the swell and then open during the course of measures 42 and 43. During the pause add whatever stops you may consider proper for the closing combination.

On the organ, the simple sustaining of the bass note in measures 47 and 48 has a better effect than the trill, which was probably intended more especially for performance on the cembalo.

XV. Prelude in A Minor. (Page 104-109.)

This piece, known traditionally as a prelude, is in reality a Chaconne, and as such is a counterpart of the Passacaglia in *C* minor. Its style being that of a series of variations, a registration worked out on broad lines is not to be thought of. In the Passacaglia, which was written later, the successive variations plainly exhibit the outlines of an architectonic design; whereas in this Prelude we have merely a simple concatenation of changeful variations. On the other hand, the changes of manual in this piece are so clearly indicated by the mode of notation, that it may be used as an instructive example. Where the pedal coöperates, Bach played on the great-organ; where it rests, he went over to choir or swell. Every such transition is to be made on the second eighth-note of the measure in question.

This piece tempts one to "modernize." It will certainly bear various effects of registration otherwise inappropriate for Bach. But do not go too far in this direction; and consider, that the frequent changes of manual provide, in themselves, a great deal of variety.

The registration of the great organ should doubtless be altered as little as possible. In fact, it is conceived in the same color and volume of tone throughout. The player may, then, if it suits his fancy, registrate the episodes with all the more freedom. But all experimentation will more probably lead to the conviction, that their effect is also best with the fewest changes in color. The swell-box will find abundant employment.

For the interpretation of this piece foundation stops would seem, as a general thing, to be best suited. Towards the close an augmentation is supposable, but not absolutely demanded. This is not a case of building up, as in an ordinary prelude.

The player's chief aim should be to guide the hearer through the details of the interesting harmony by a plastic interpretation and a delicate shading of the tempo, that his fancy may rove, as it were through a blooming garden.

XVI. Fantasia con Imitatione, in B Minor. (Page 110-113.)

The first section of the Fantasia is very effective when the two highest parts are played with flute-registers on one manual, and the middle part with Gambas and Salicionals on the other.

On the first sixteenth of measure 16, couple the two manuals together, and play on one of them with both hands.

Probably the Imitatio is also to be performed with foundation stops only. Begin on the great-organ. In measure 23 both the highest parts go over to the choir, returning to the great on the second quarter-note in measure 34.

After the first quarter of measure 38, both hands leave the great-manual; they return to it on the second quarter of measure 43, and leave it again on the second quarter of measure 47. The two highest parts again go over to the great on the second quarter of measure 55, the middle part in measure 57. On the second quarter of measure 65 the right hand goes over to the choir with the highest part, alto and tenor following on the third quarter and returning to

the great on the second quarter in measure 69; the right hand follows them in measure 71.

In measure 81 the two highest parts change to the choir-manual, while the tenor remains on the great. In measure 85, on the third beat, the tenor also goes over to choir. The swell-box closes during the course of the four measures following. From the third quarter of measure 91 to the close, both hands are on the great-organ.

In this manner the responsorial character of this grandly naïve piece will be most appropriately set forth. The registration—a skilfully blended combination of foundation stops—is retained from beginning to end, as the logic of the composition requires no change.

XVII. Fugue in B Minor. (Page 114-119.)

The fugue which Corelli wrote on this theme, numbered thirty-nine measures; Bach carries his through more than one hundred.

Begin on the great-organ, with the foundation stops of all the manuals coupled together. In measure 11 beware of going over to the choir with soprano and alto under the pretext that the tenor will thus be brought out better; that would be an offence to the shade of Bach.

On the last quarter in measure 24, soprano and alto are transferred to the choir; the tenor will follow most fittingly on the first half-note in measure 25, its first count being struck on the great-manual, while for the second count one stretches over to the choir. During the course of this episode, the swell-box closes gradually.

The *tutti* reënters in measure 31. With the second eighth-note of the measure the alto returns to the great, soprano and tenor following on the second quarter.

On the third quarter of measure 41, throw off either a few of the great-organ stops or the couplers, so that you can use the softened great-organ as a subsidiary manual, until, with the second eighth in measure 45, a good opportunity offers to bring both hands over to the choir.

In measure 49 the theme enters, as a solo, on the great (still reduced as above); the left hand follows on the second eighth of measure 51. On the second eighth in measure 54 the great-organ is augmented to its former registration.

On the last quarter of measure 57, the mixtures of the swell may be brought on while the swell-box is closed; then open it during the course of the four succeeding measures.

With the second eighth of measure 62 go over to the choir, and at the beginning of measure 65 draw the mixtures of the choir.

In order to bring out the theme in the alto well, one may proceed as follows: Throw off the registers of the pedal, couple it to the choir-manual, and play the tenor part from the end of measure 67 with the feet. From measure 67 onward, the theme will be played by the left hand on the great-manual, which has been uncoupled from the others.

On the second sixteenth-note of the third count in measure 71, the right hand also goes over to the great. On the second eighth of measure 74 draw the couplers again. The pedal registers will, of course, be ready for the entrance of the theme.

The volume of tone in which the Fugue closes must be reached with the last quarter of measure 90. Augmentations may be introduced on the last eighth of measure 76, during the rests in measures 84 and 85, and on the second eighth of measure 87.

PRELUDES AND FUGUES OF THE YOUTHFUL PERIOD

I
Fantasie in C-Dur

Manual

Pedal

Printed in the U.S.A.

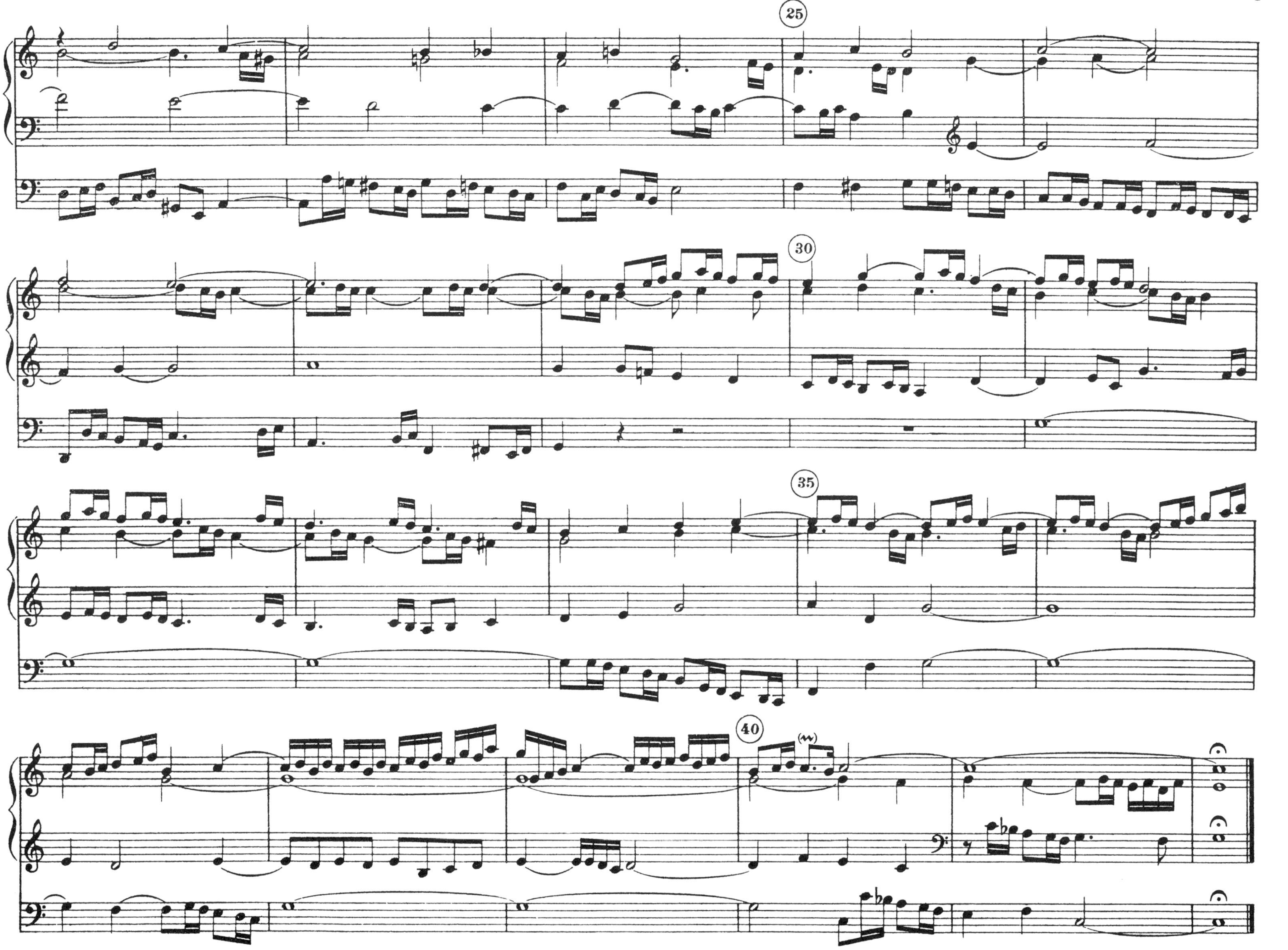

25
30
35
40

II
Praeludium und Fuge in C-Moll

Praeludium

Manual

Pedal

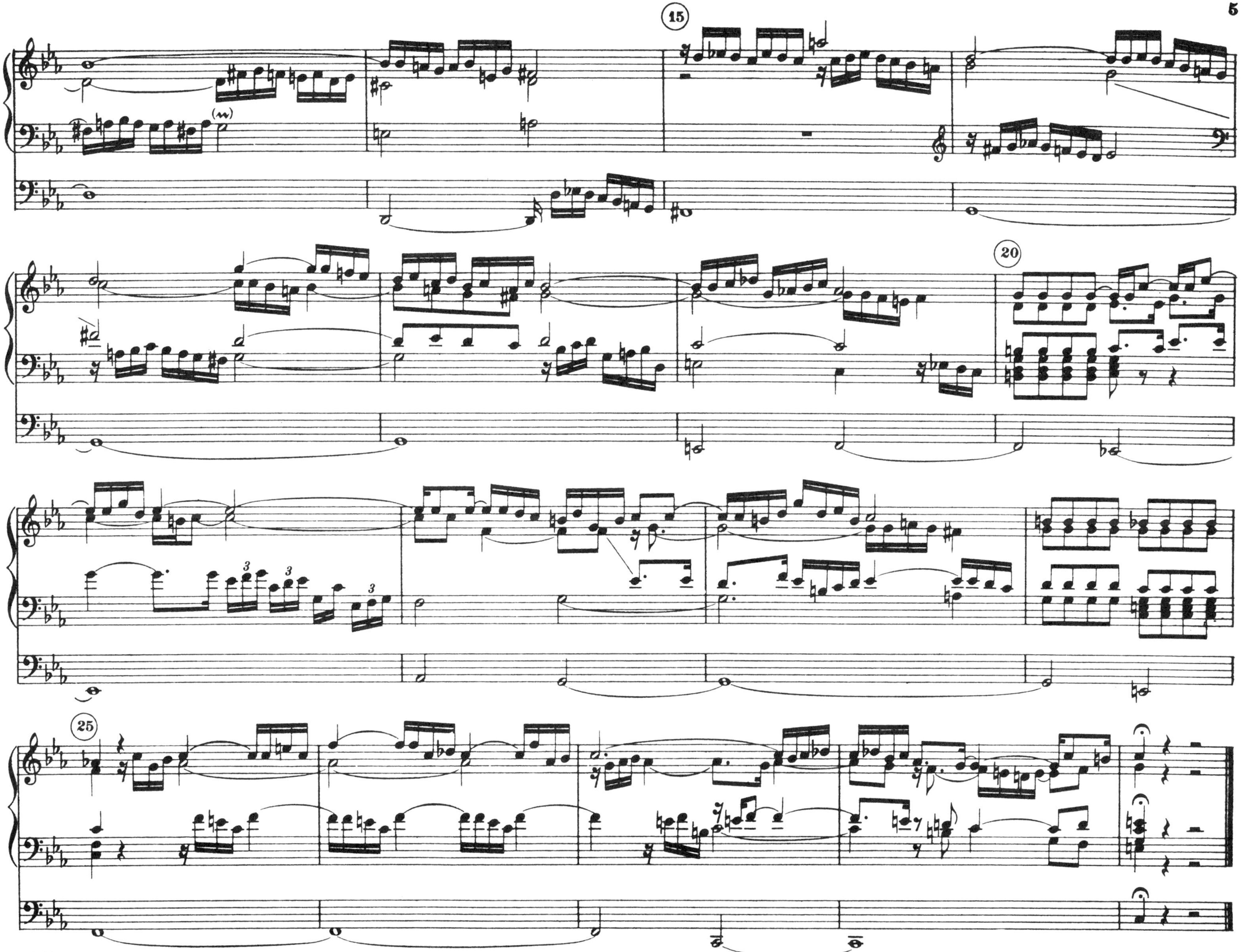
15
20
25

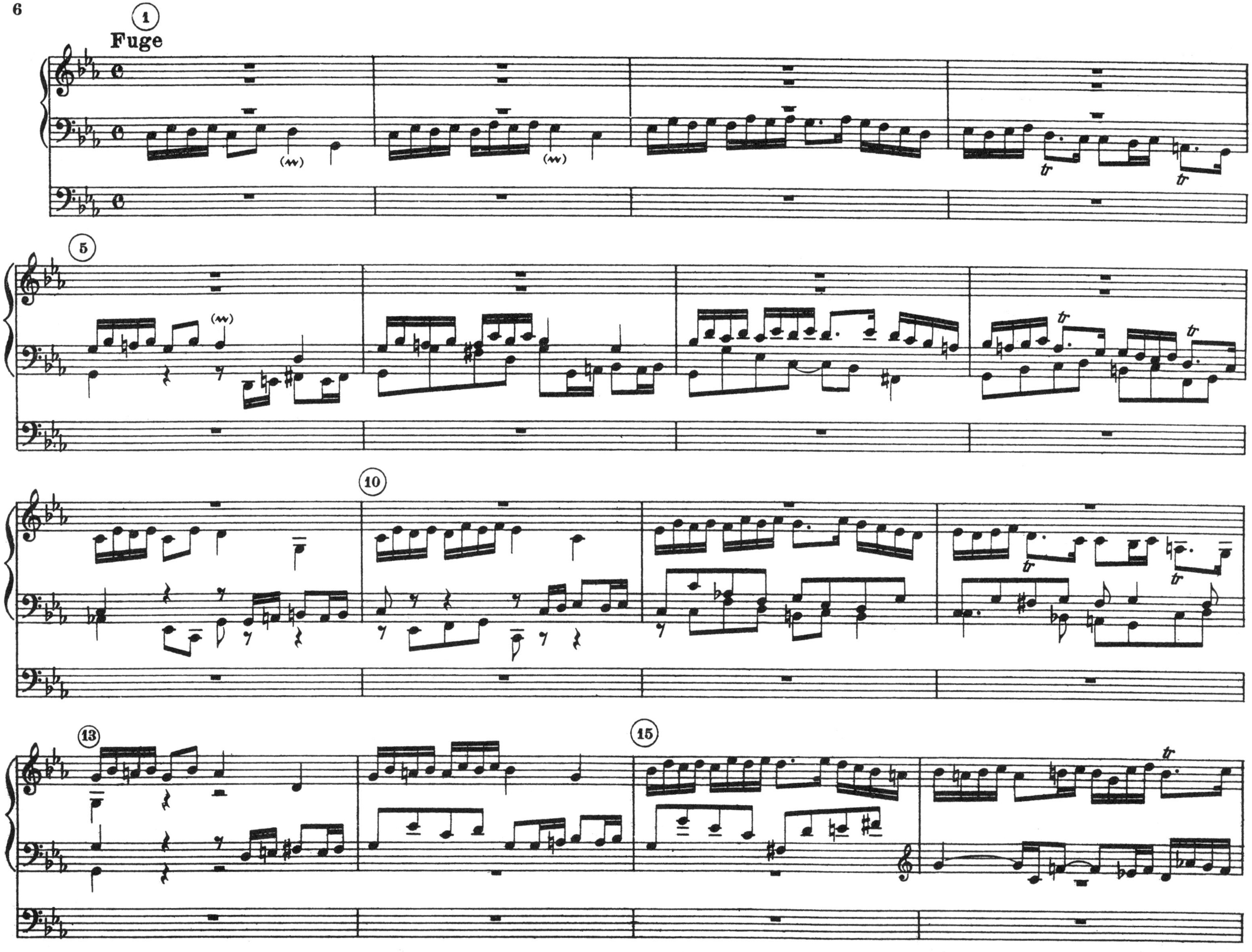
Fuge

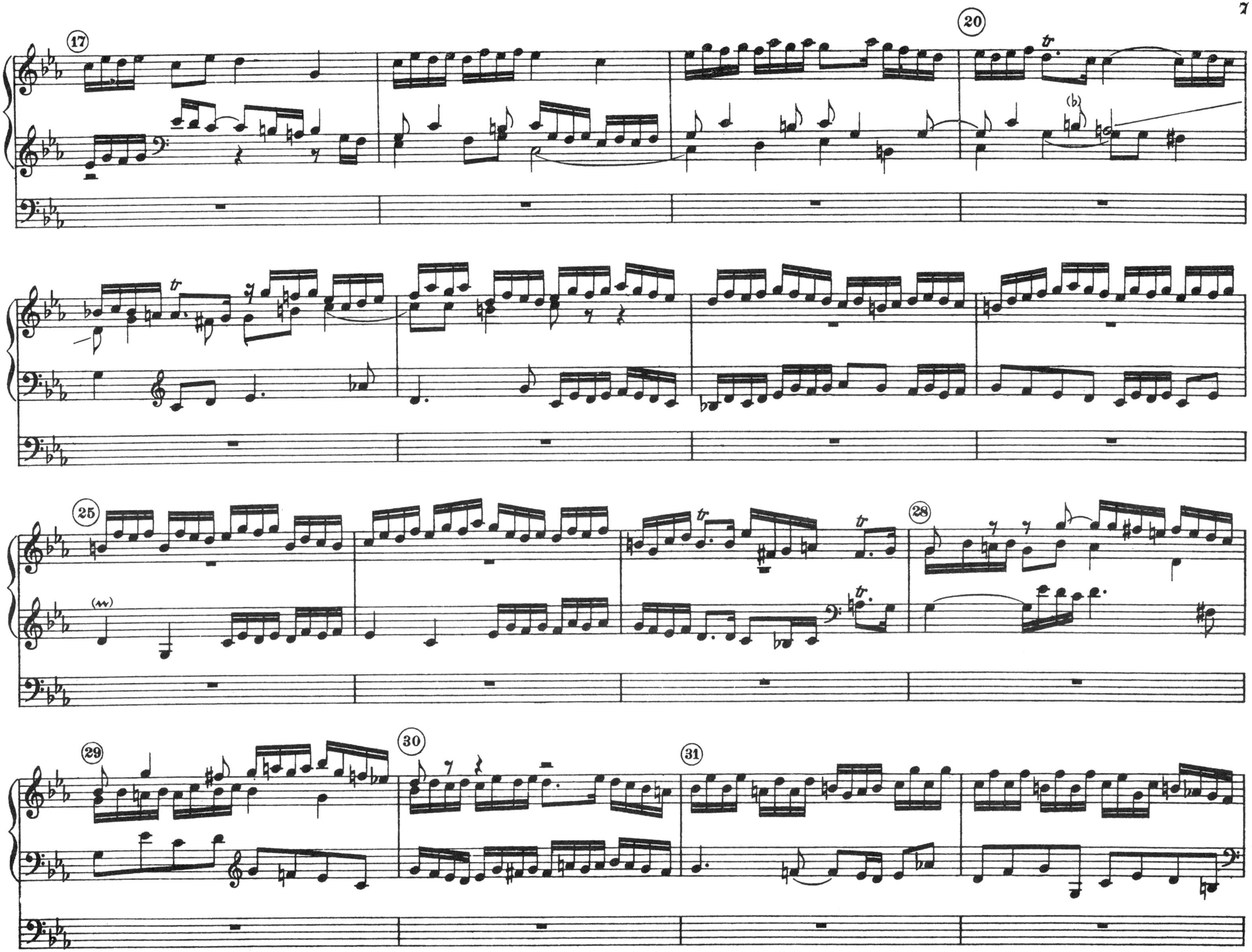
17
20
25
28
29
30
31
tr

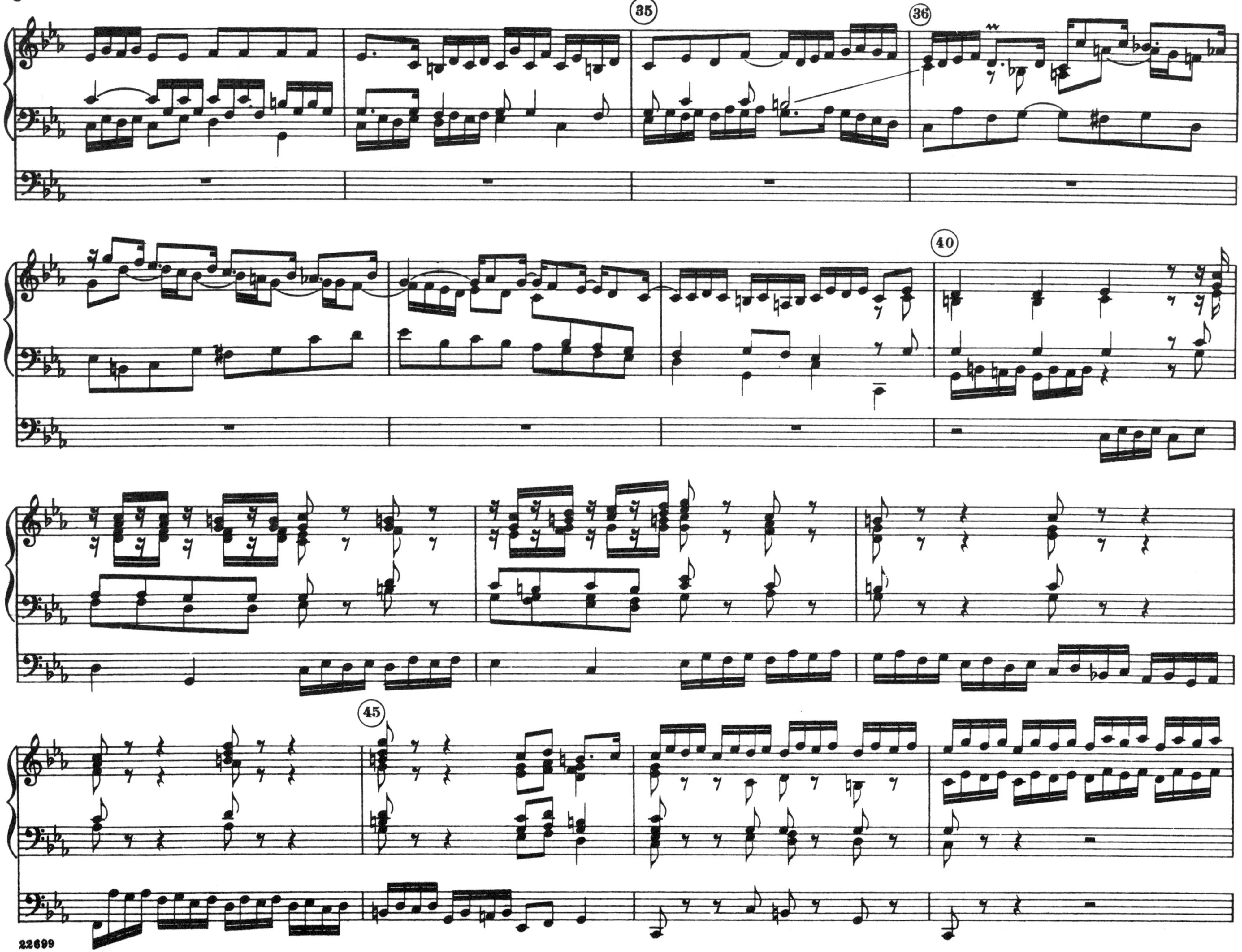
35
36
40
45

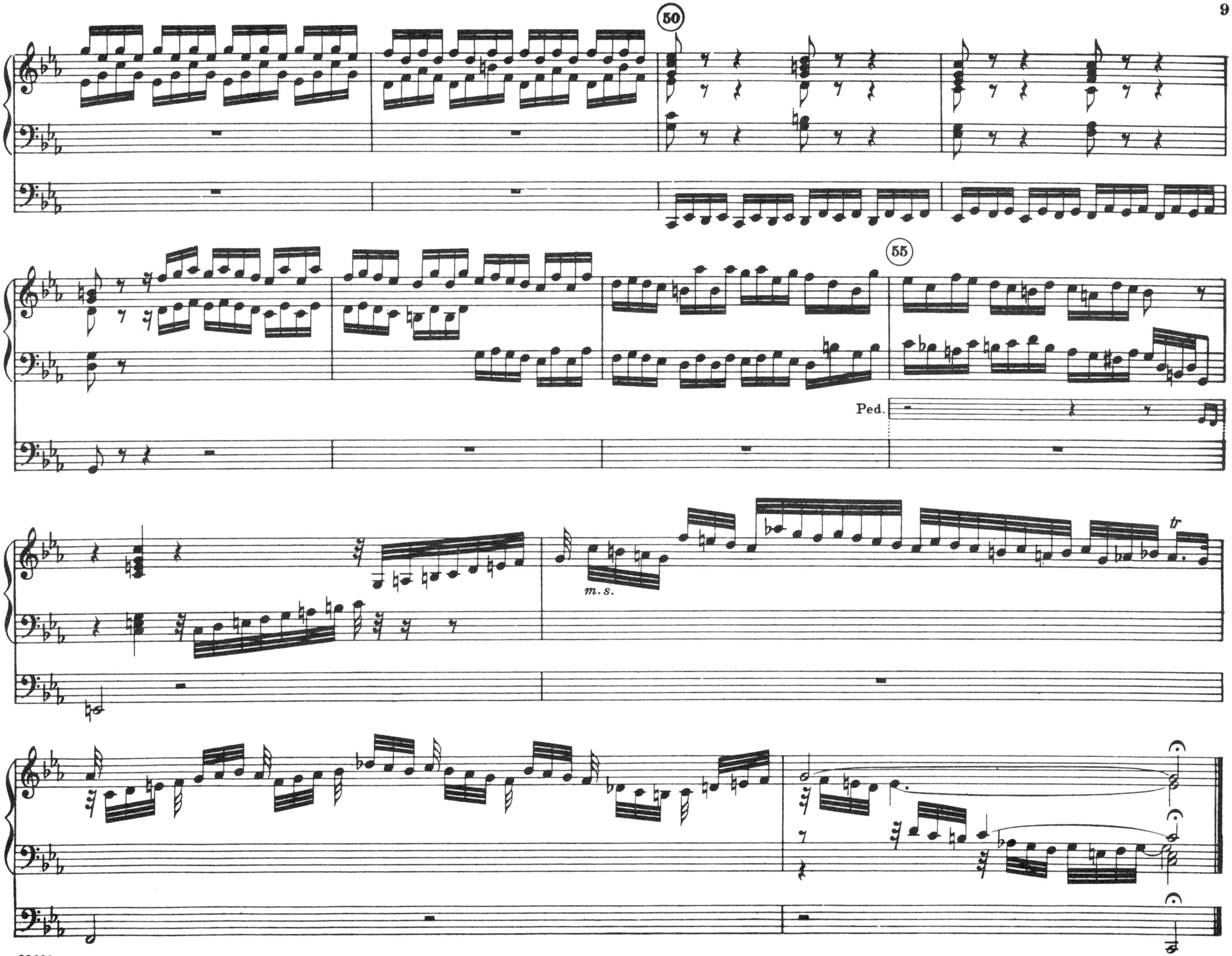
50
55
Ped.
m.s.
tr

III
Fuge in C-Moll

Über ein Thema von Legrenzi (1625-1690)

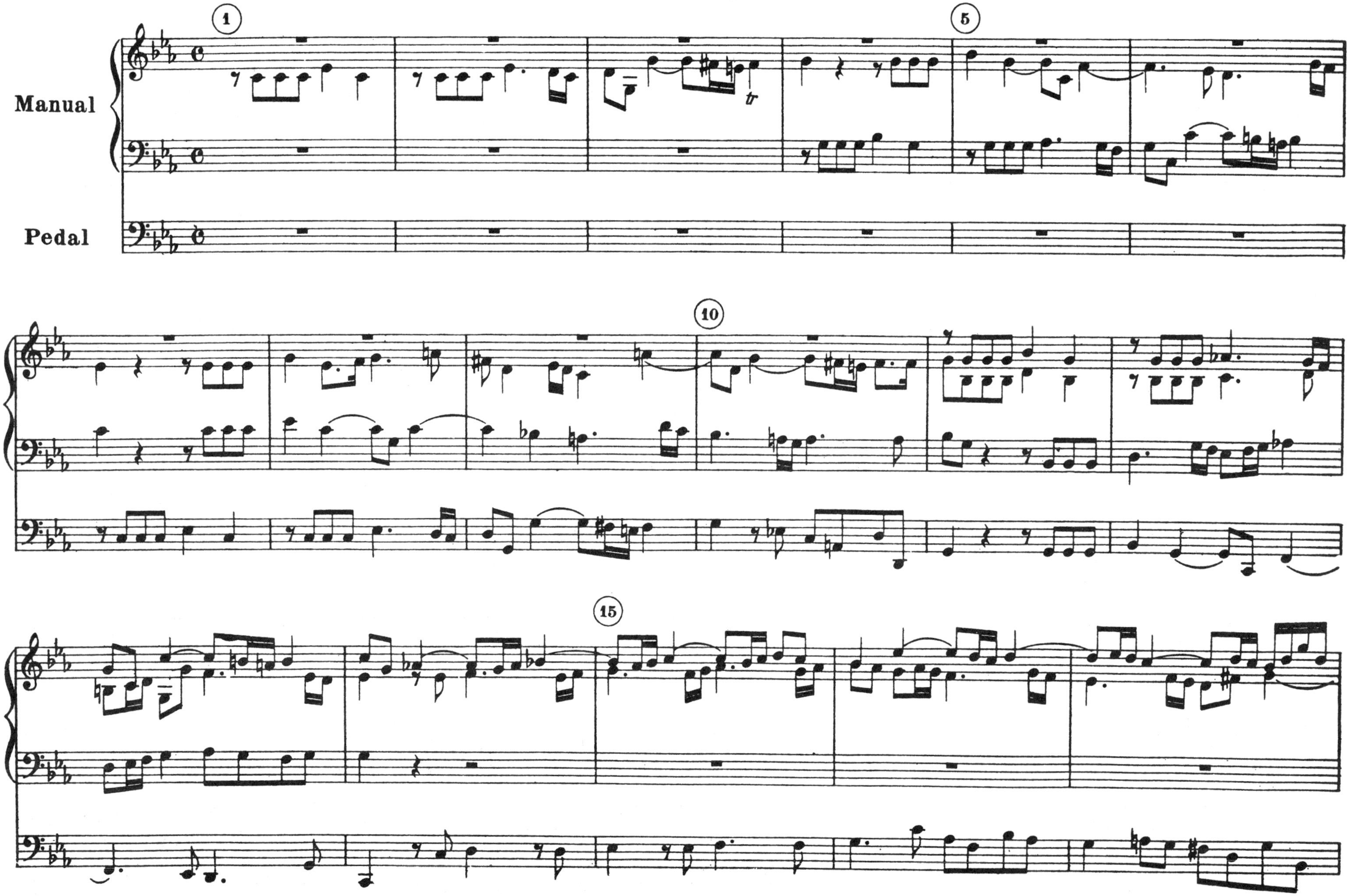

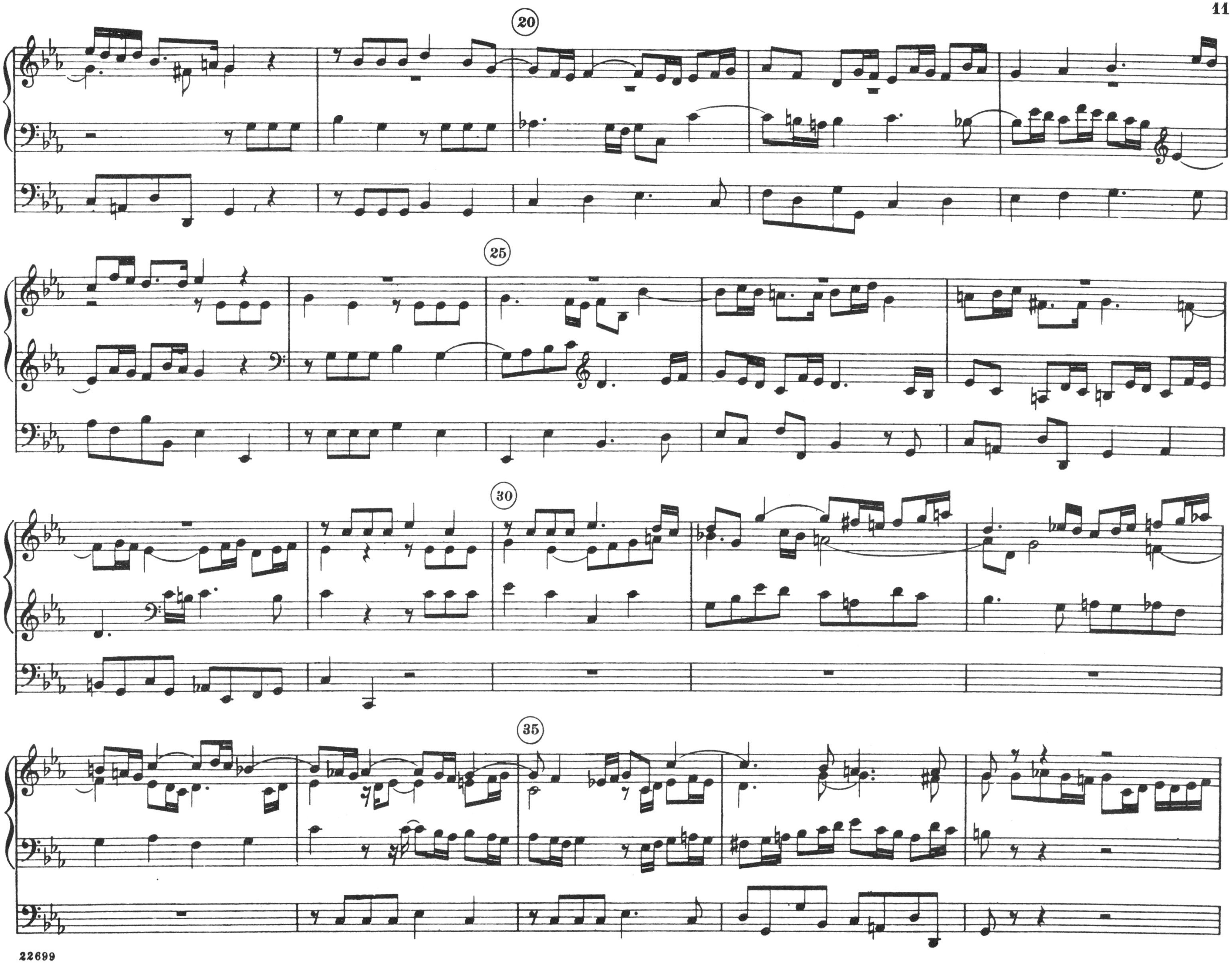

20
25
30
35

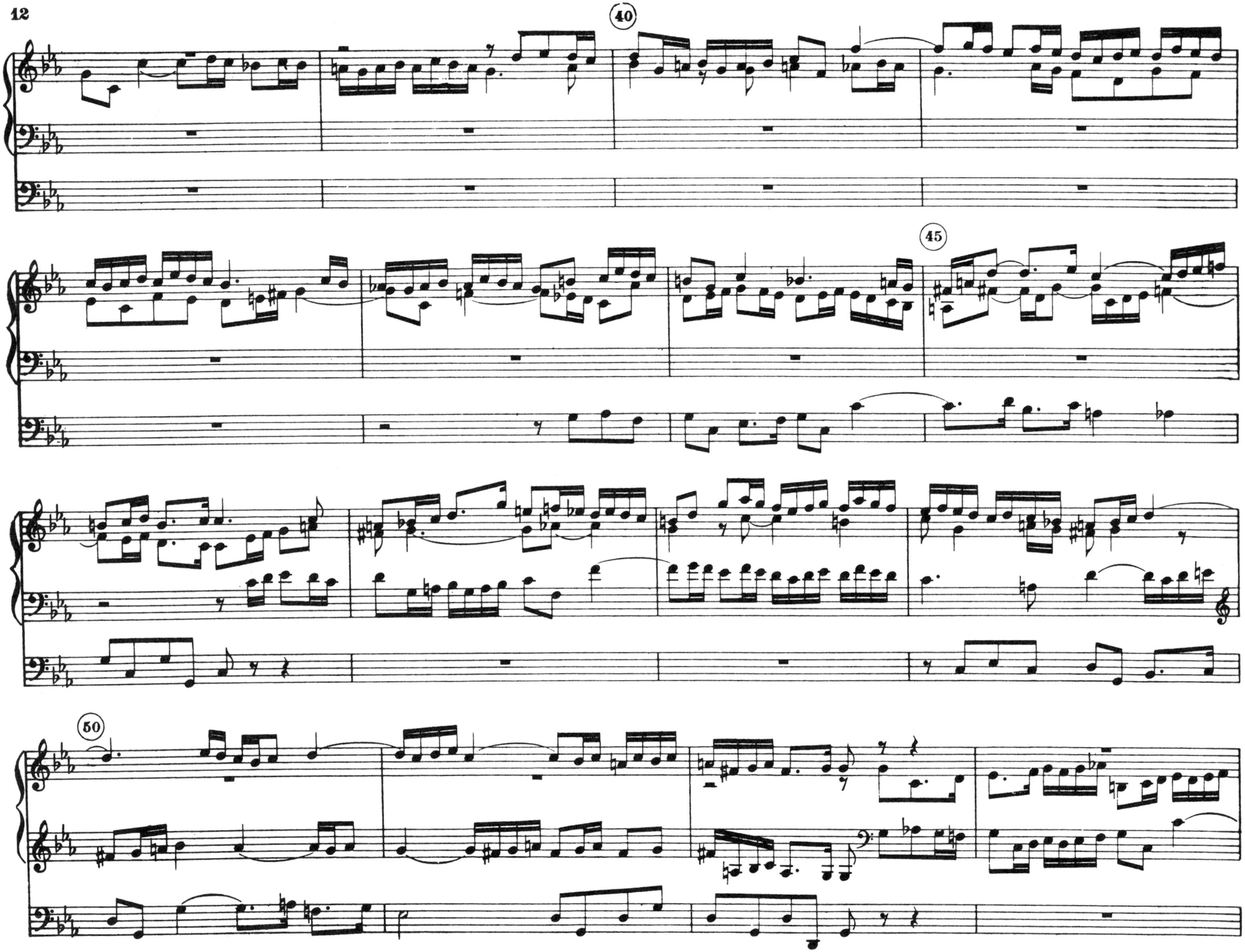
40
45
50

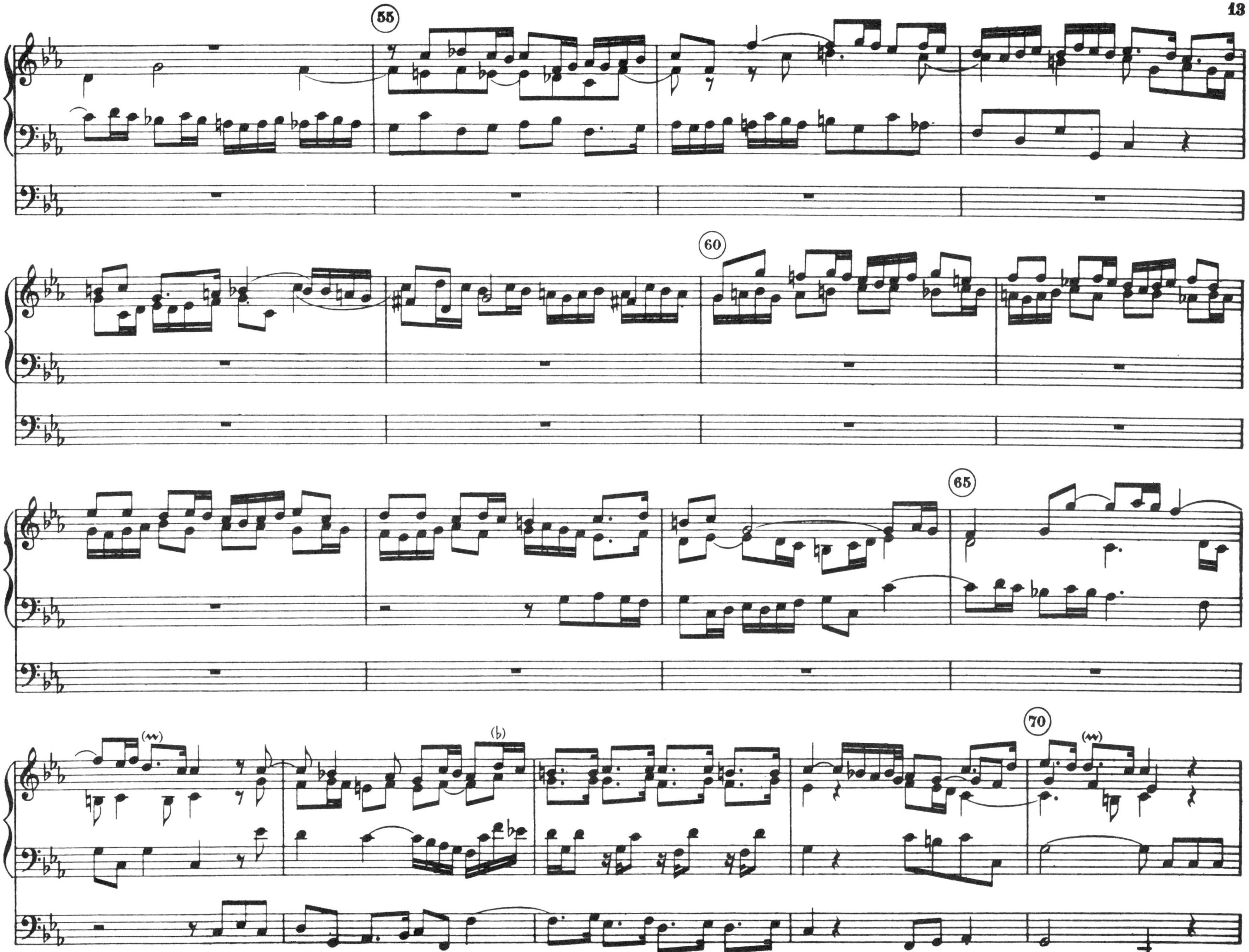
55
60
65
70
(b)

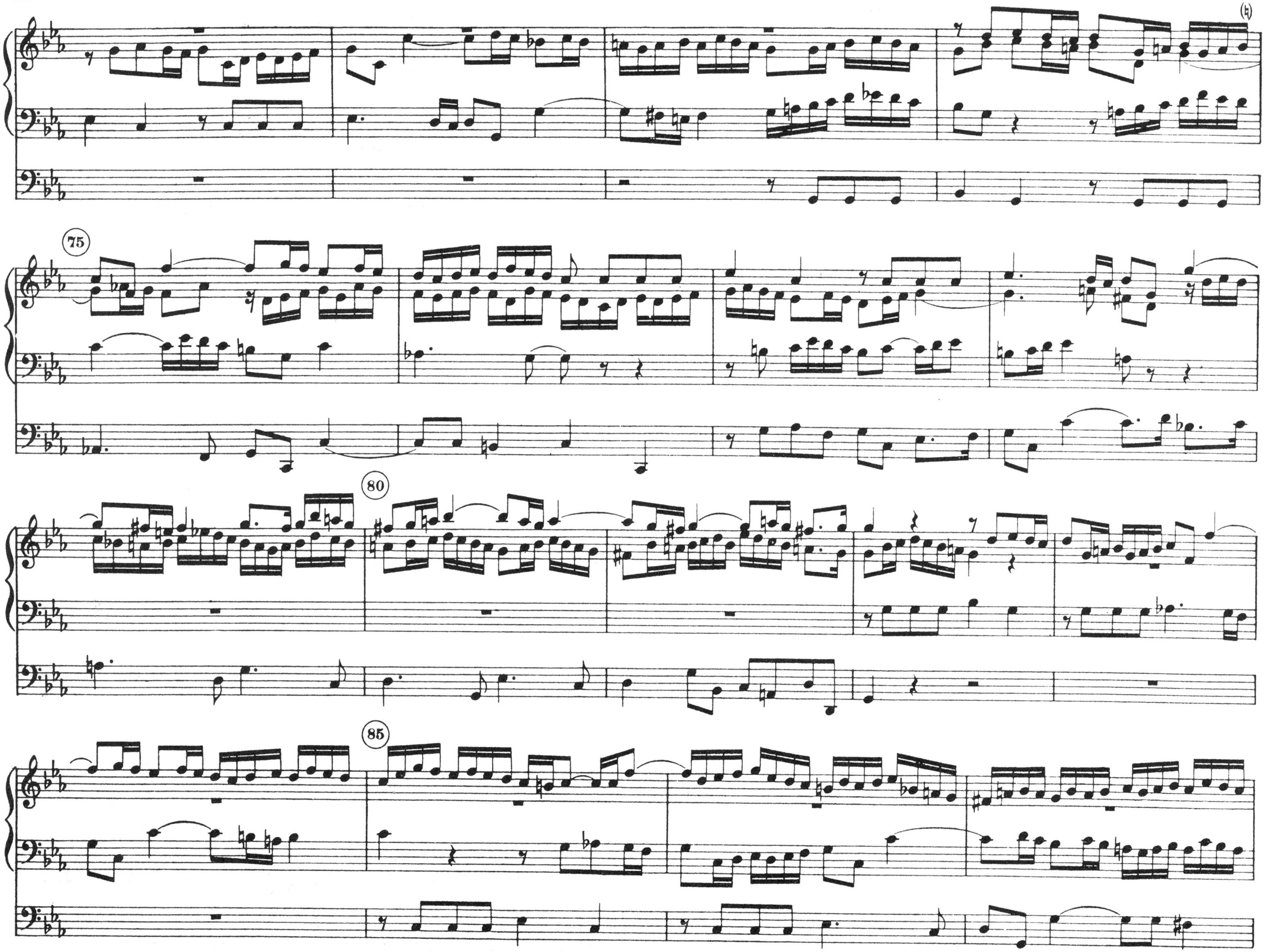
(♮)
75
80
85

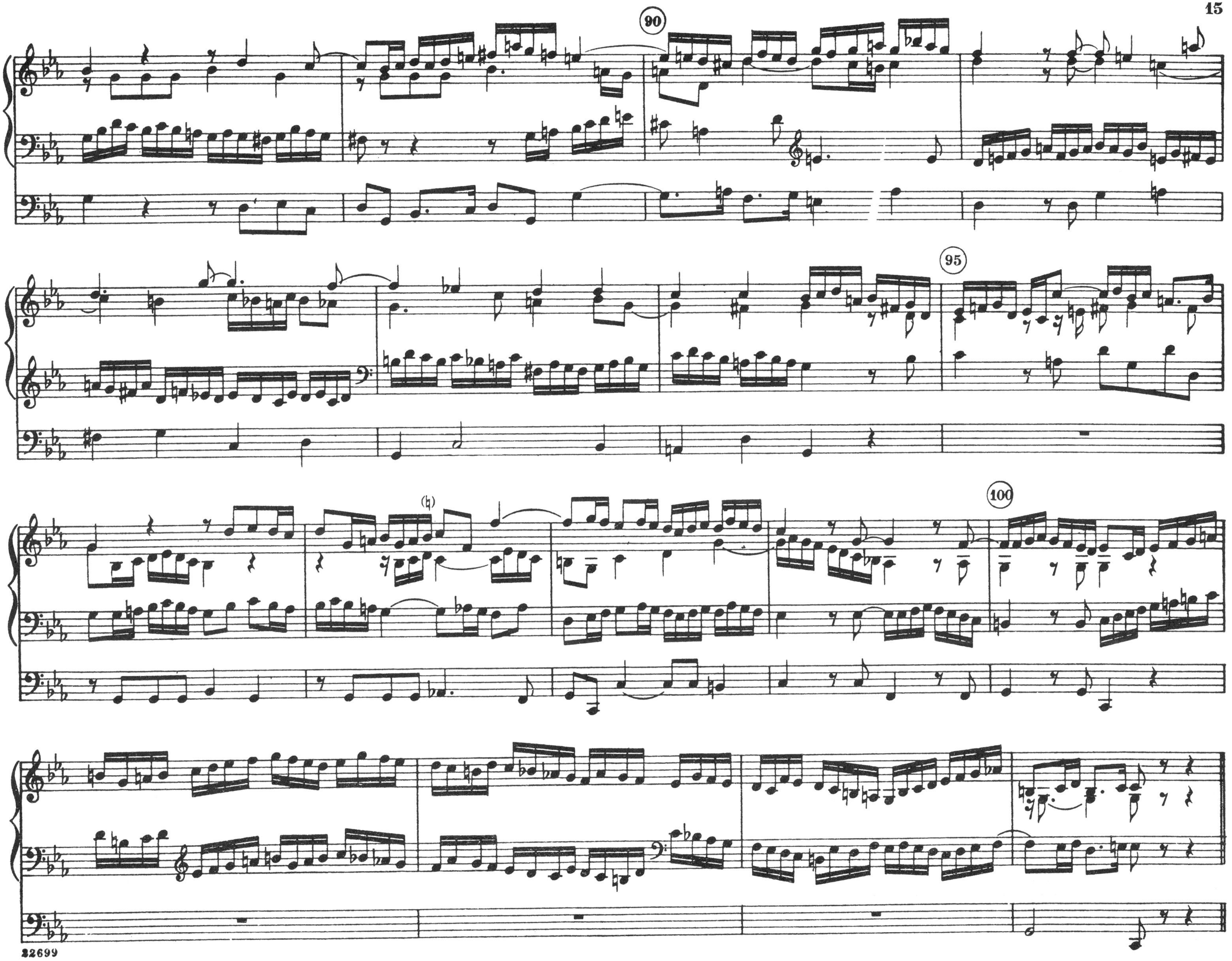
90
95
100

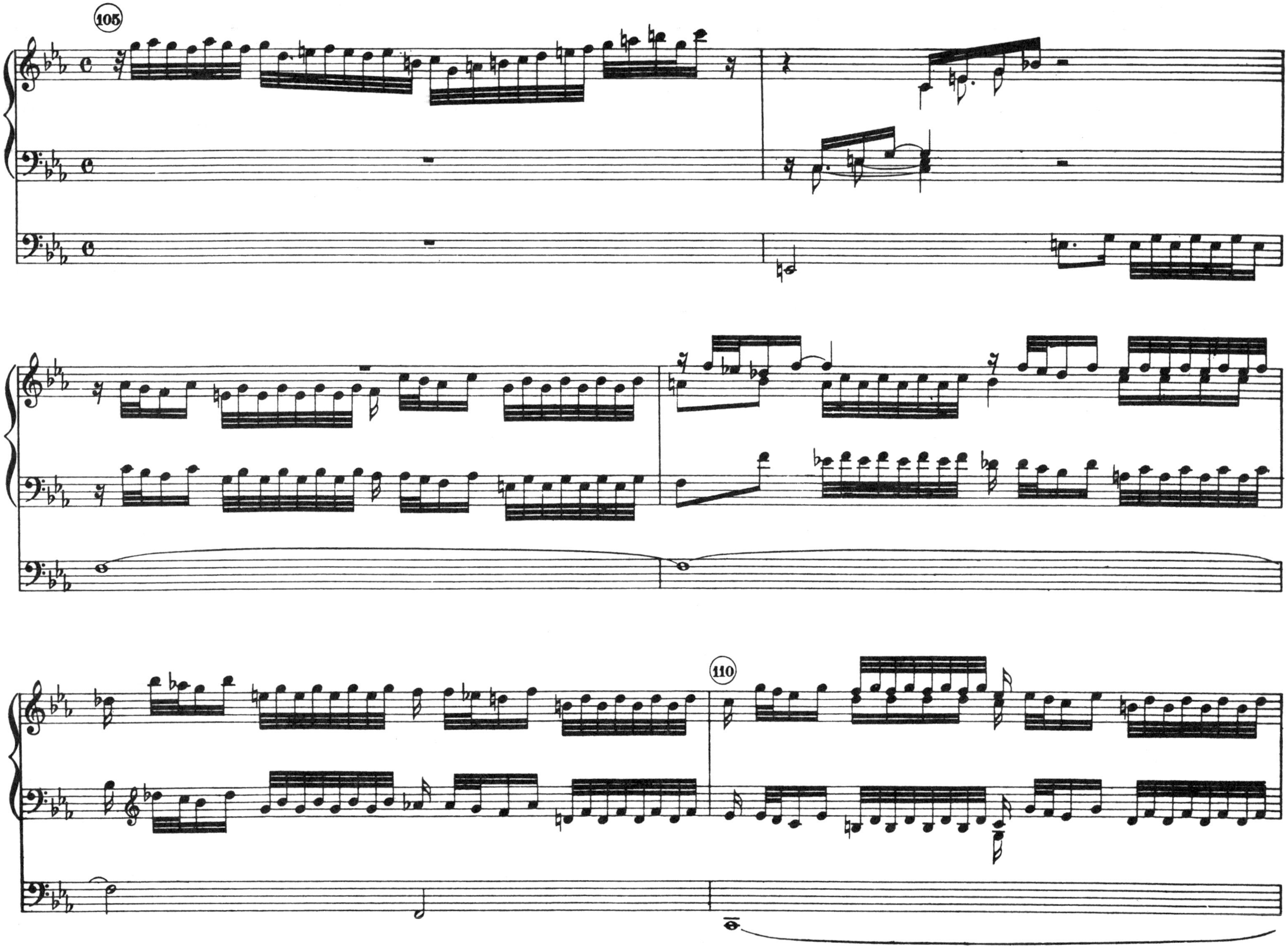
105
110

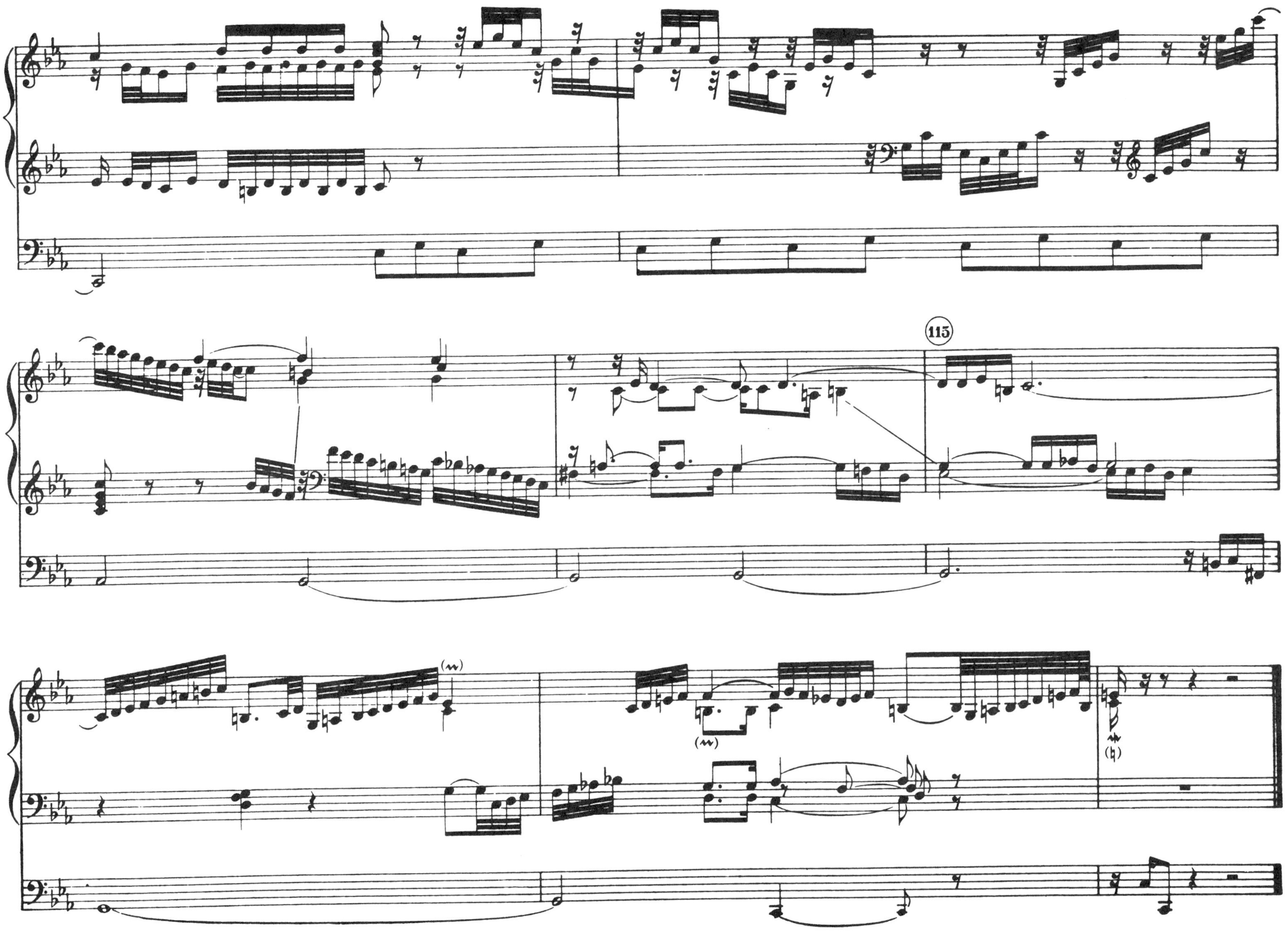
115

IV
Allabreve in D-Dur

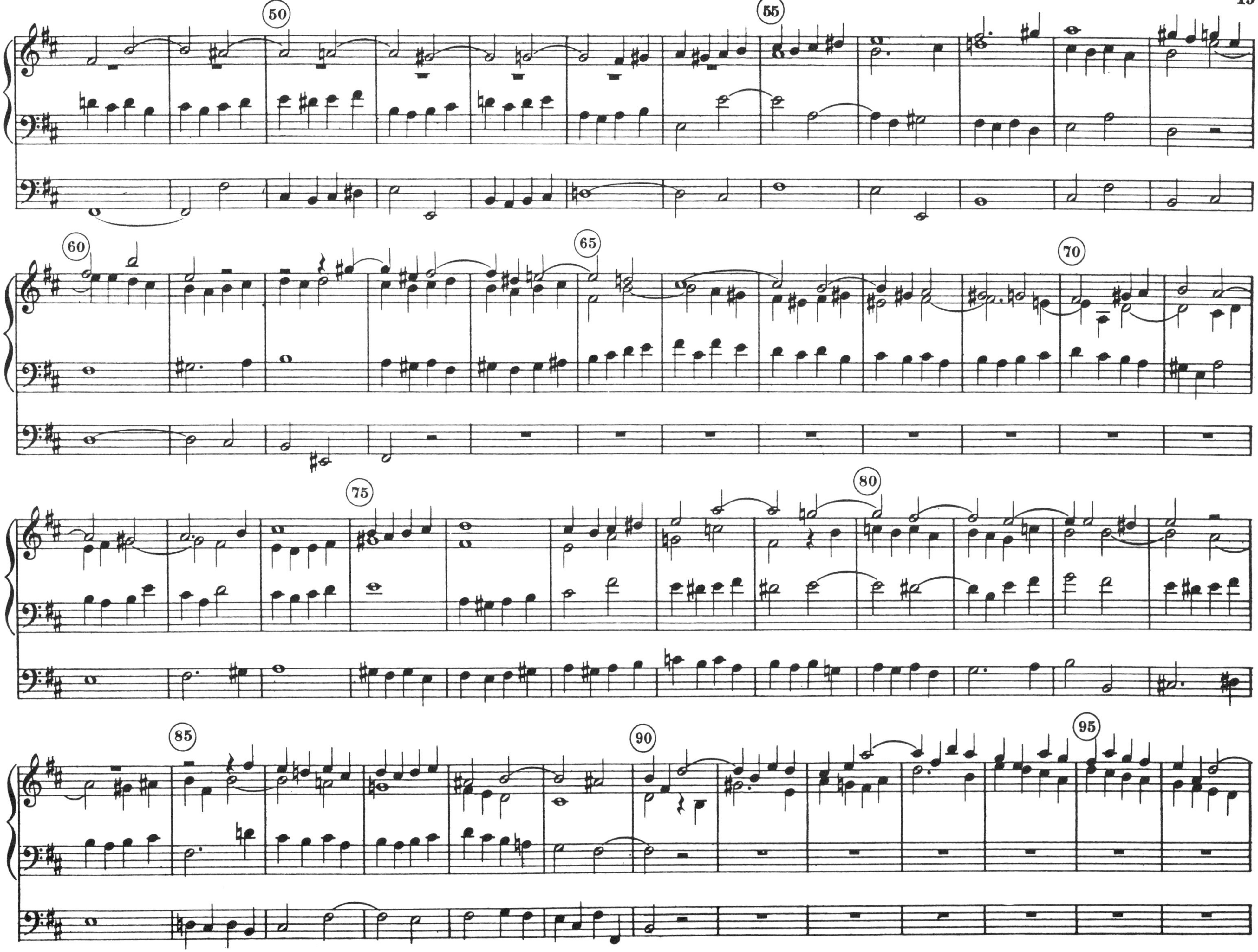
50
55
60
65
70
75
80
85
90
95

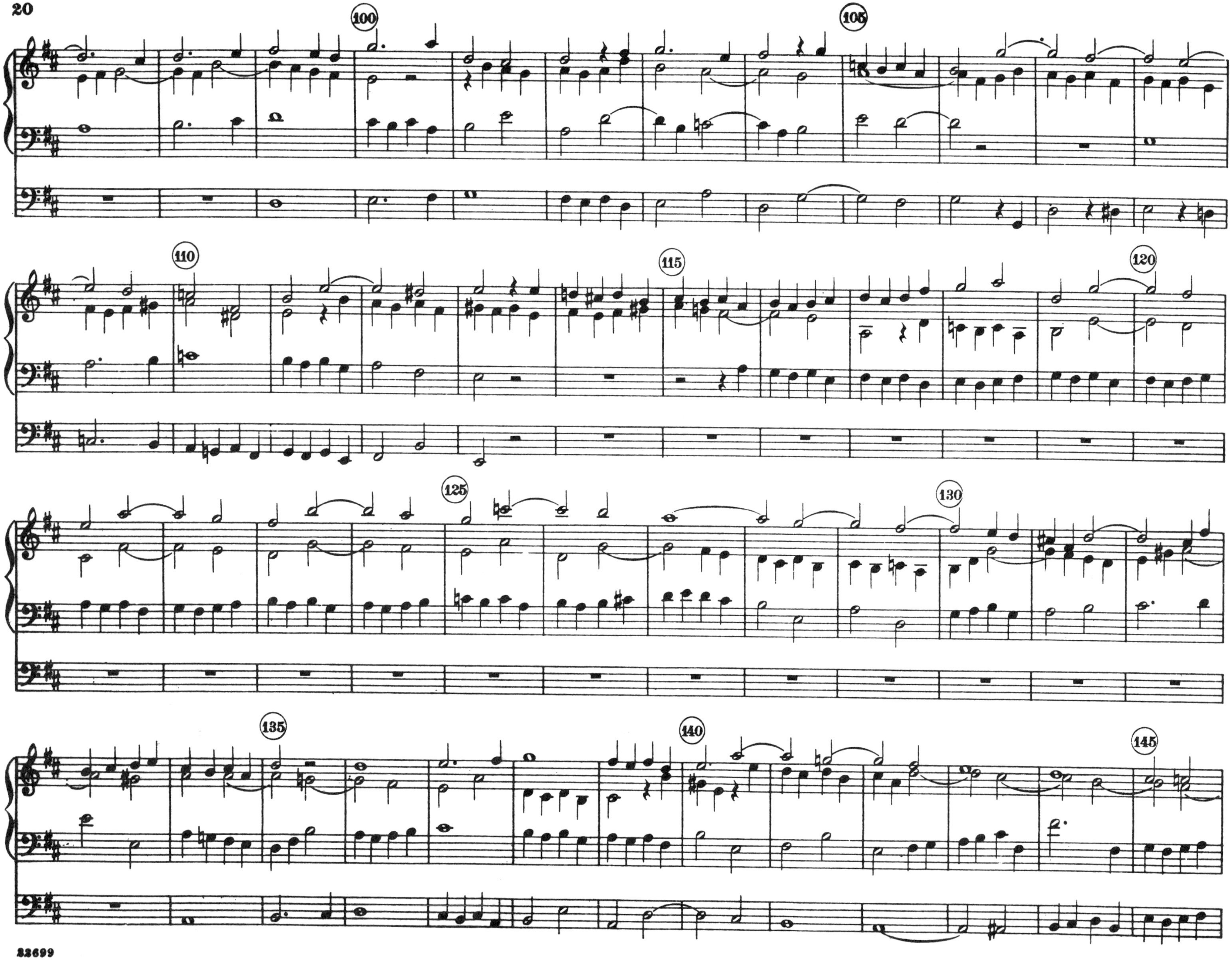
100
105
110
115
120
125
130
135
140
145

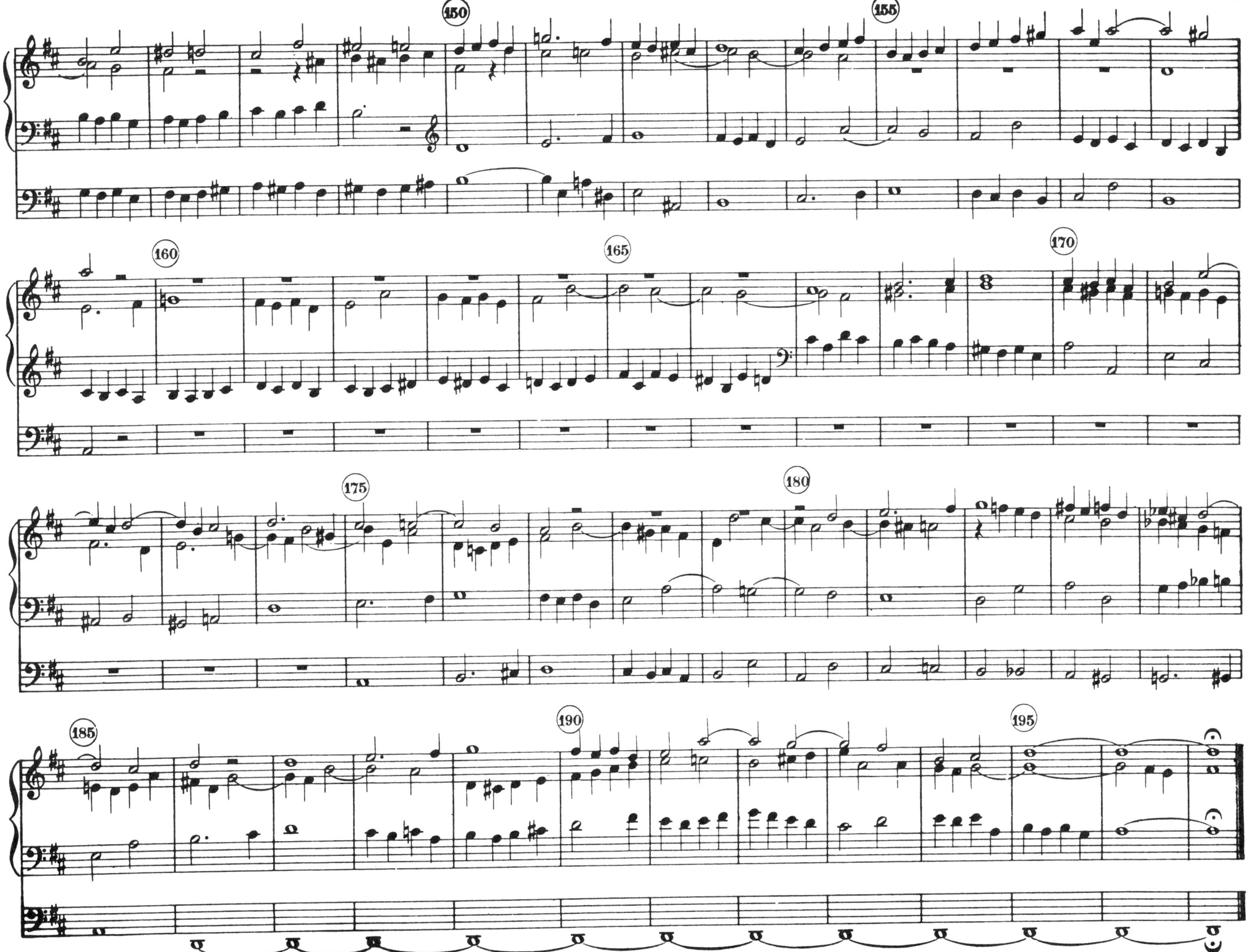
150
155
160
165
170
175
180
185
190
195

V
Toccata in E-Dur

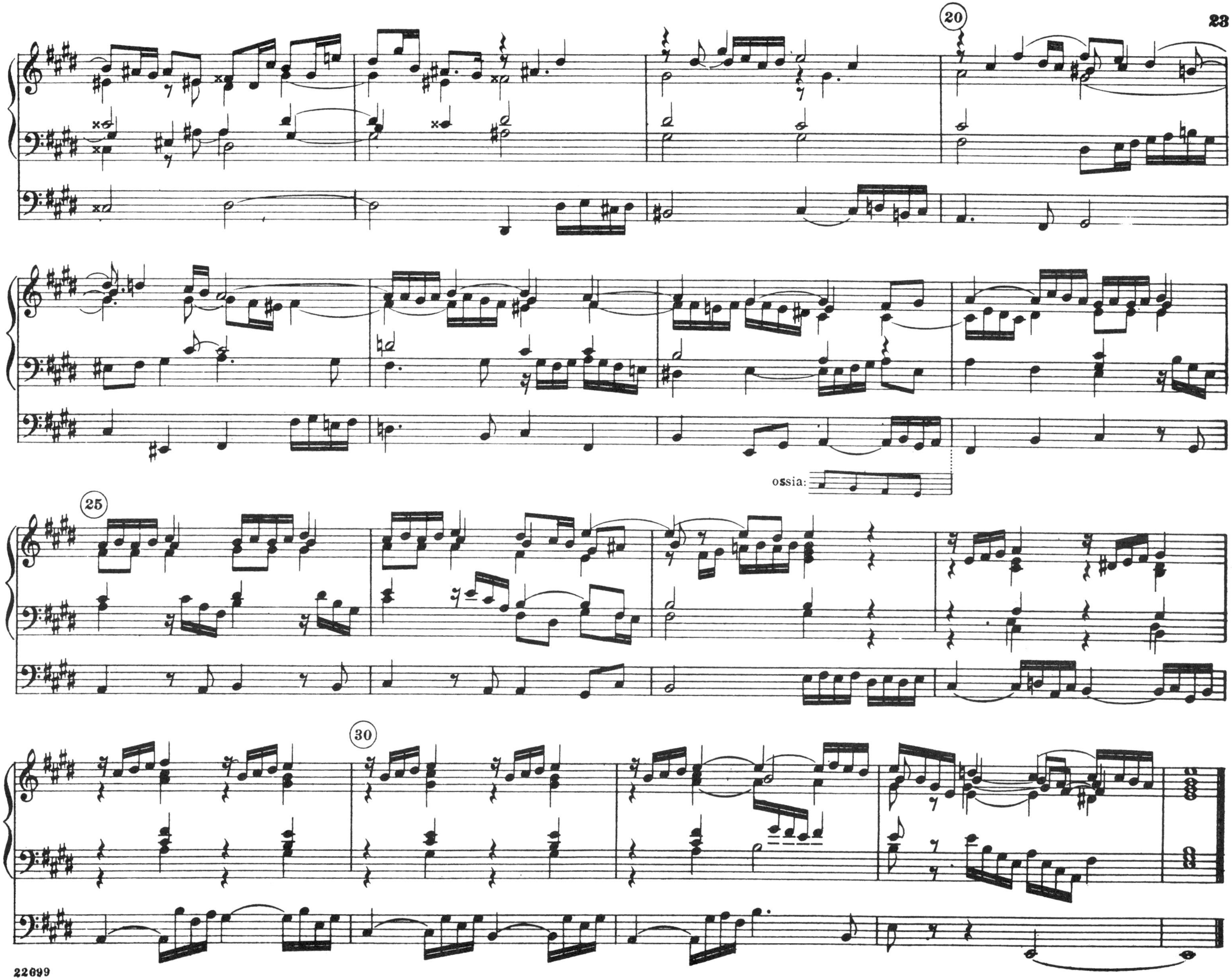
20
ossia:
25
30

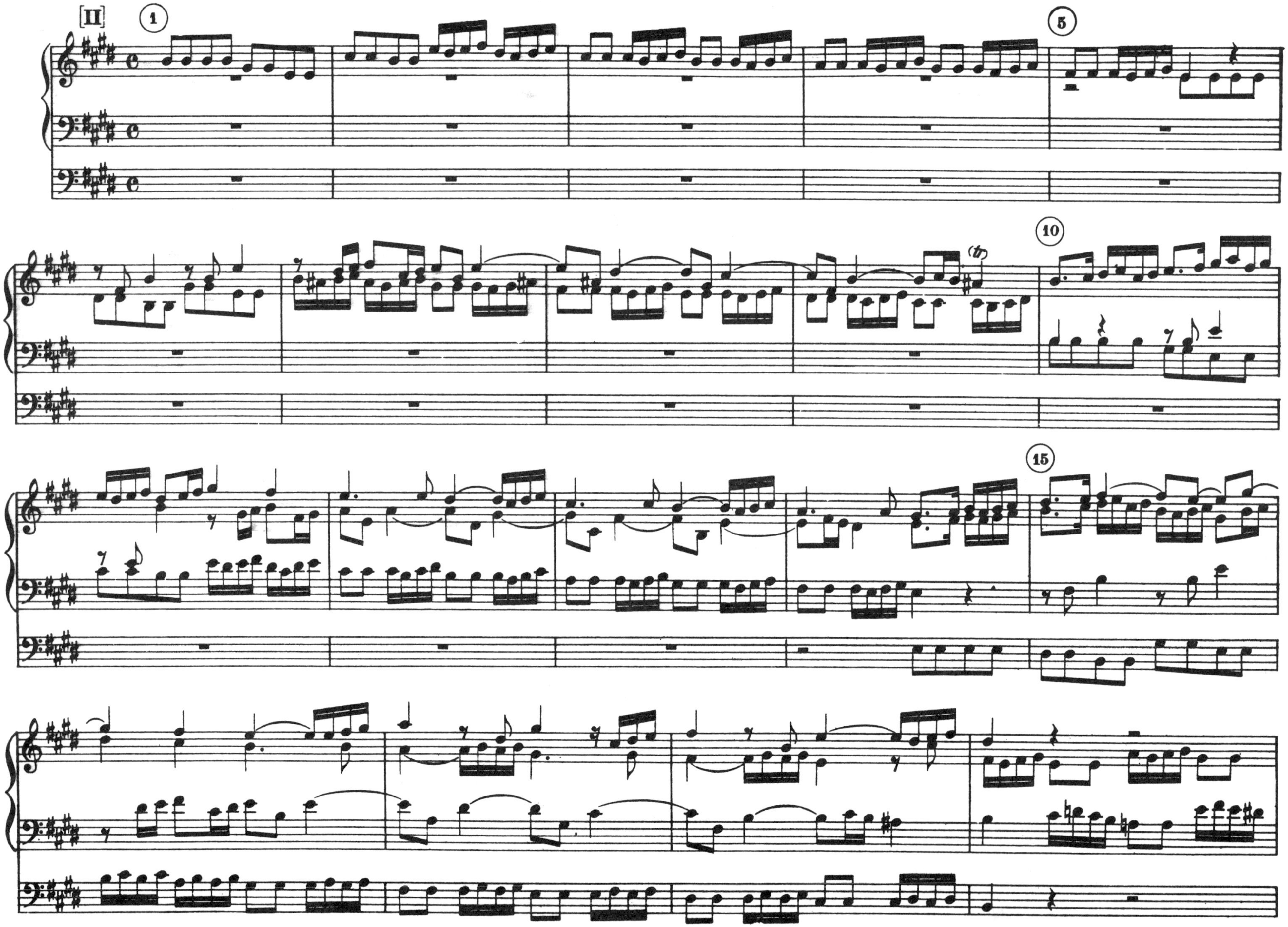
[II]
1
5
10
(tr)
15

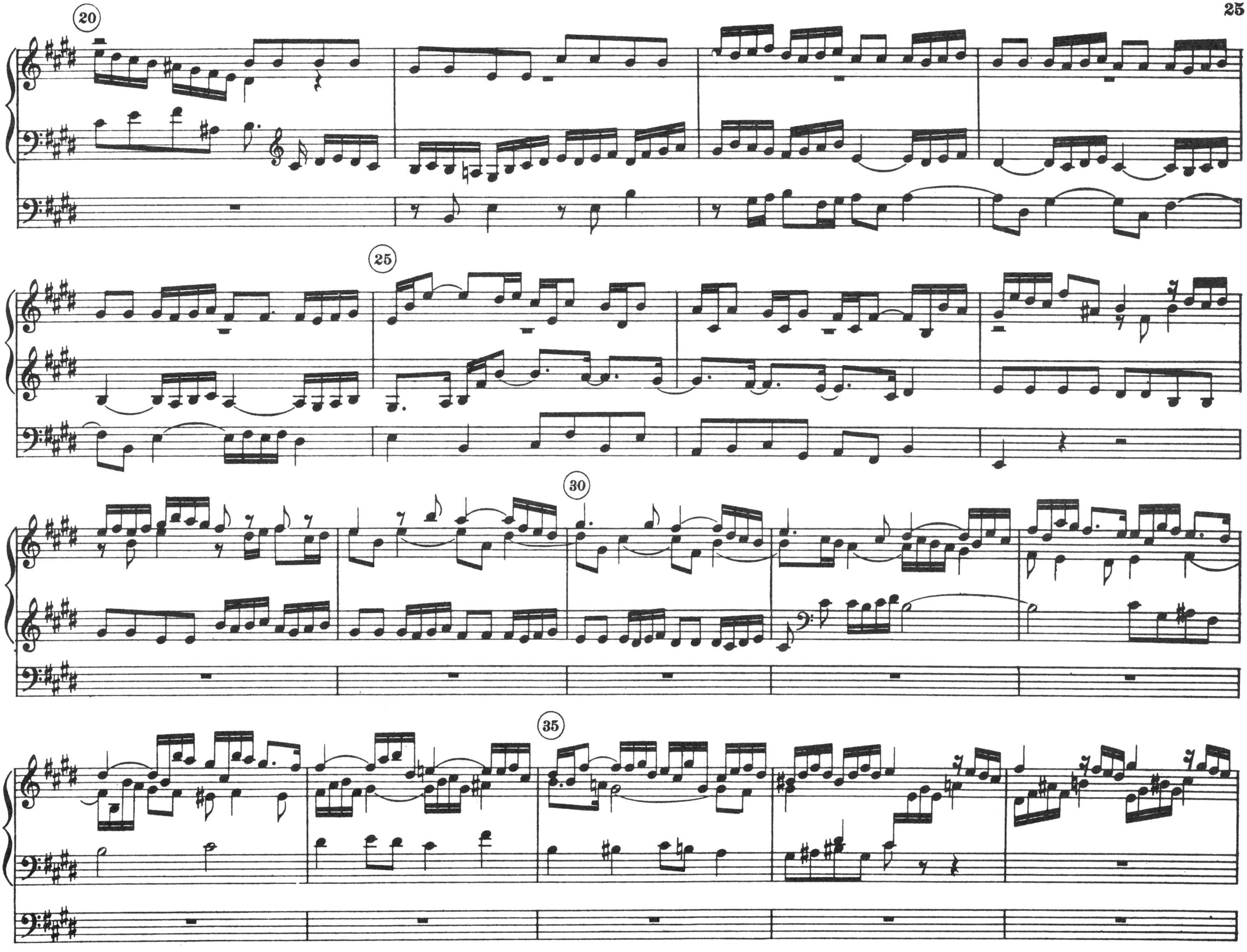

20
25
30
35

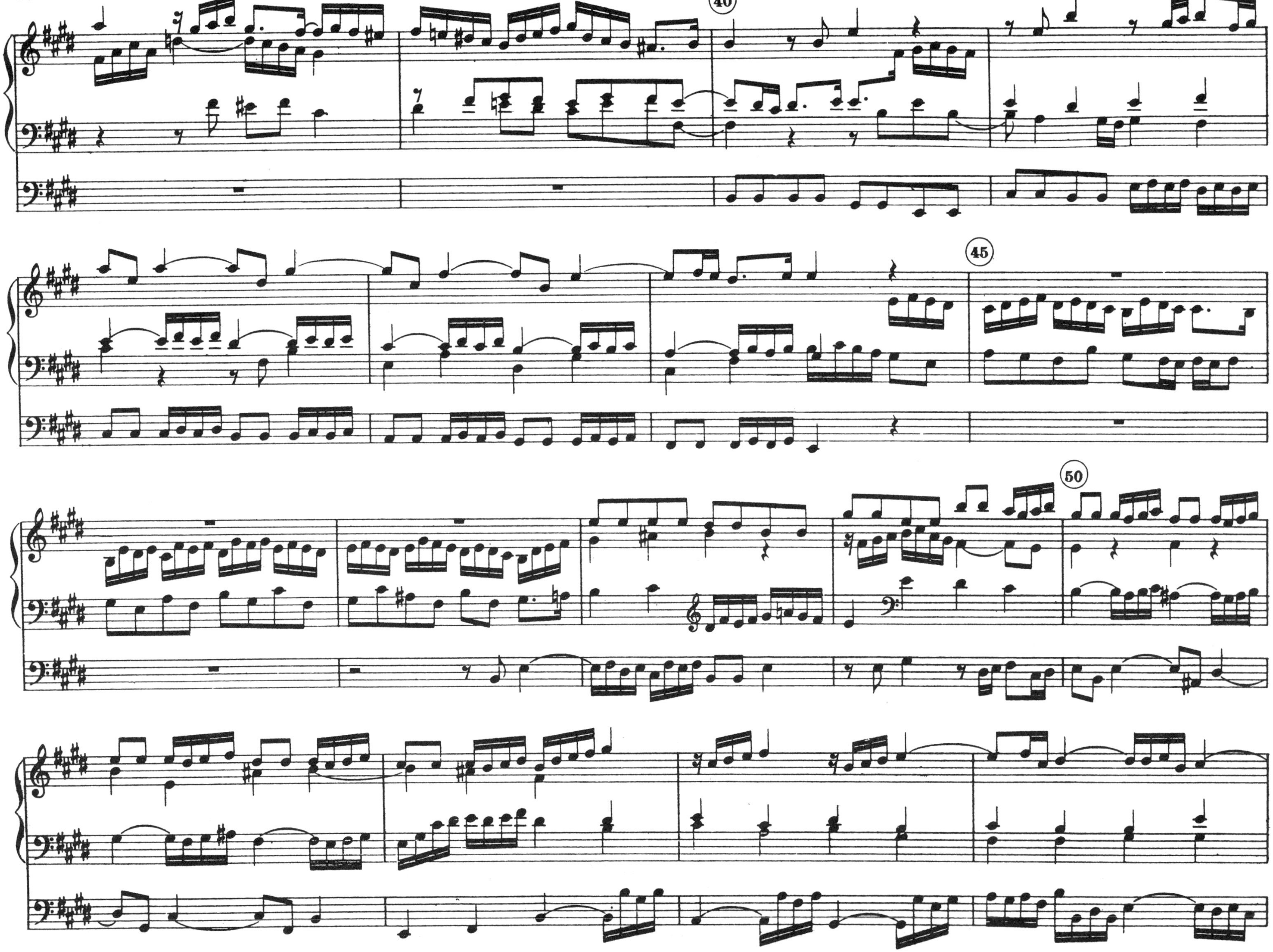
40
45
50

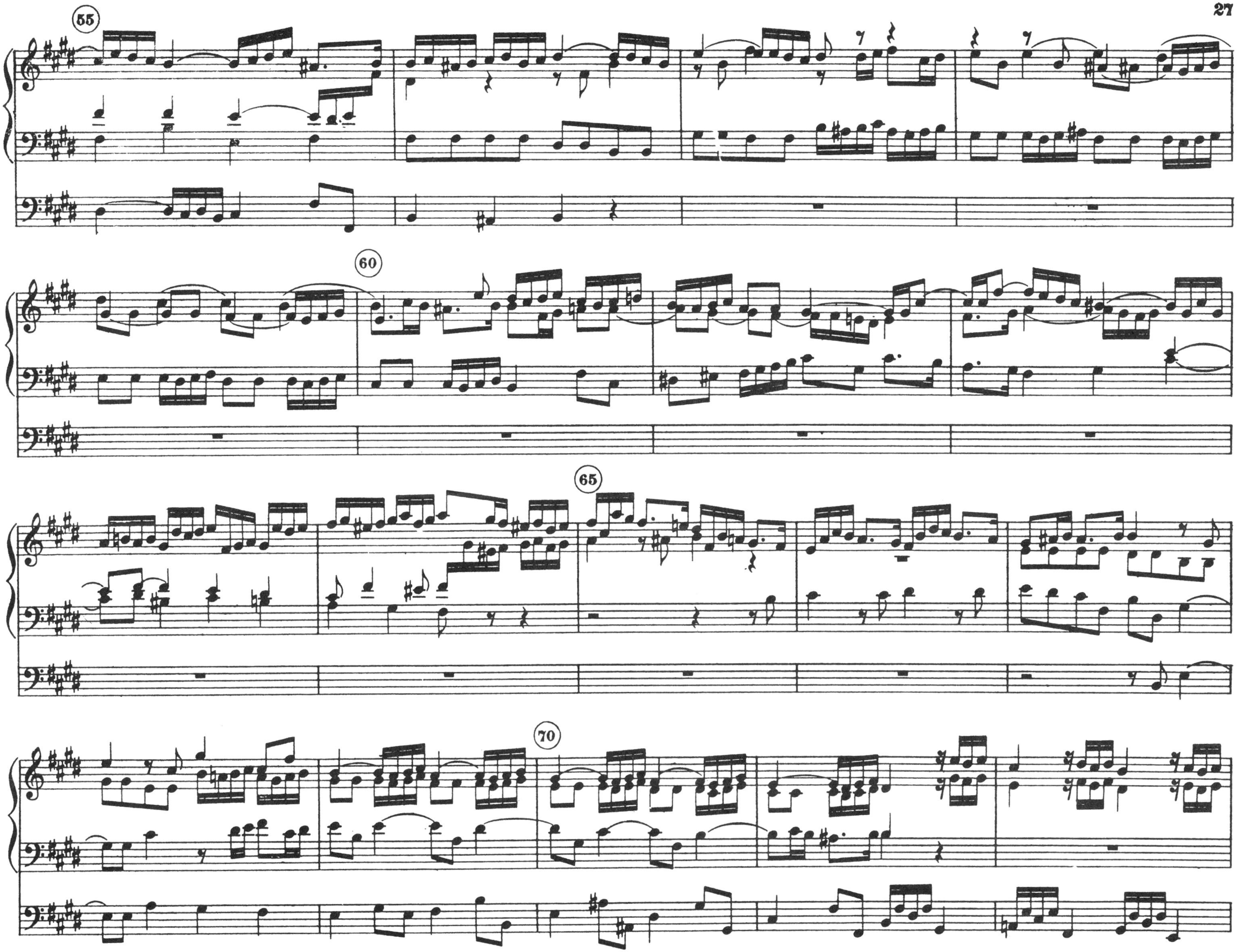
55
60
65
70

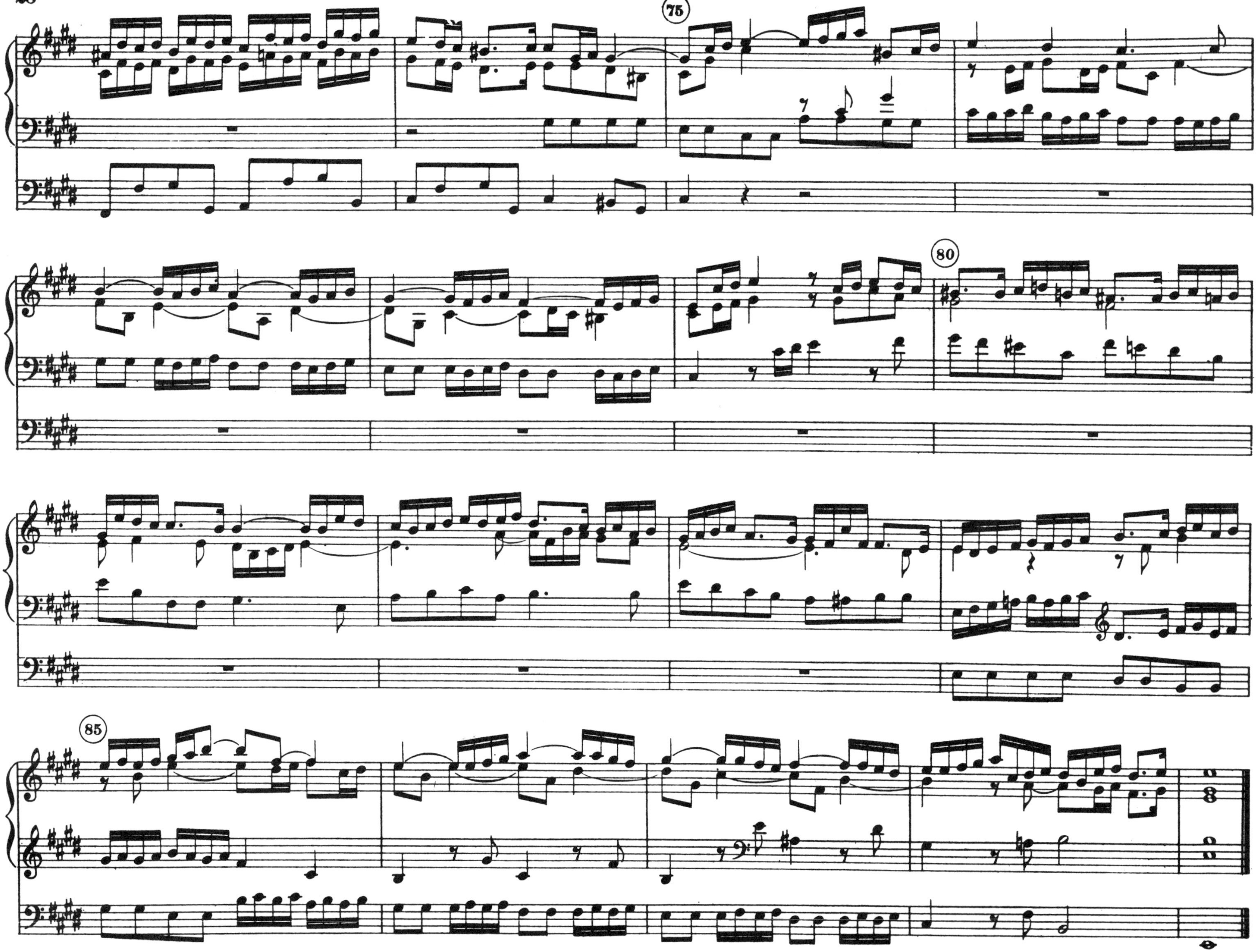
75
80
85

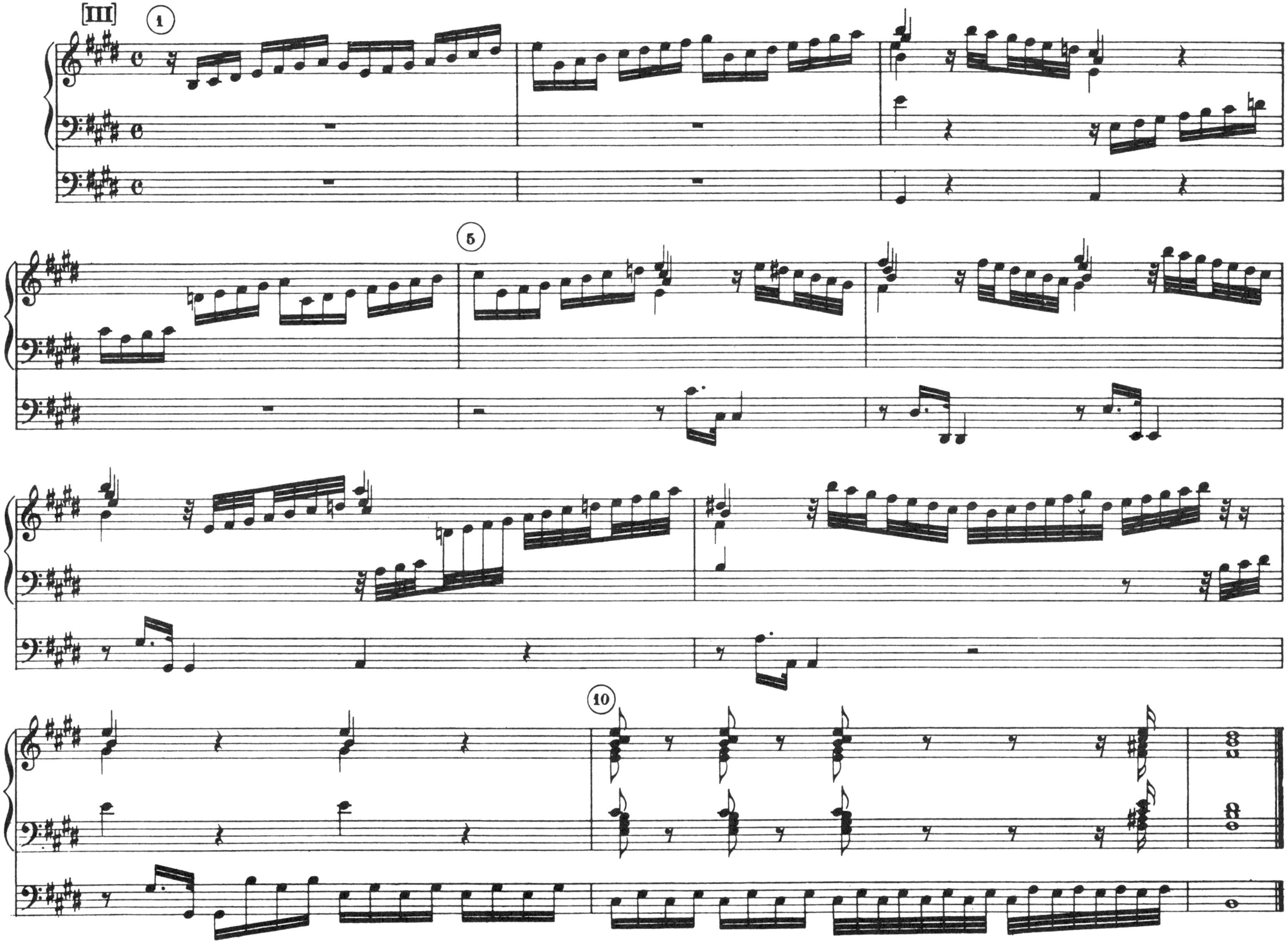
[III]
1
5
10

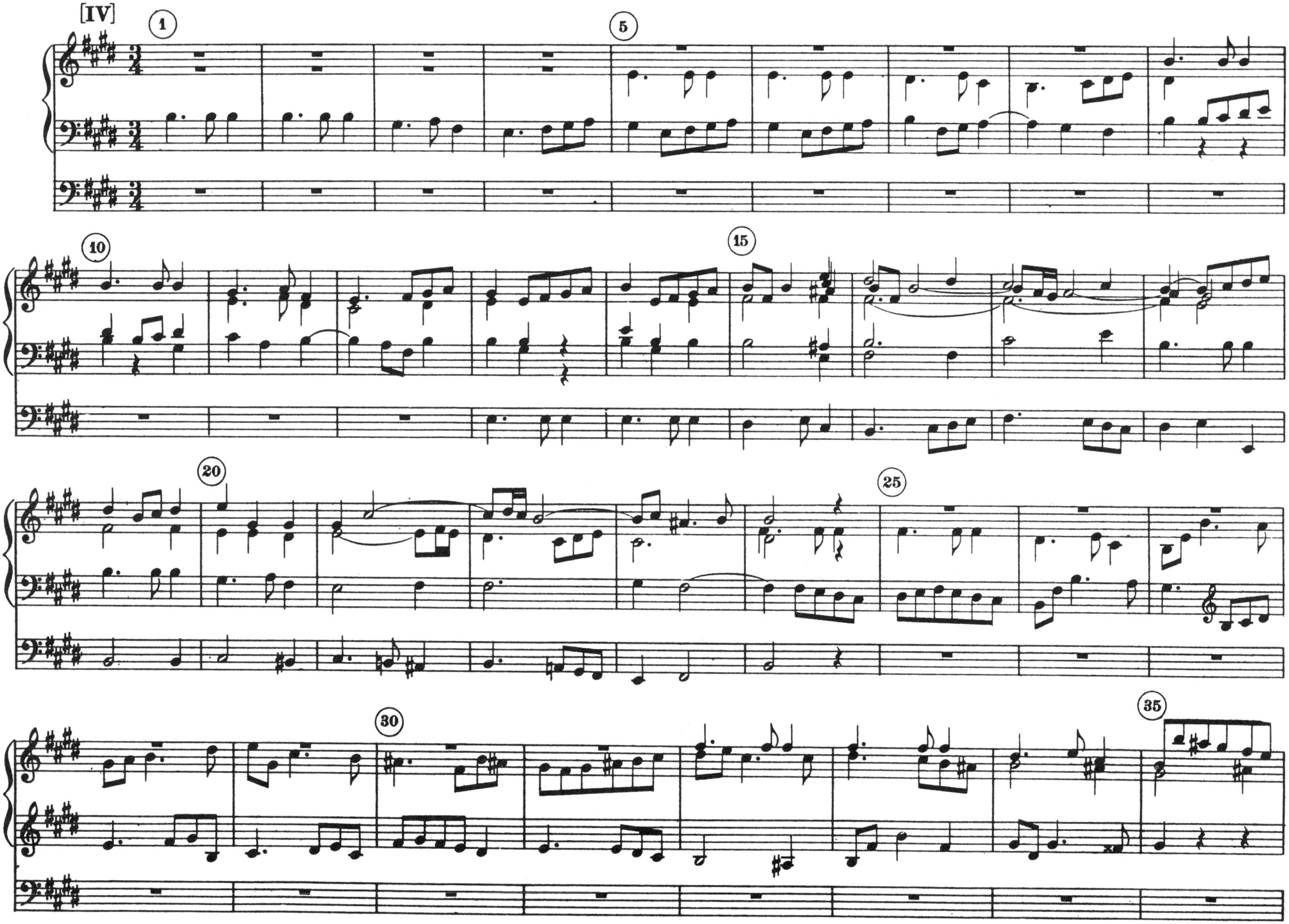
[IV]
1
5
10
15
20
25
30
35

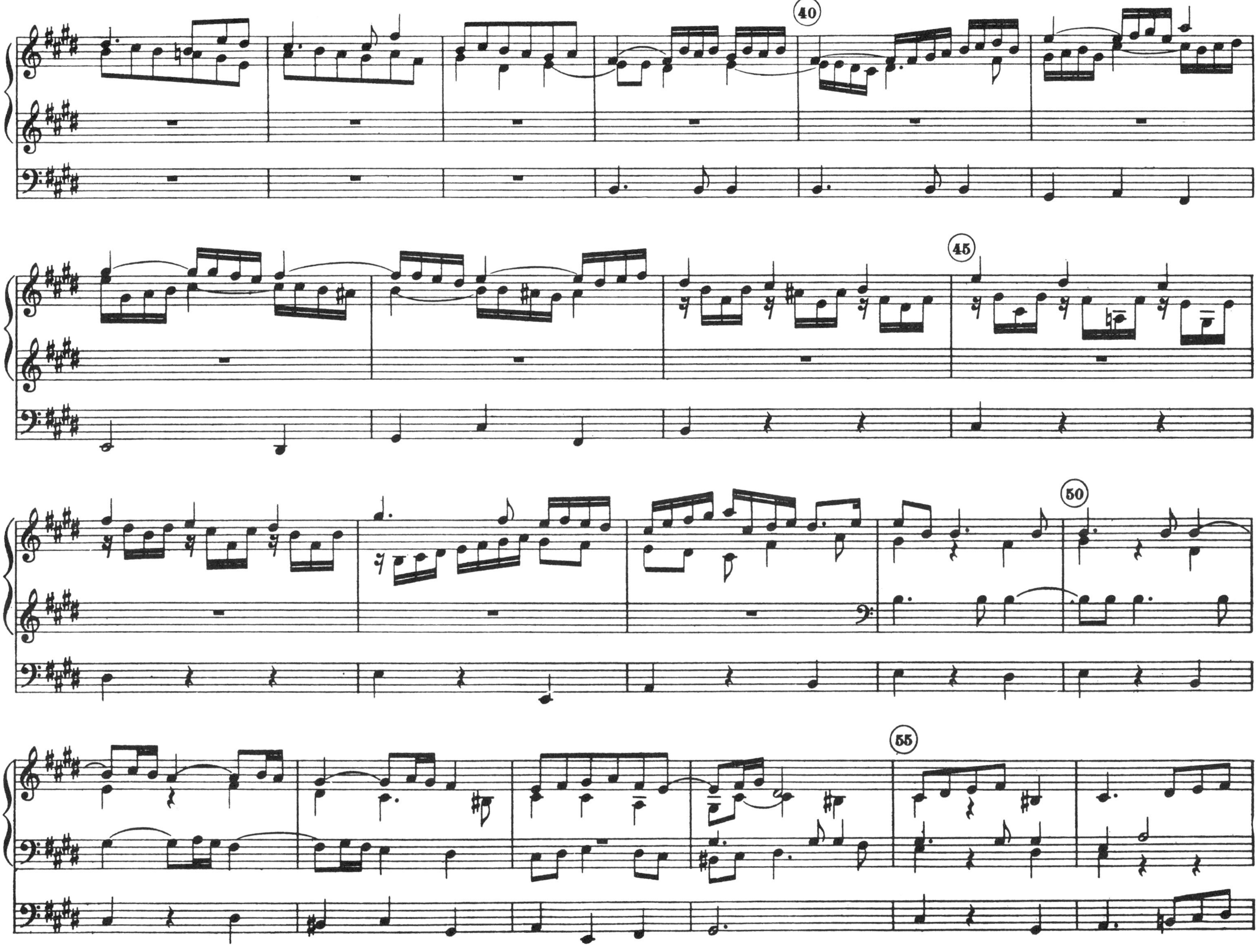
40
45
50
55

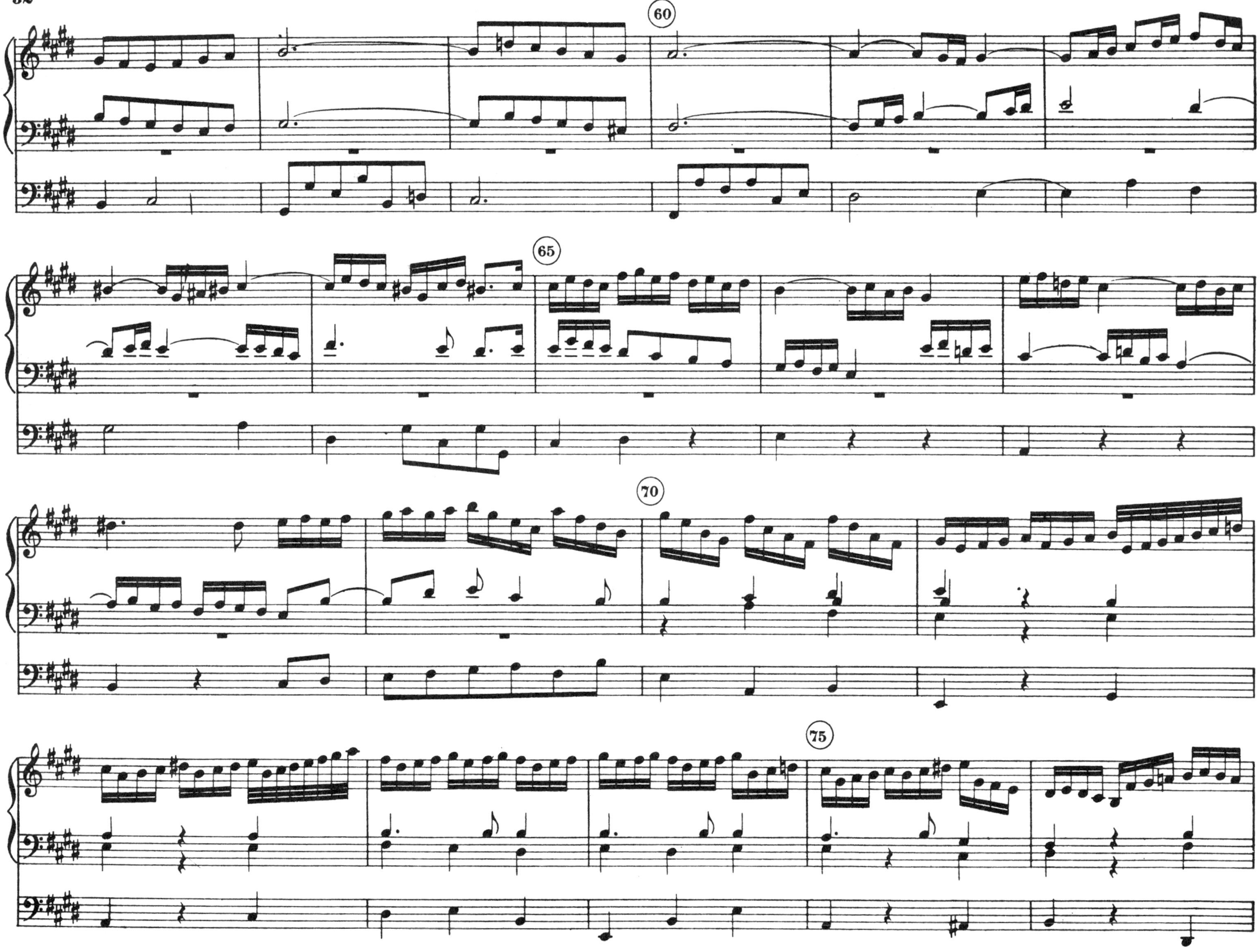
60
65
70
75

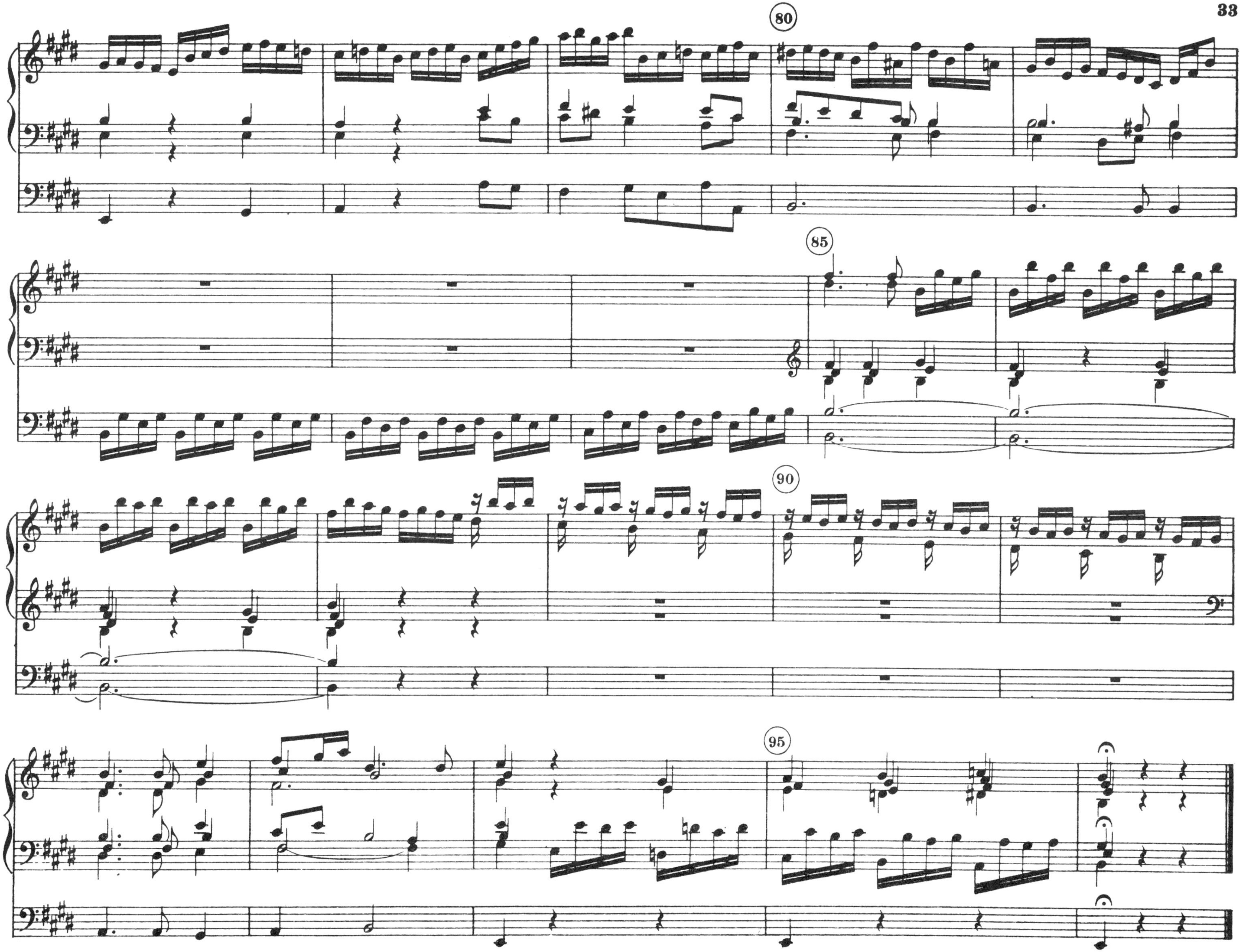
80
85
90
95

VI
Fantasie in G-Dur

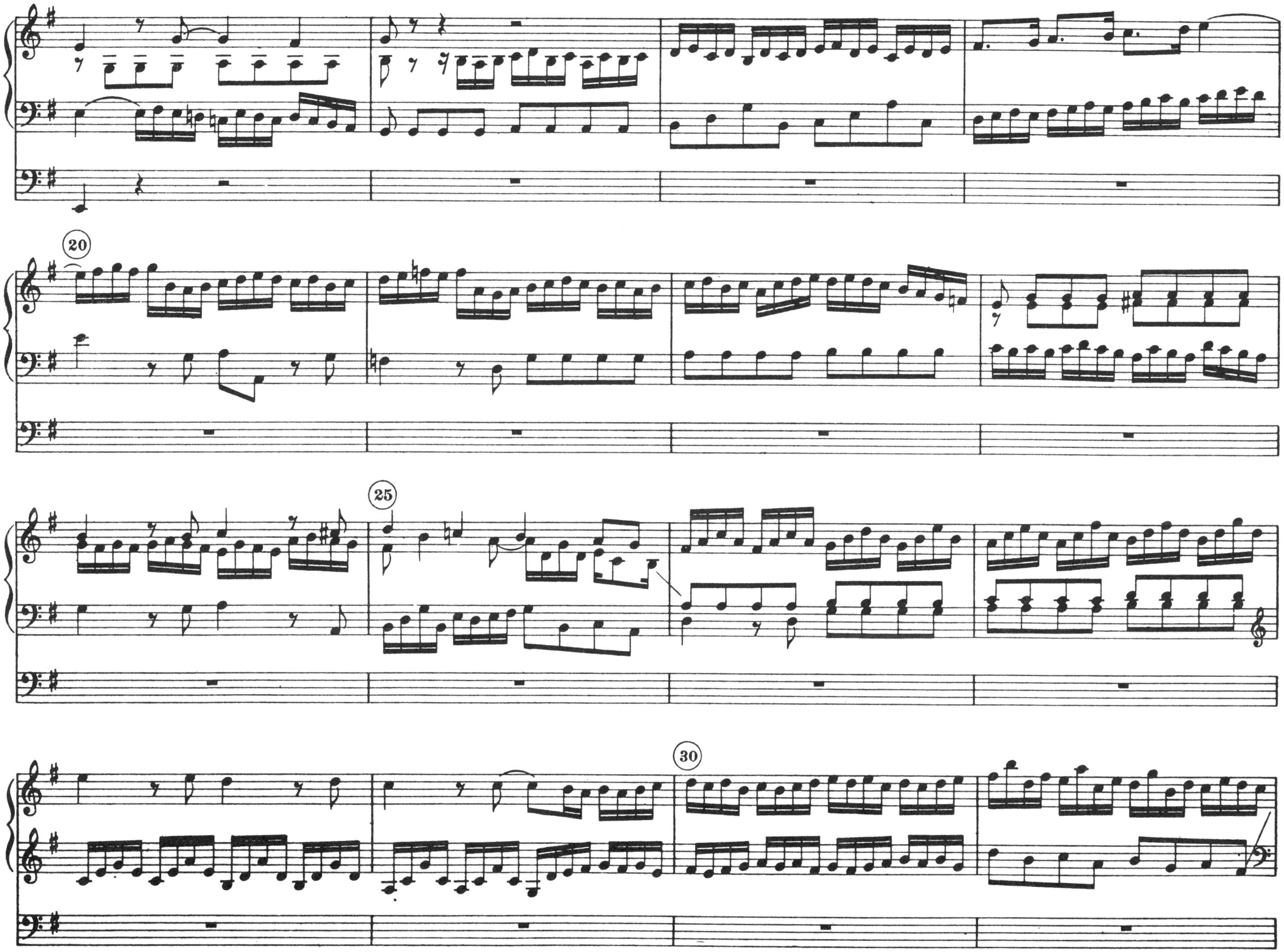
20
25
30

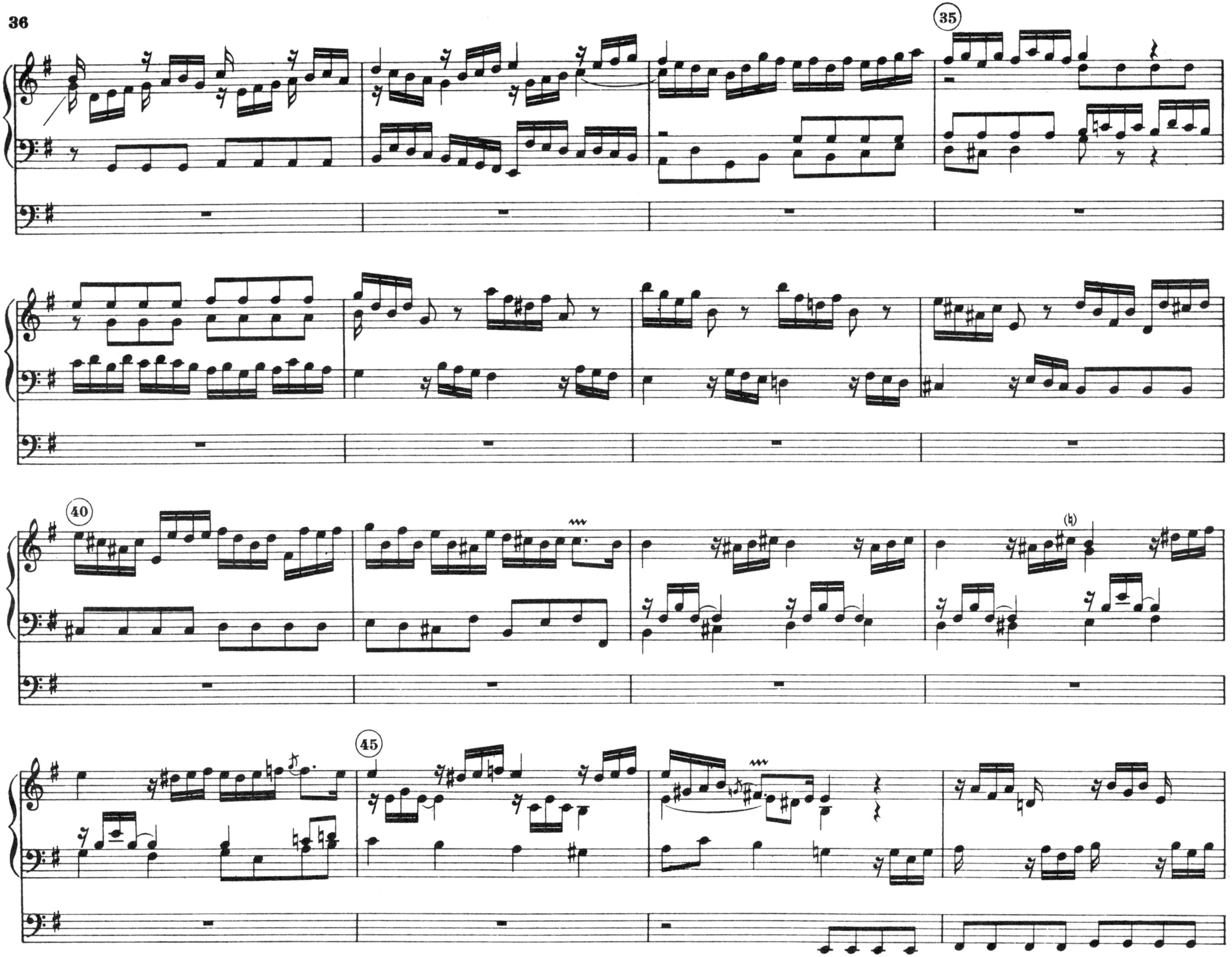
35
40
45

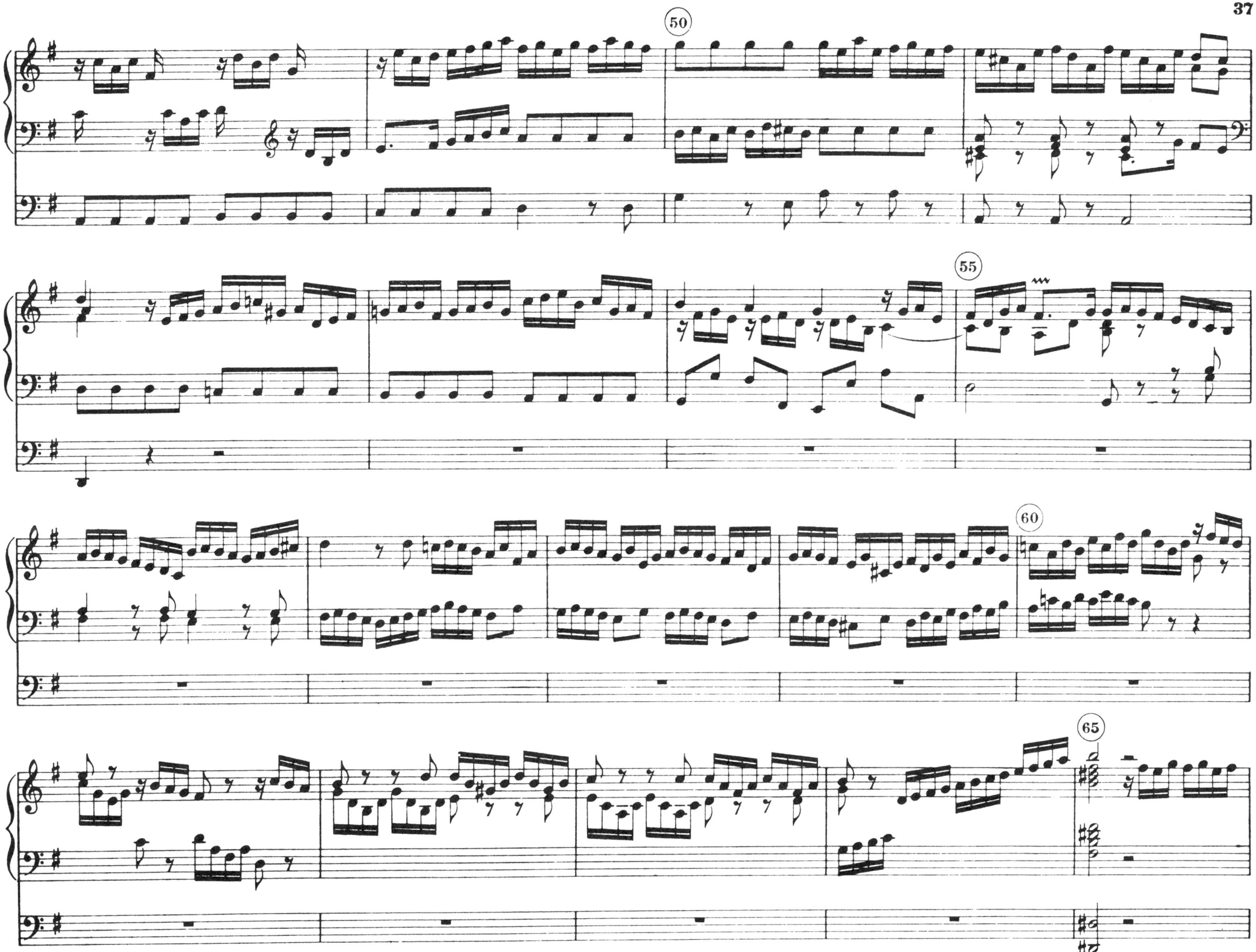
50
55
60
65

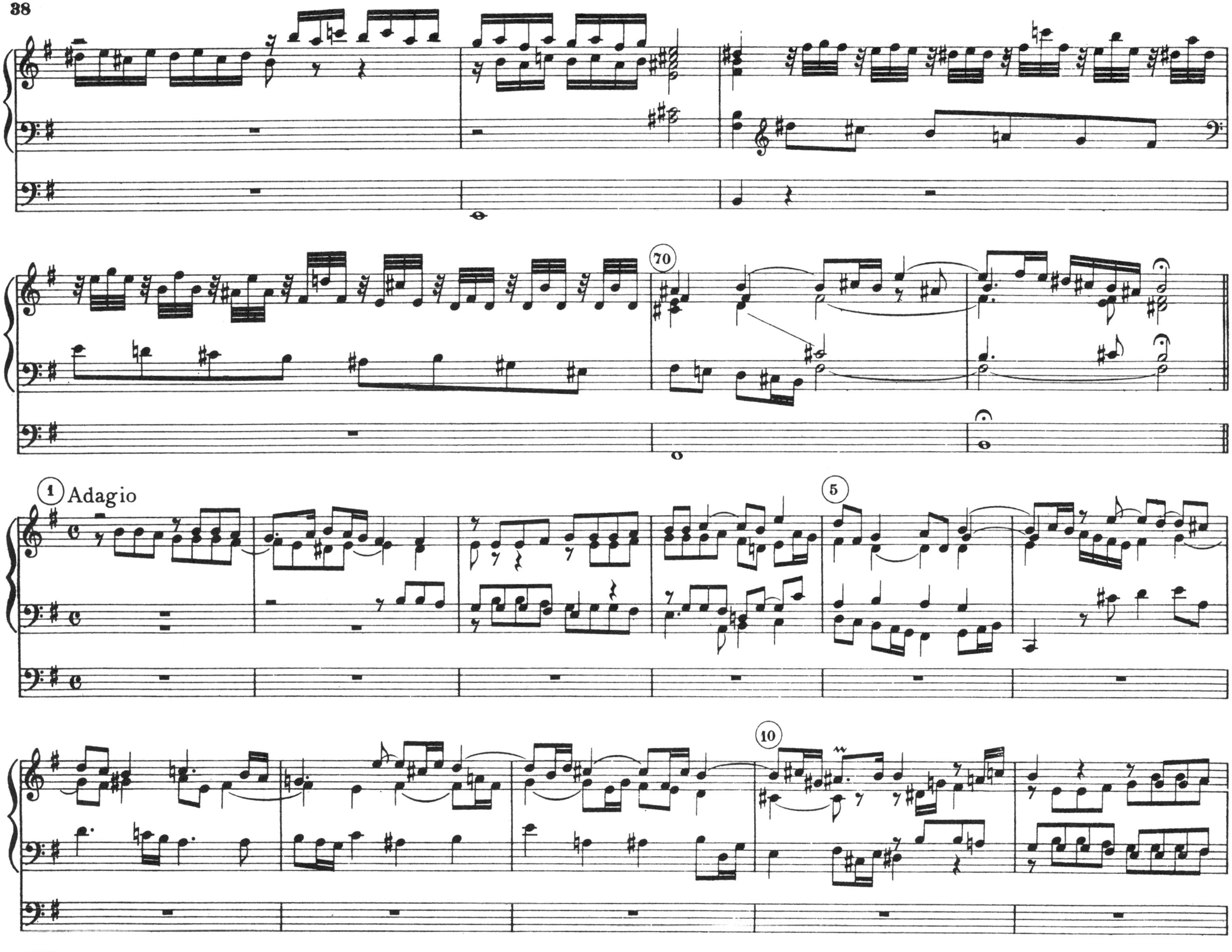
70
1
Adagio
5
10

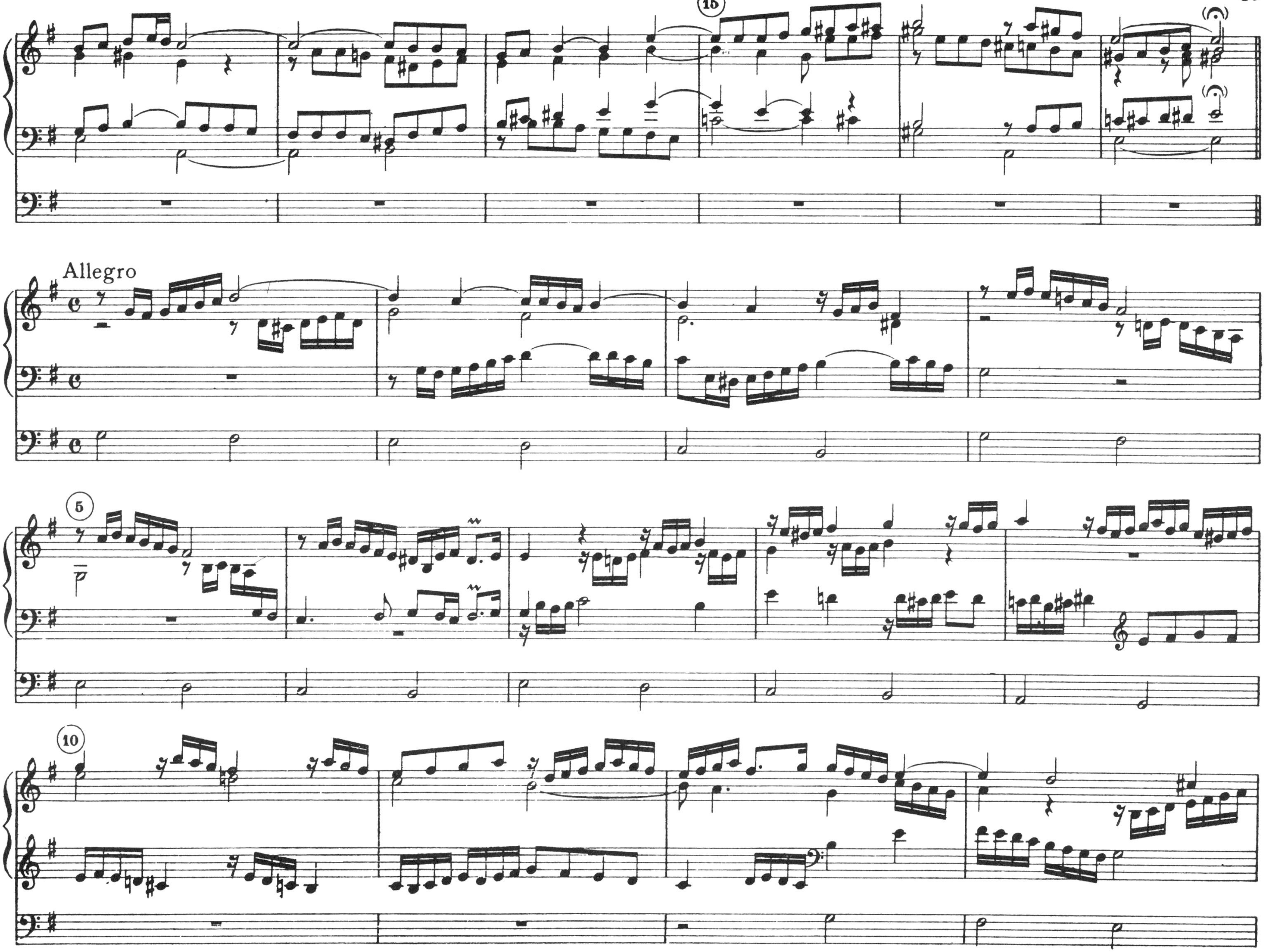
15
Allegro
5
10

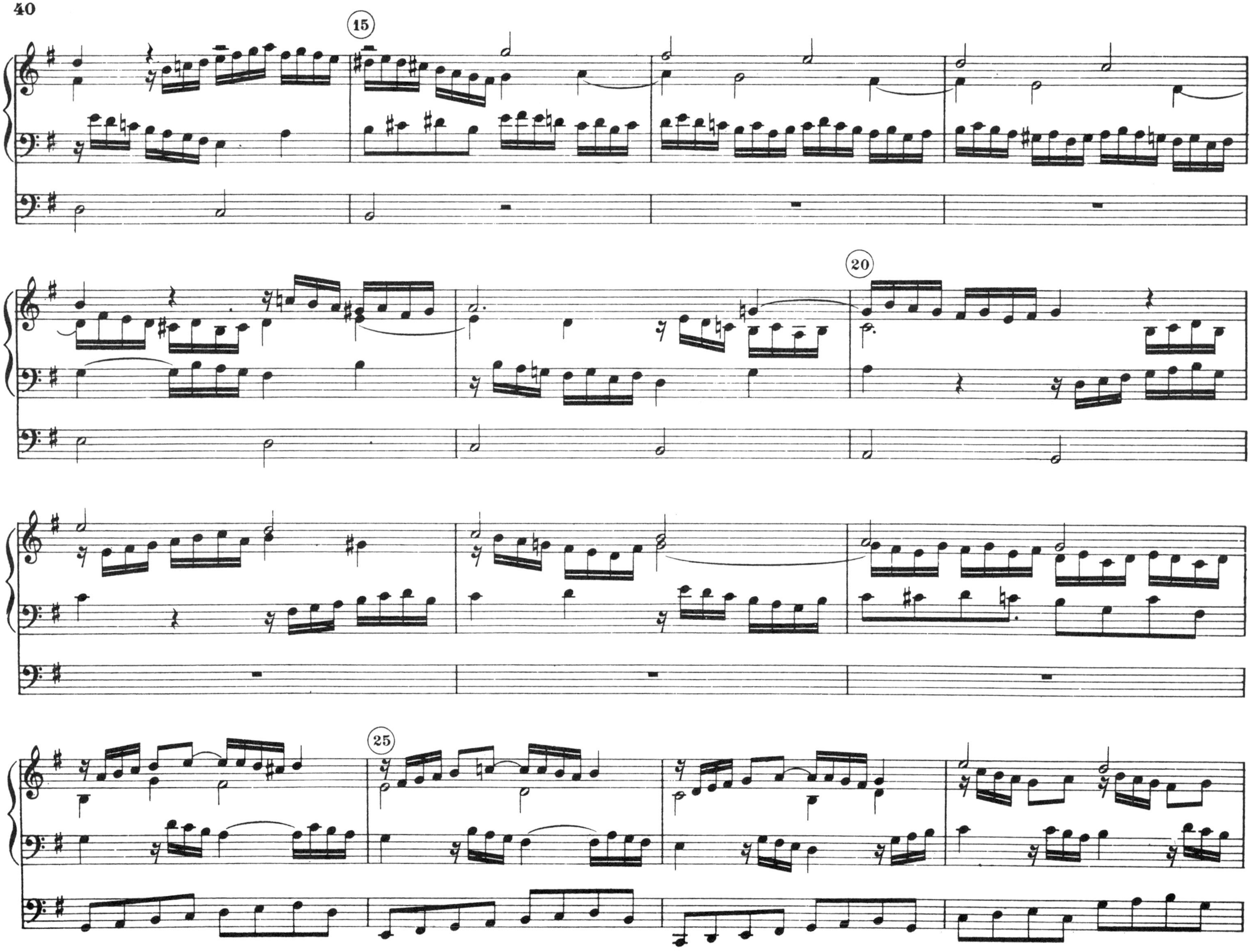
15
20
25

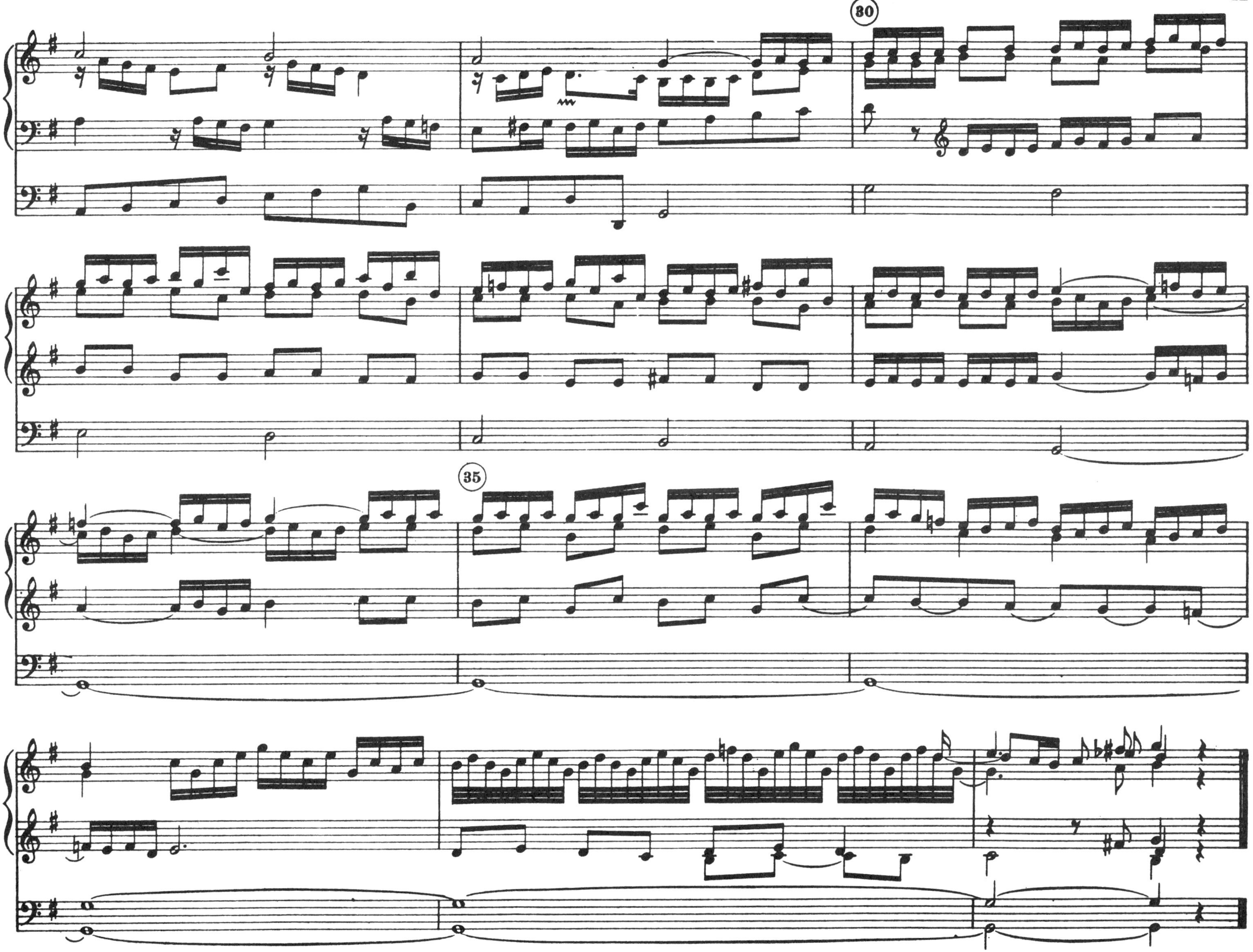
30
35

VII
Praeludium in G-Dur

Manual

Pedal

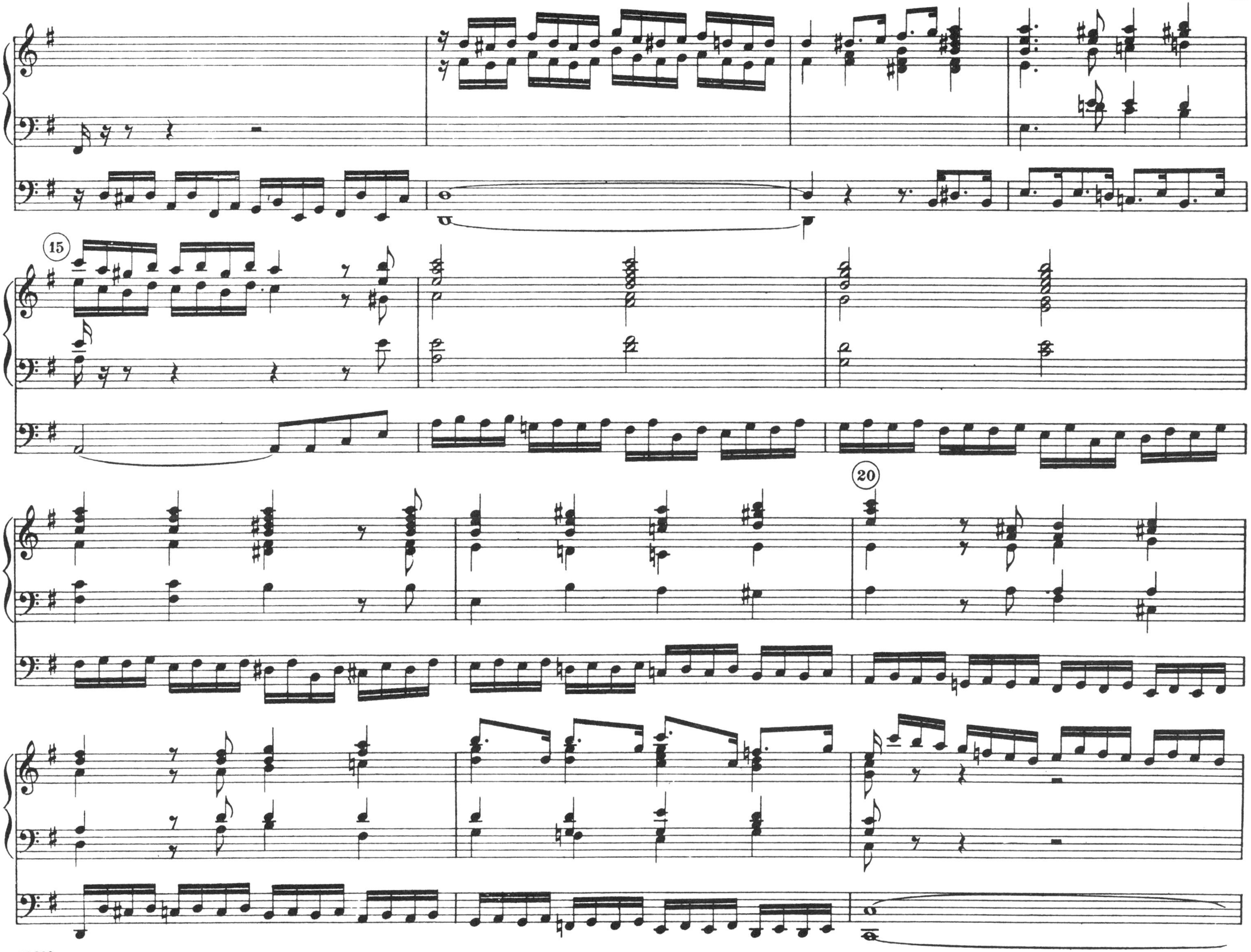
15
20

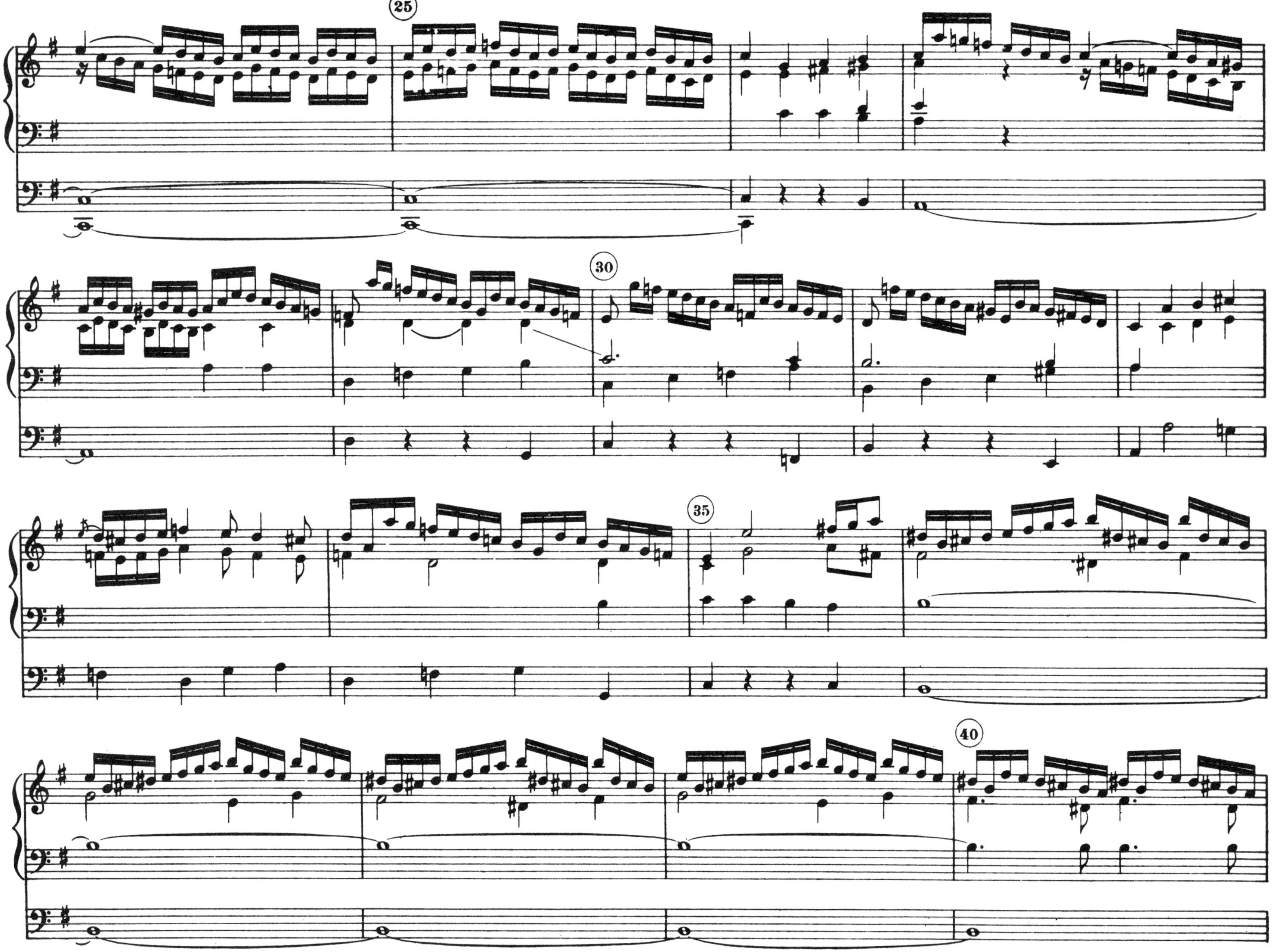
25
30
35
40

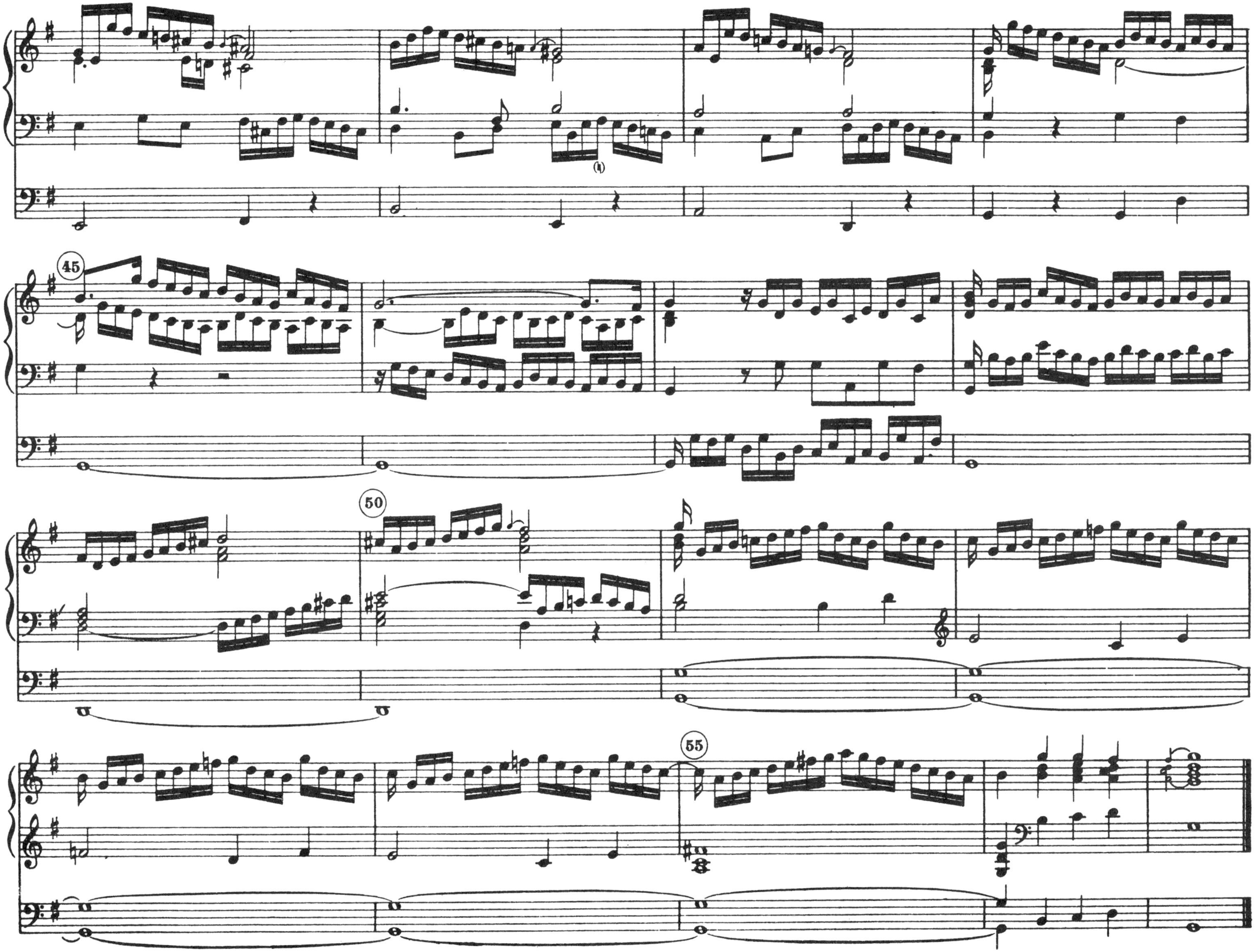
45
50
55

VIII
Fantasie in G-Dur

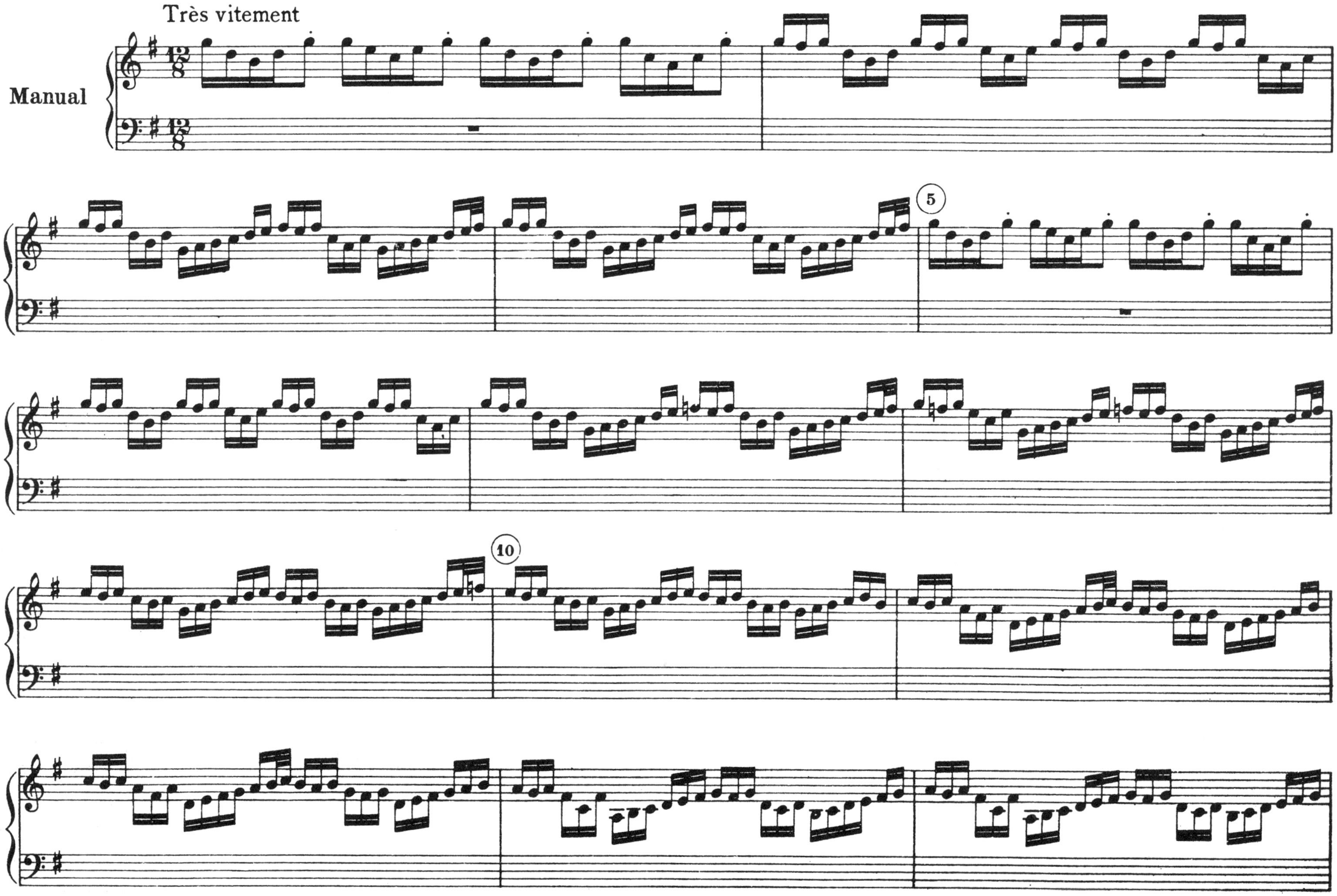

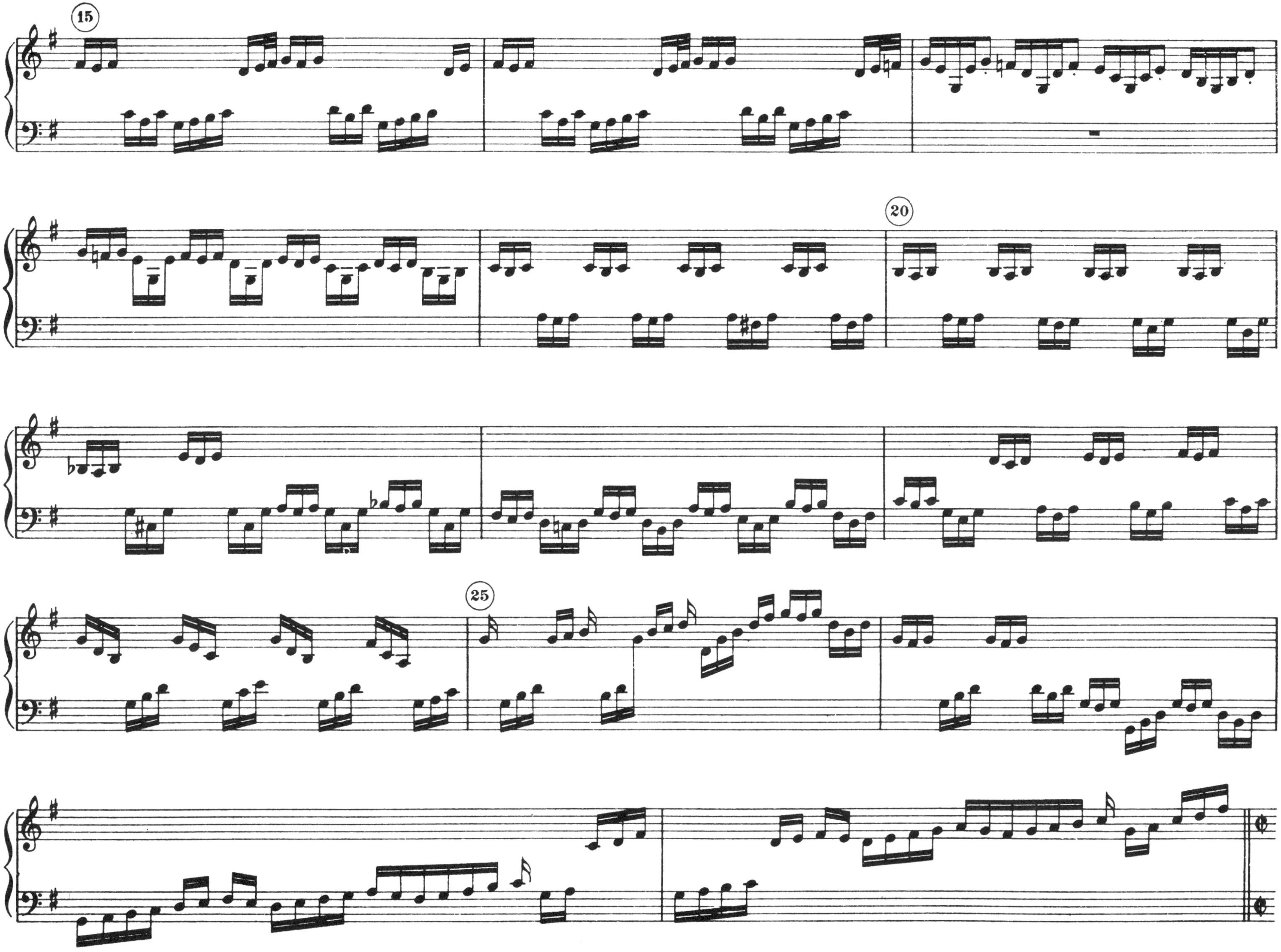
15
20
25

Gravement

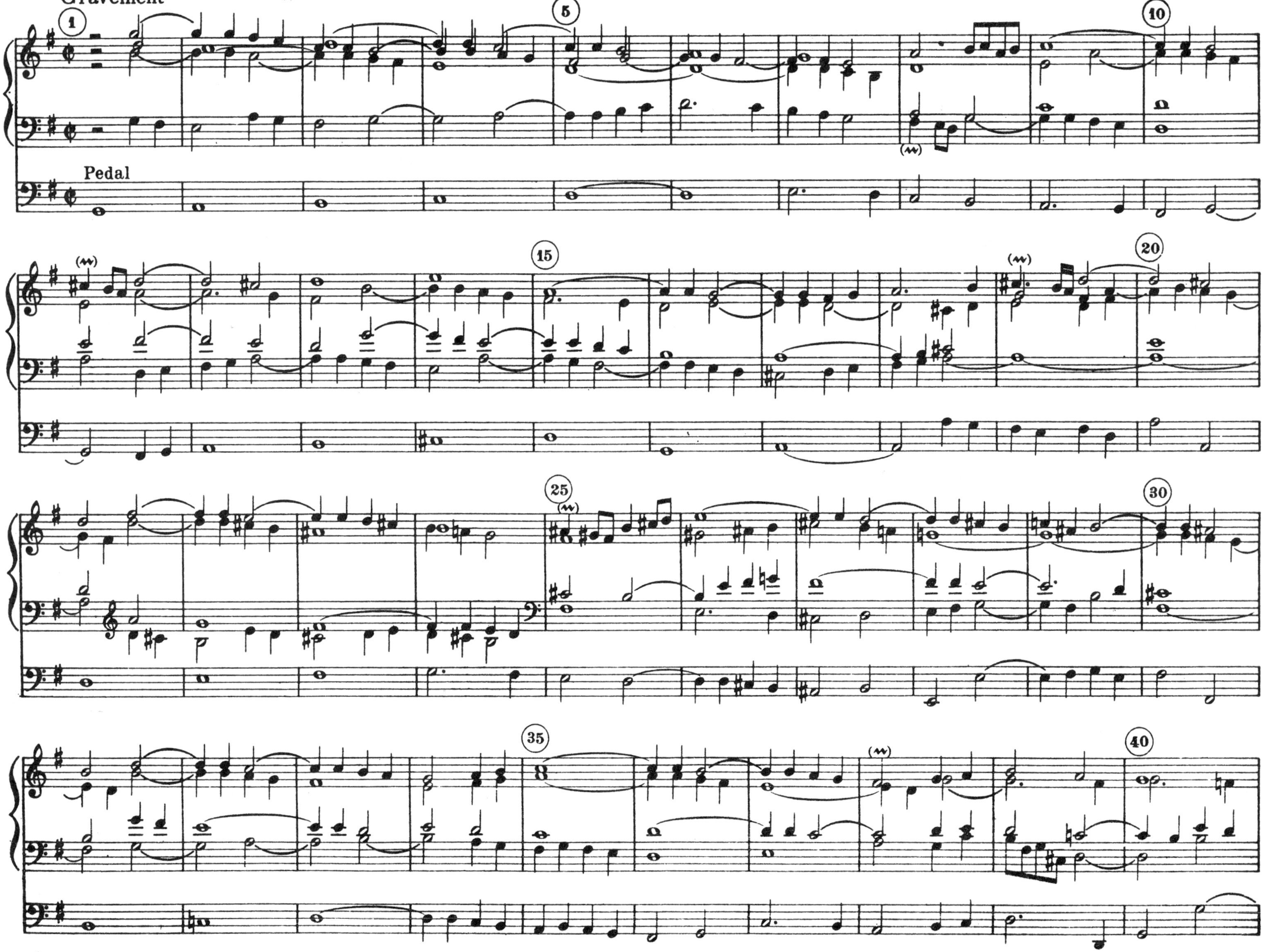

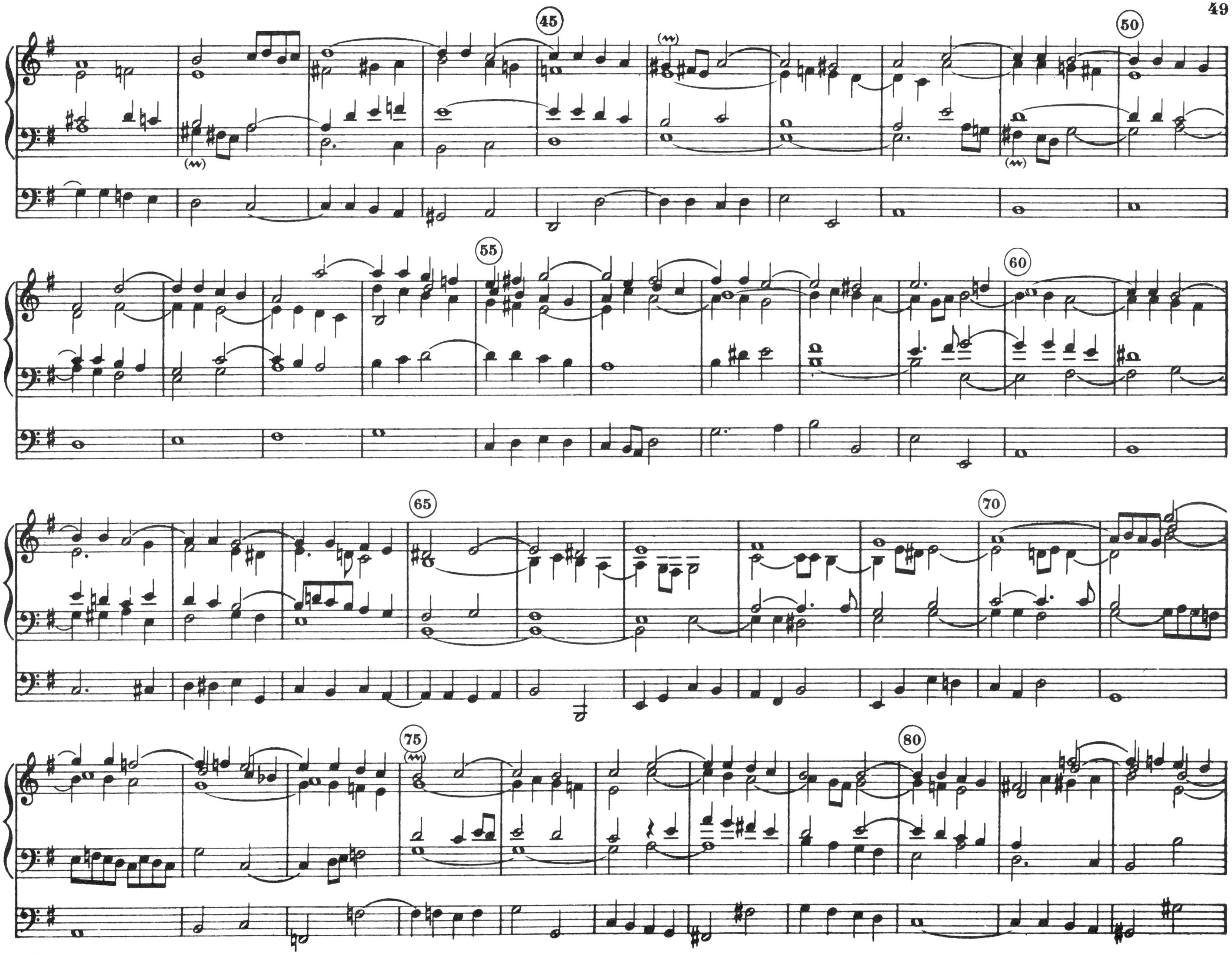
45
50
55
60
65
70
75
80

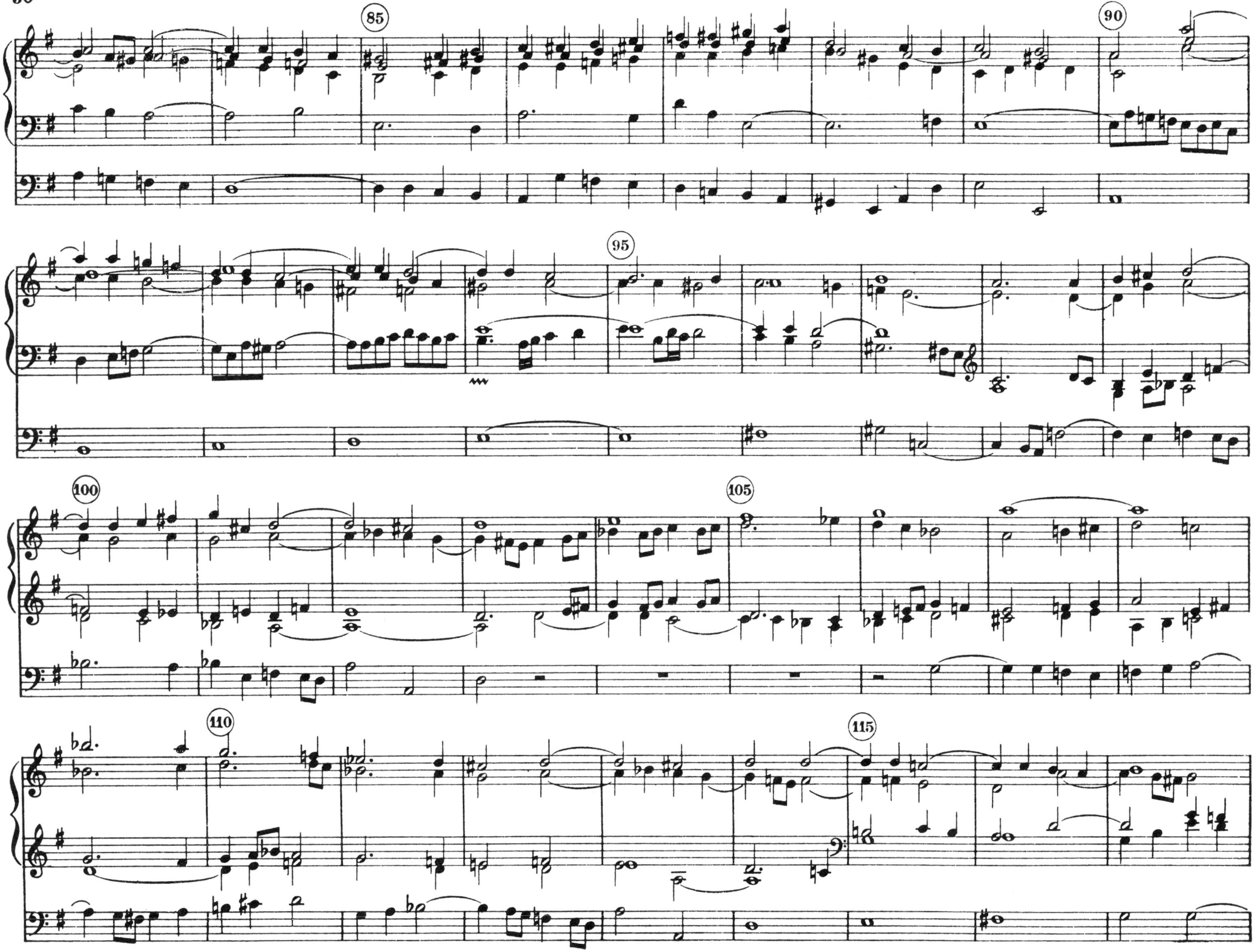
85
90
95
100
105
110
115

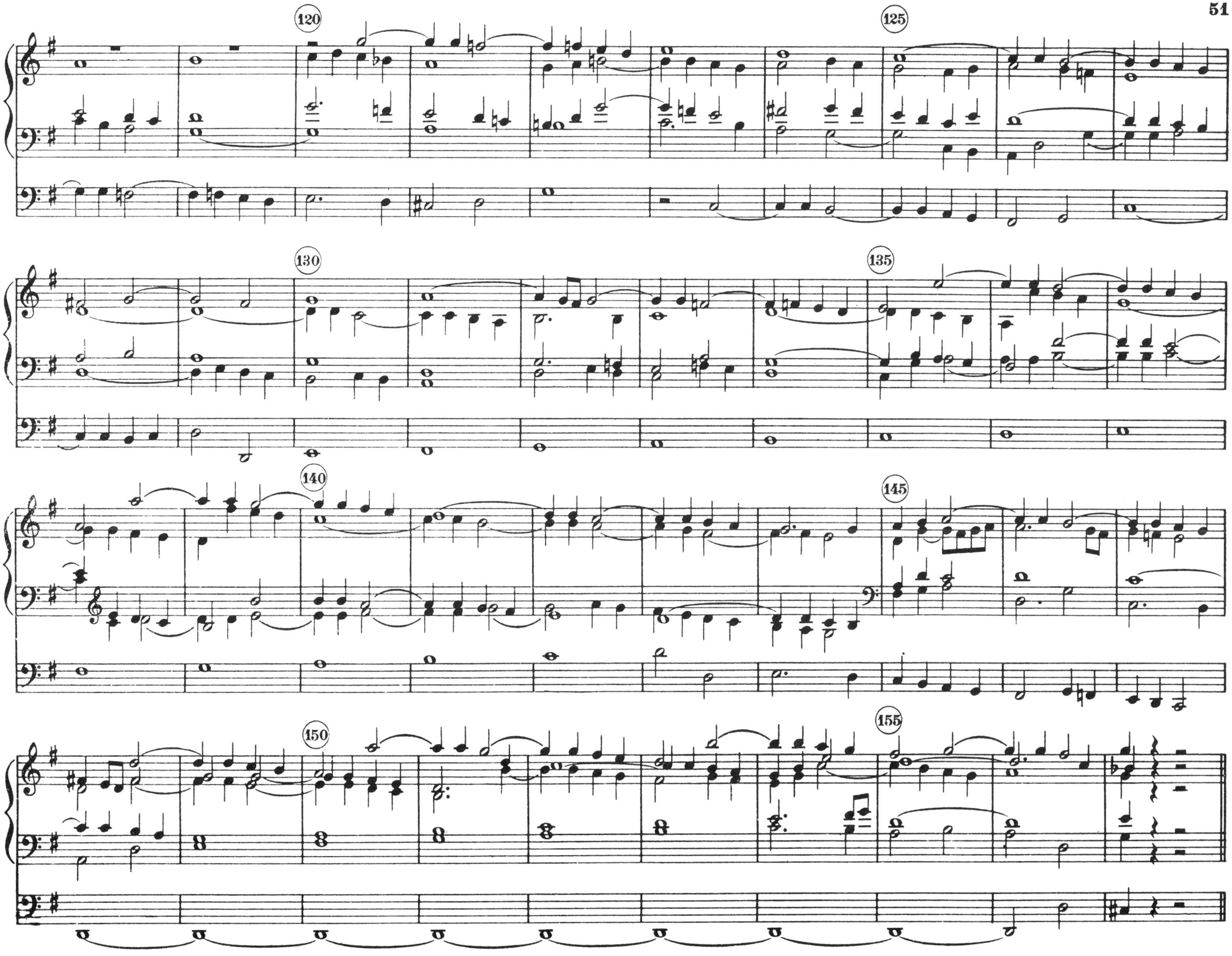
120
125
130
135
140
145
150
155

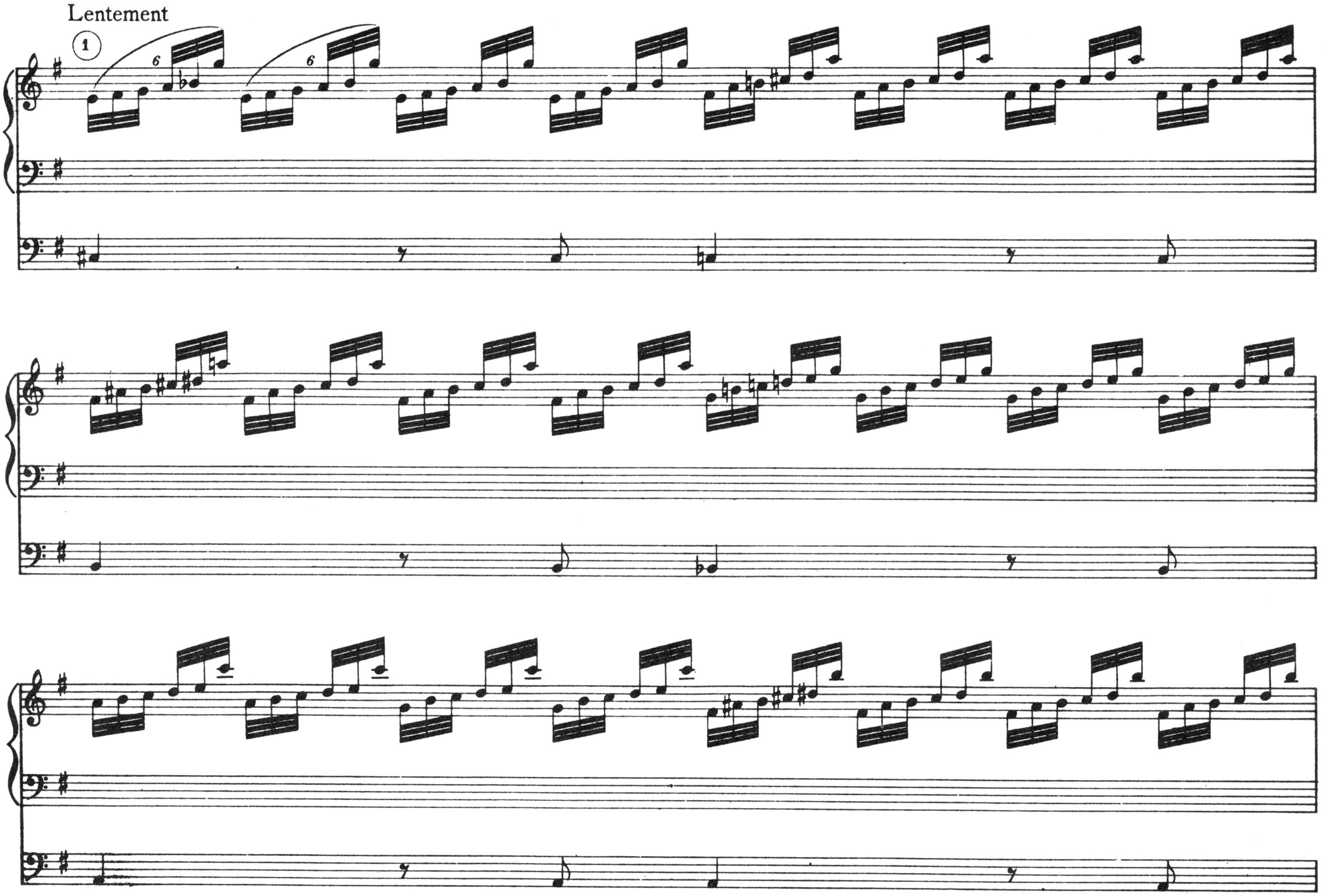
Lentement
1
6
6

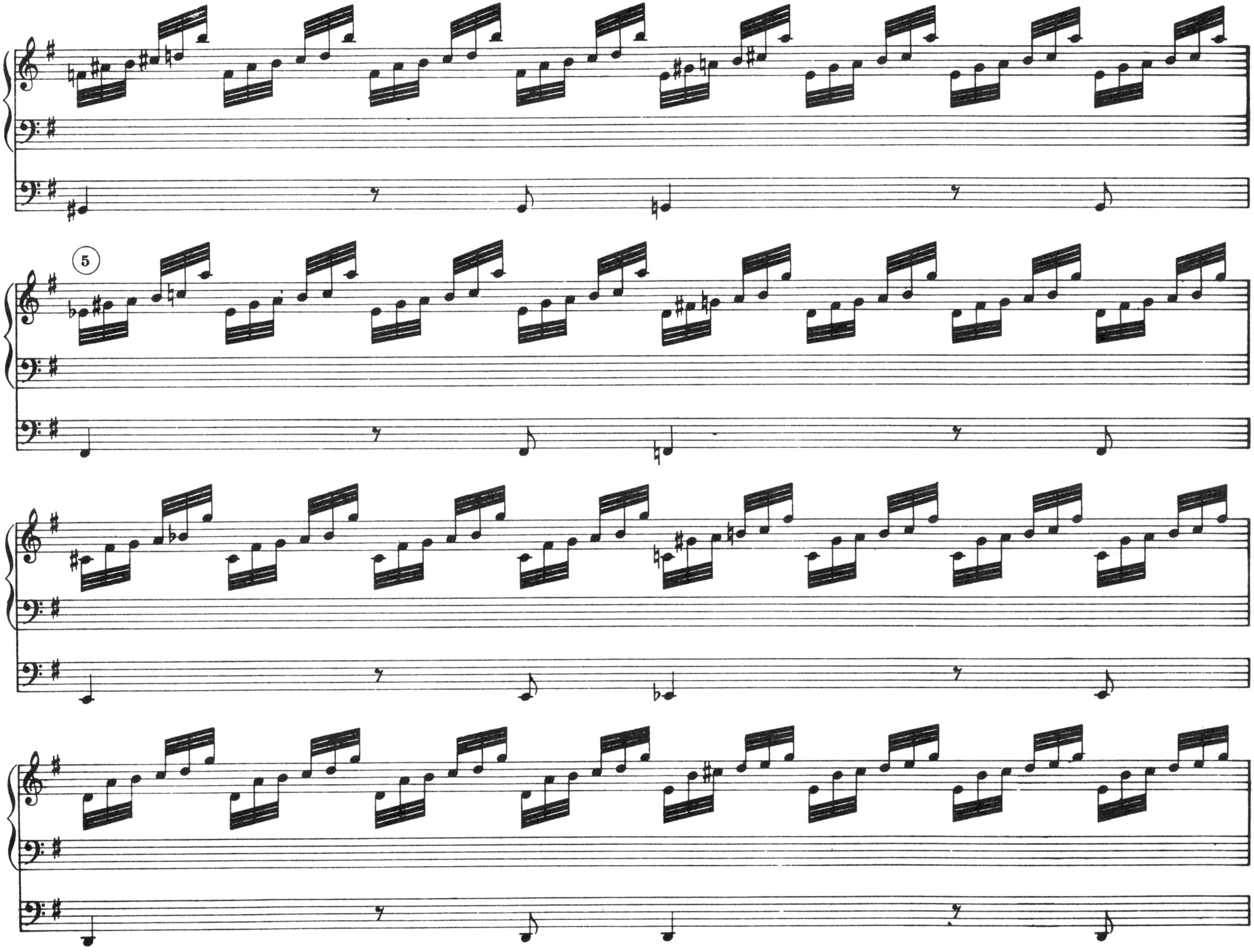
5

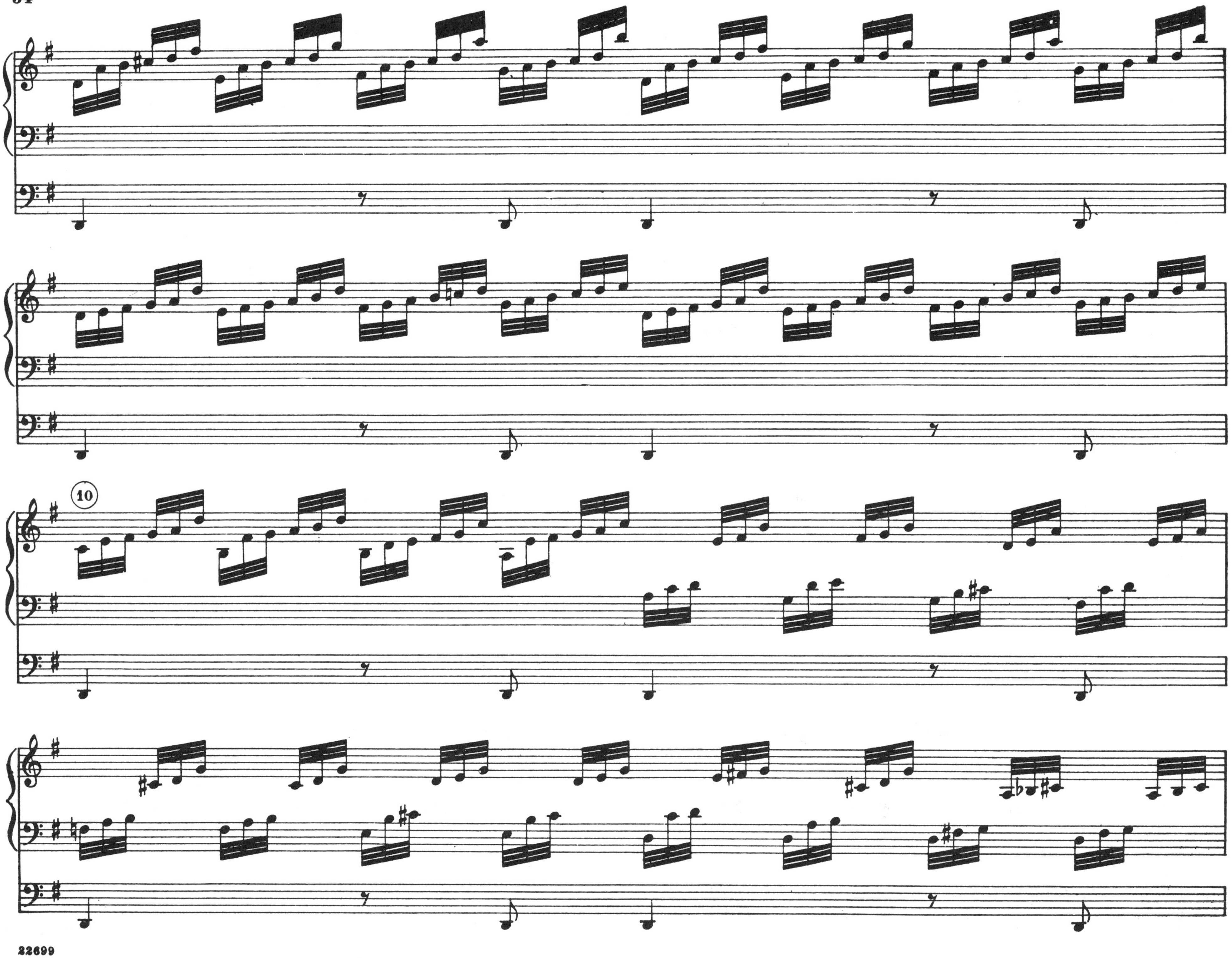
10

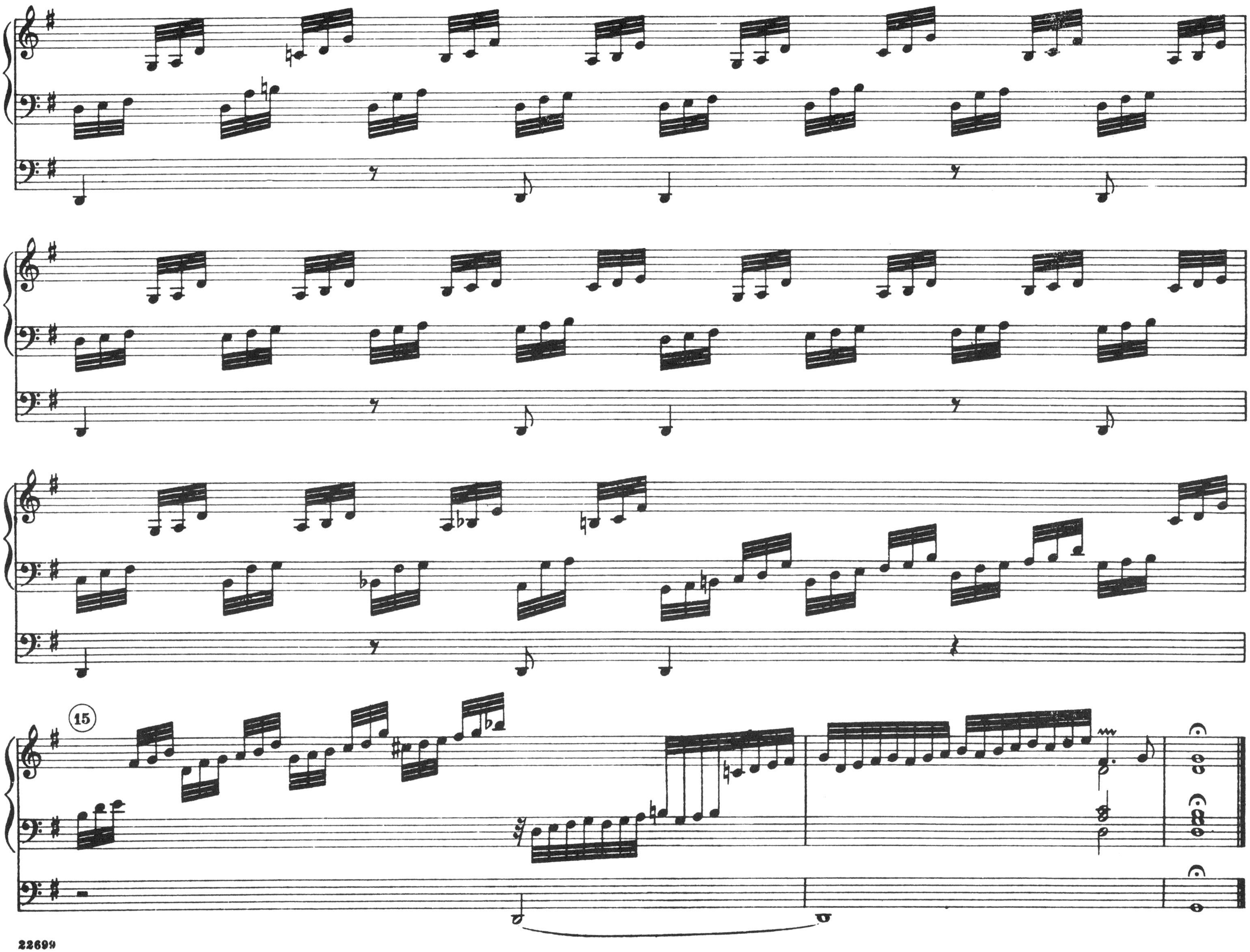
15

IX
Fuge in G-Dur

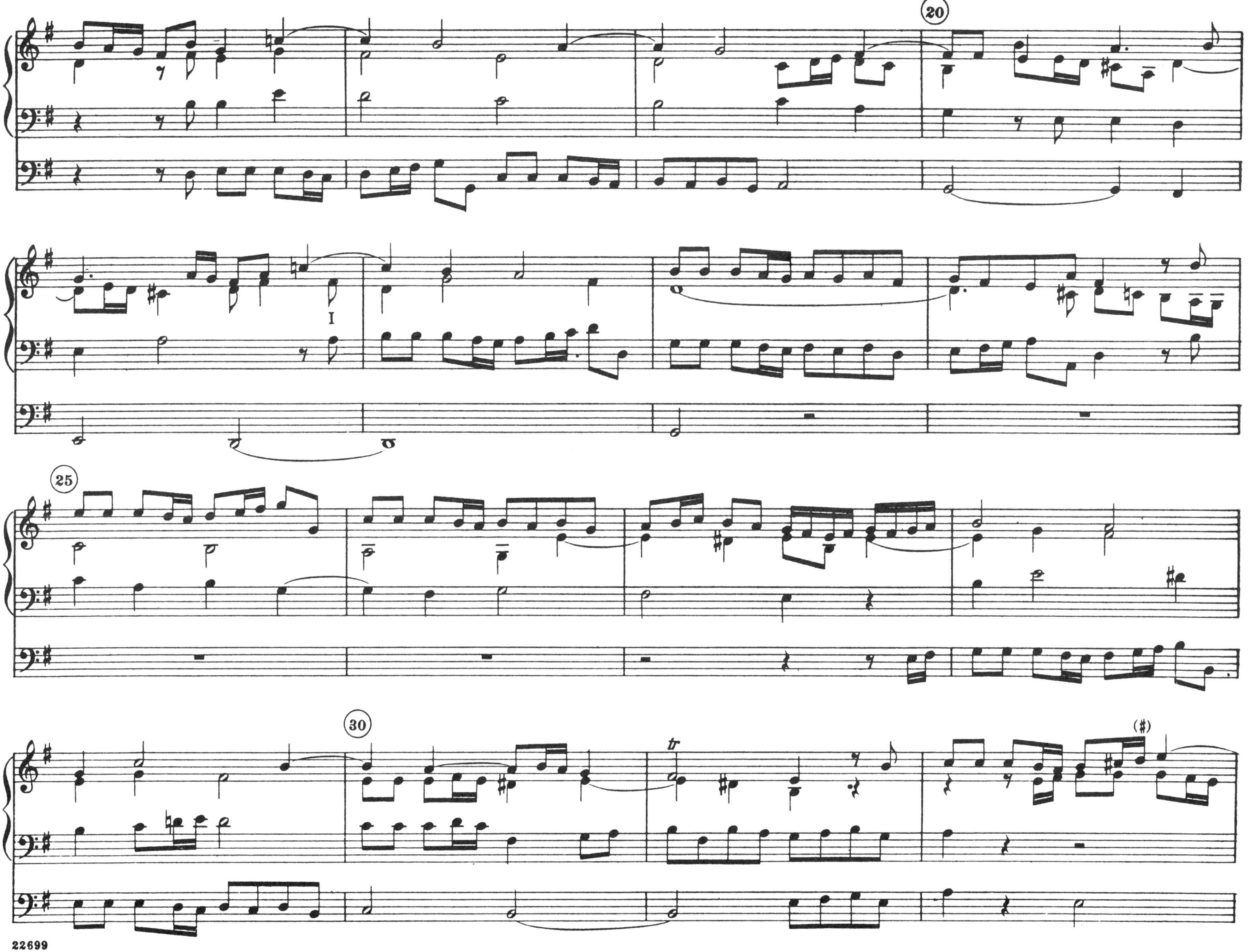
20
I
25
30
tr
(♯)

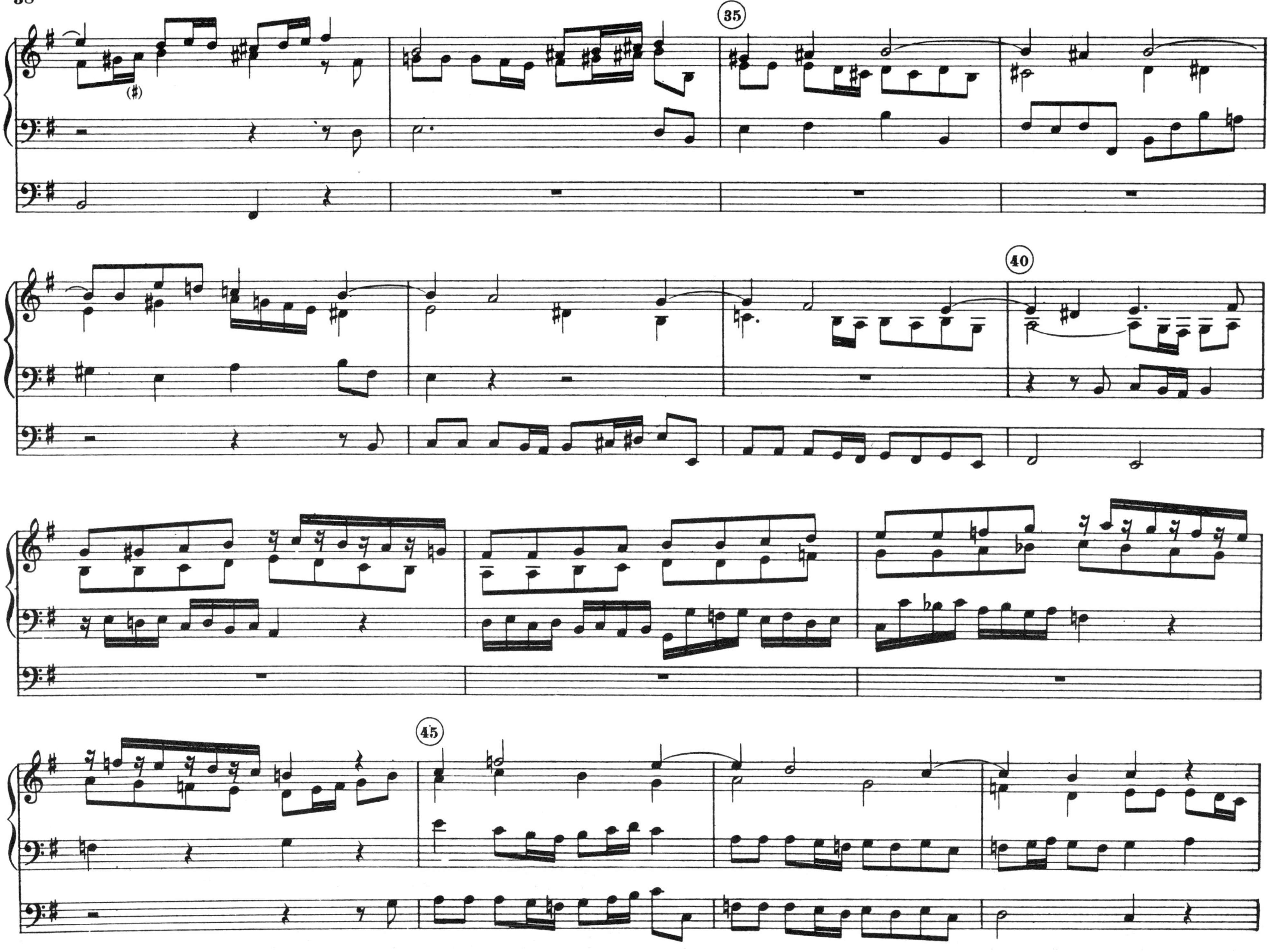
35
40
45

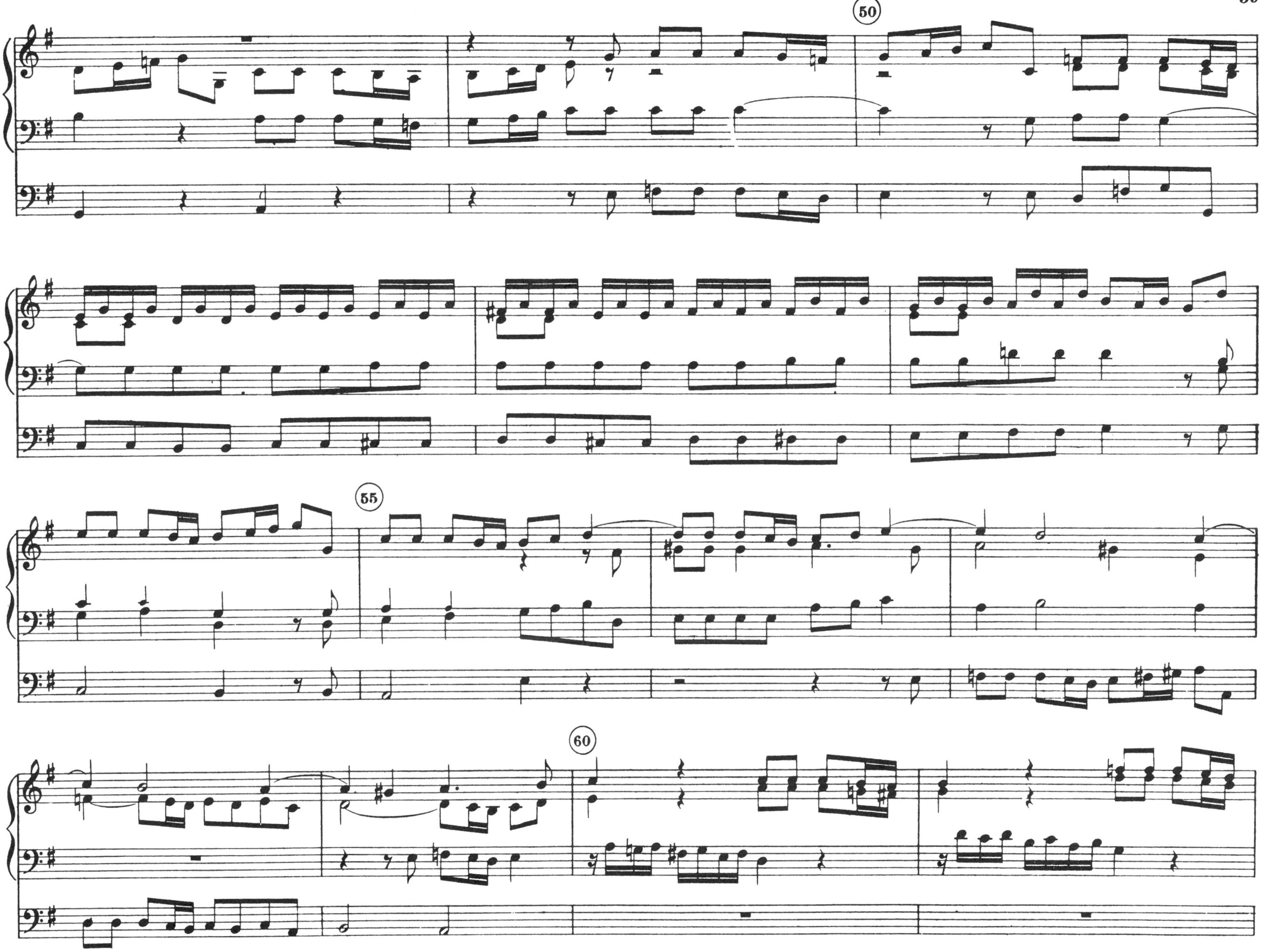

50
55
60

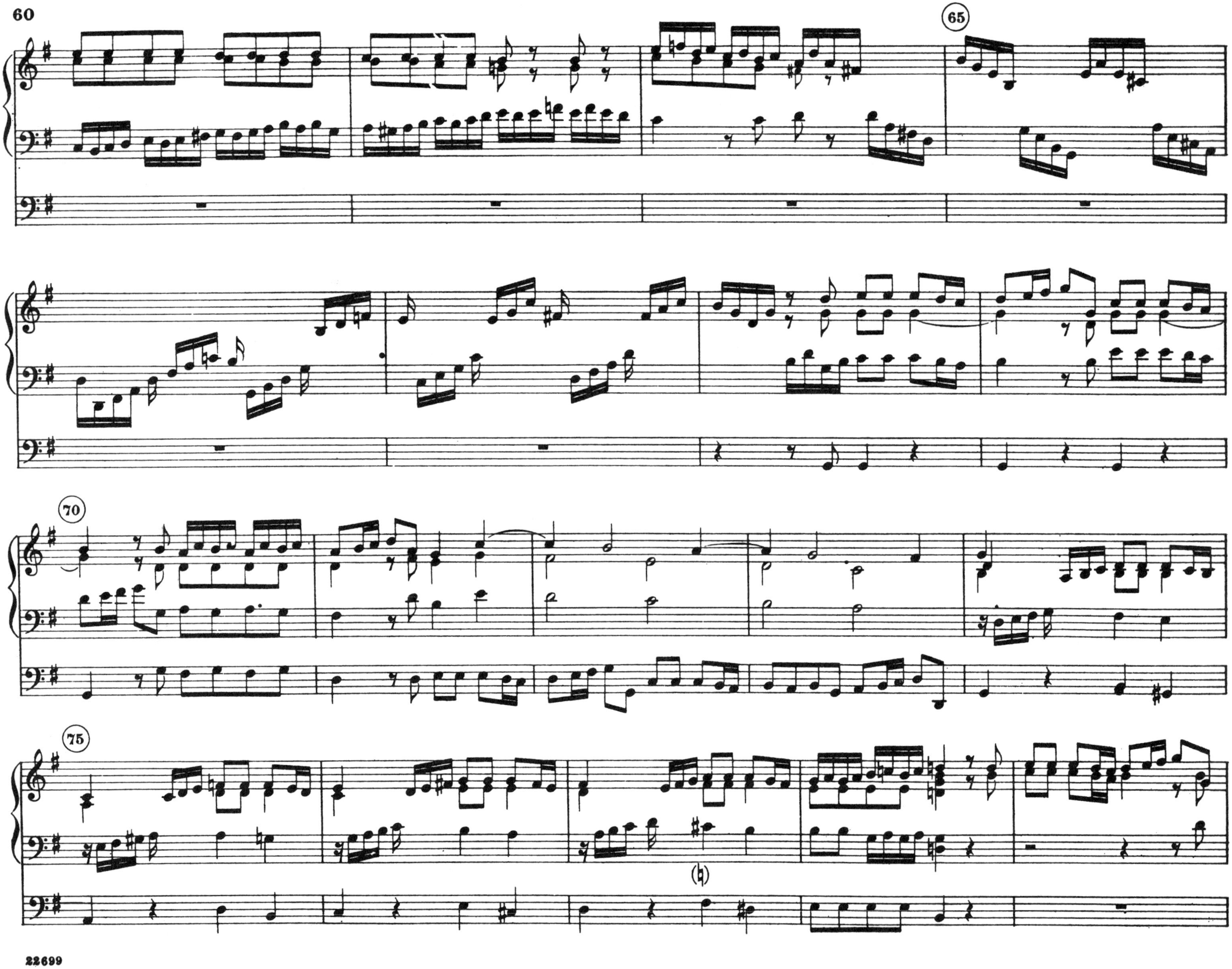
65
70
75

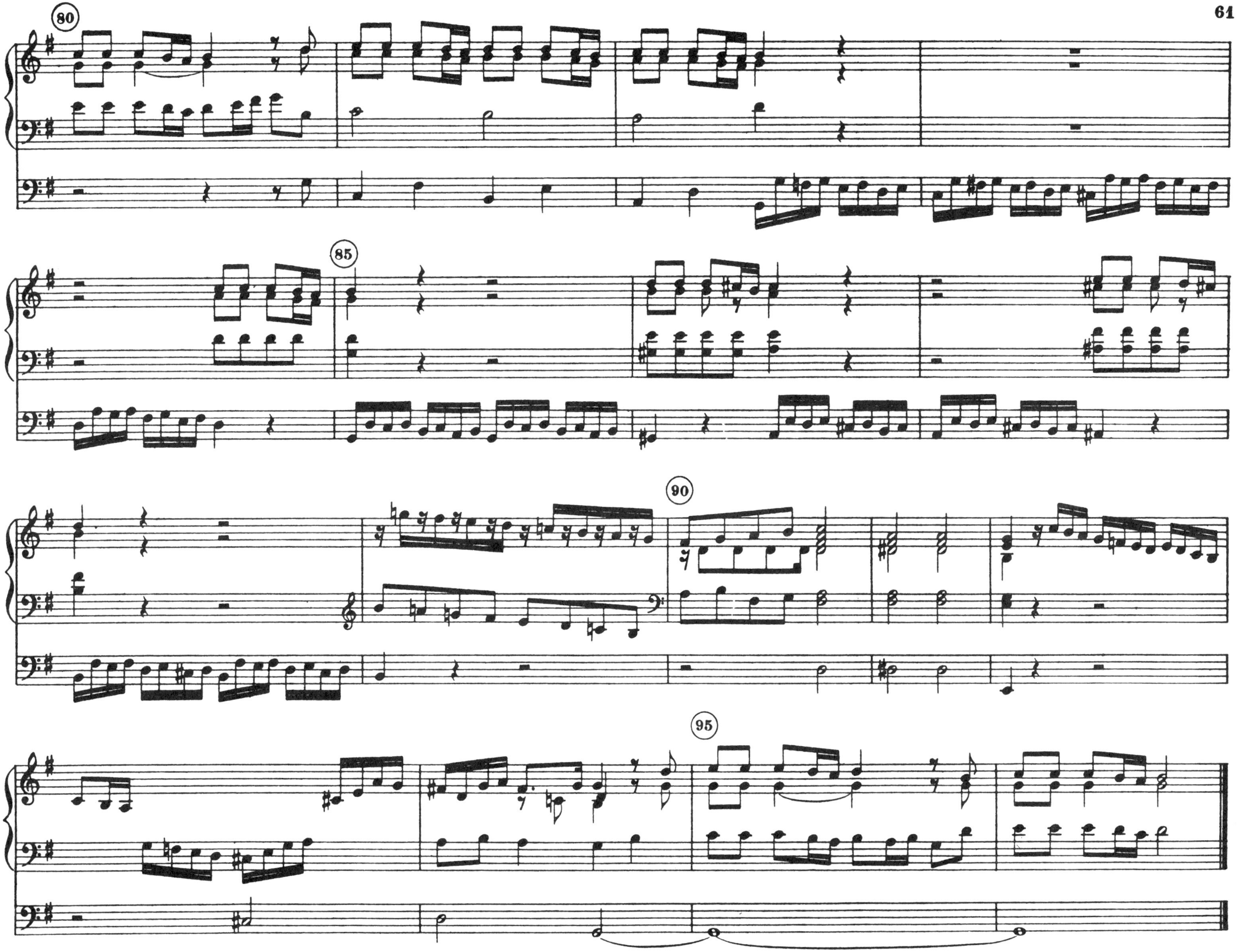
80
85
90
95

X
Fuge in G-Dur

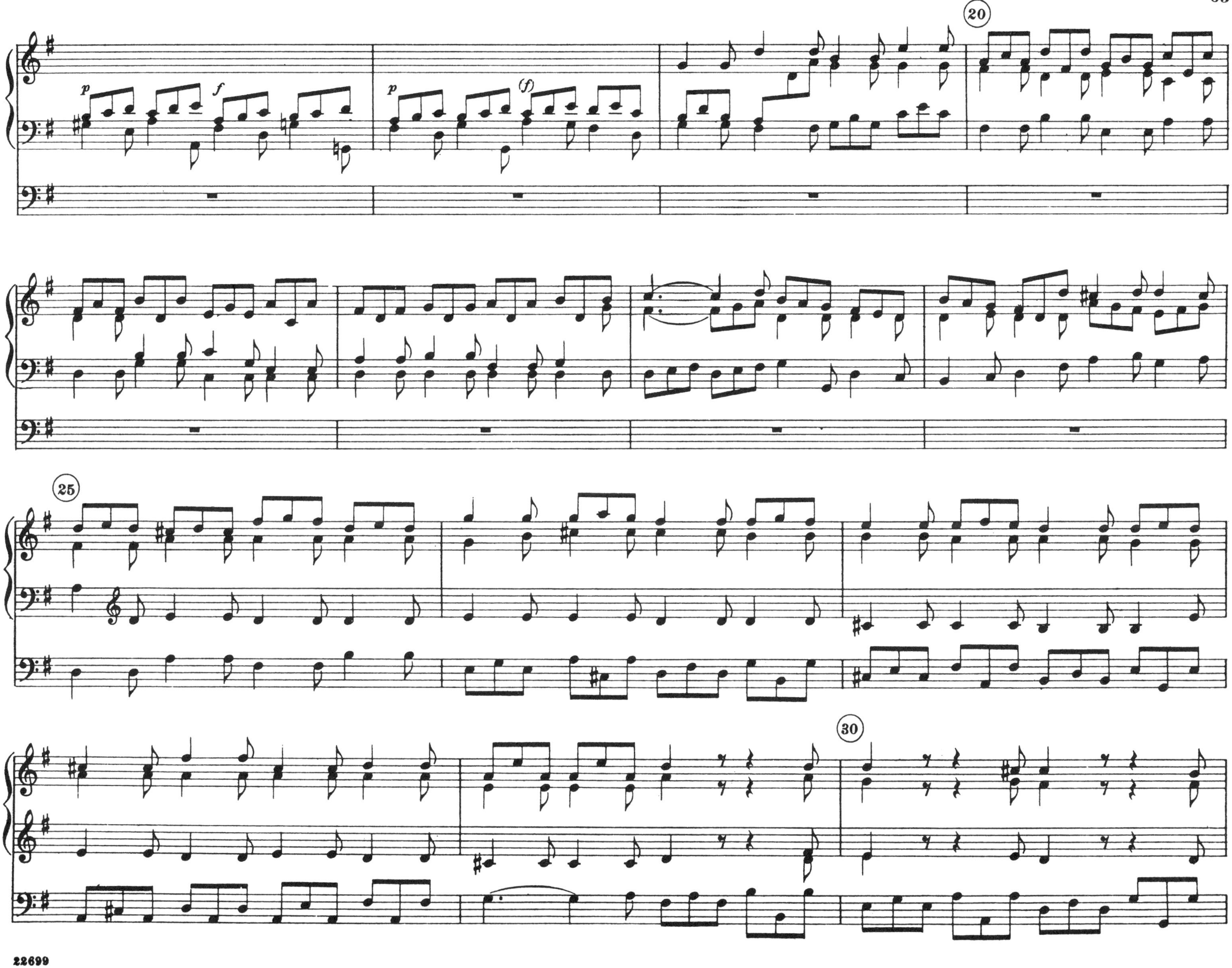
20
p
f
p
(f)
25
30

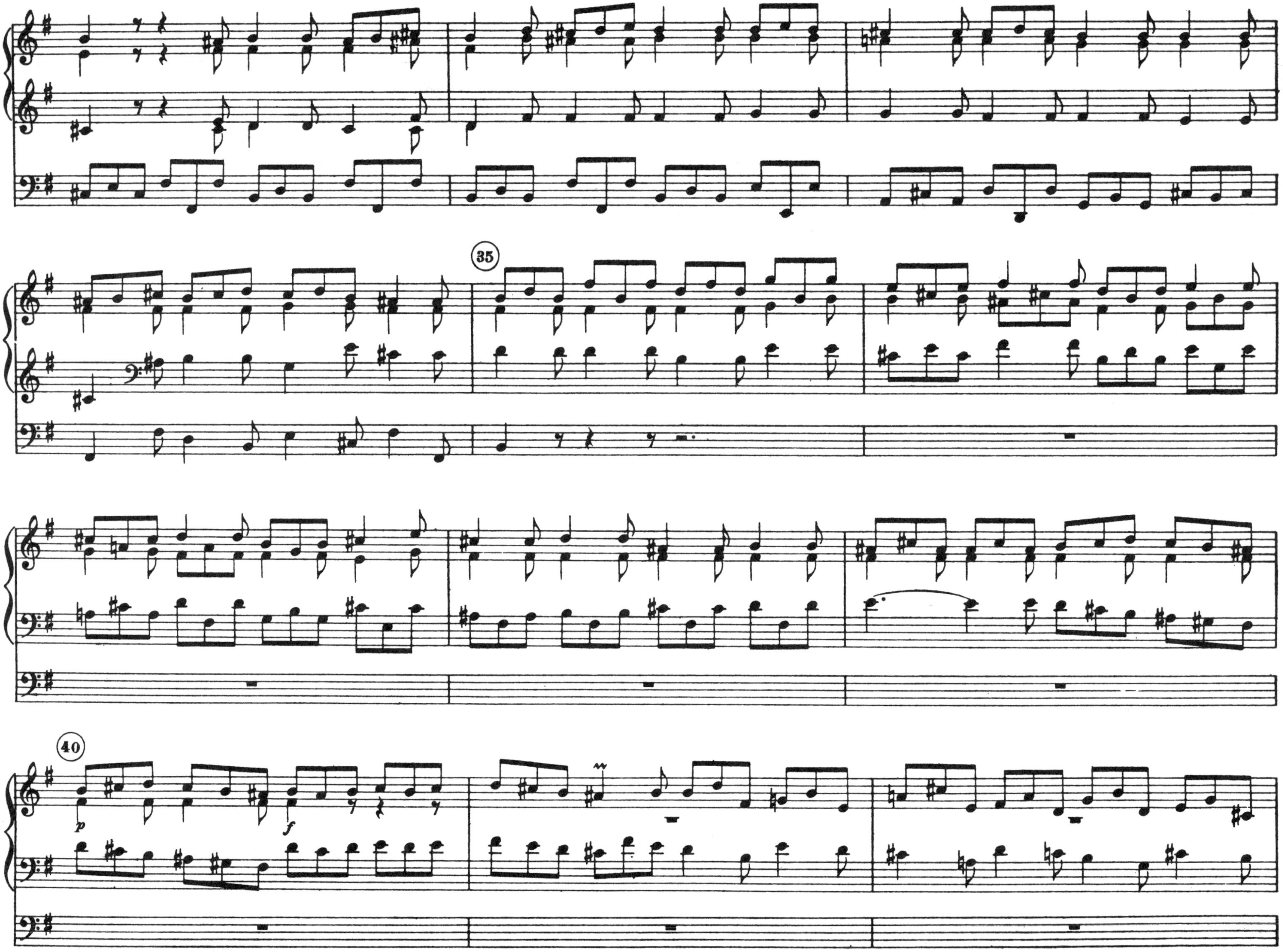
35
40
p
f

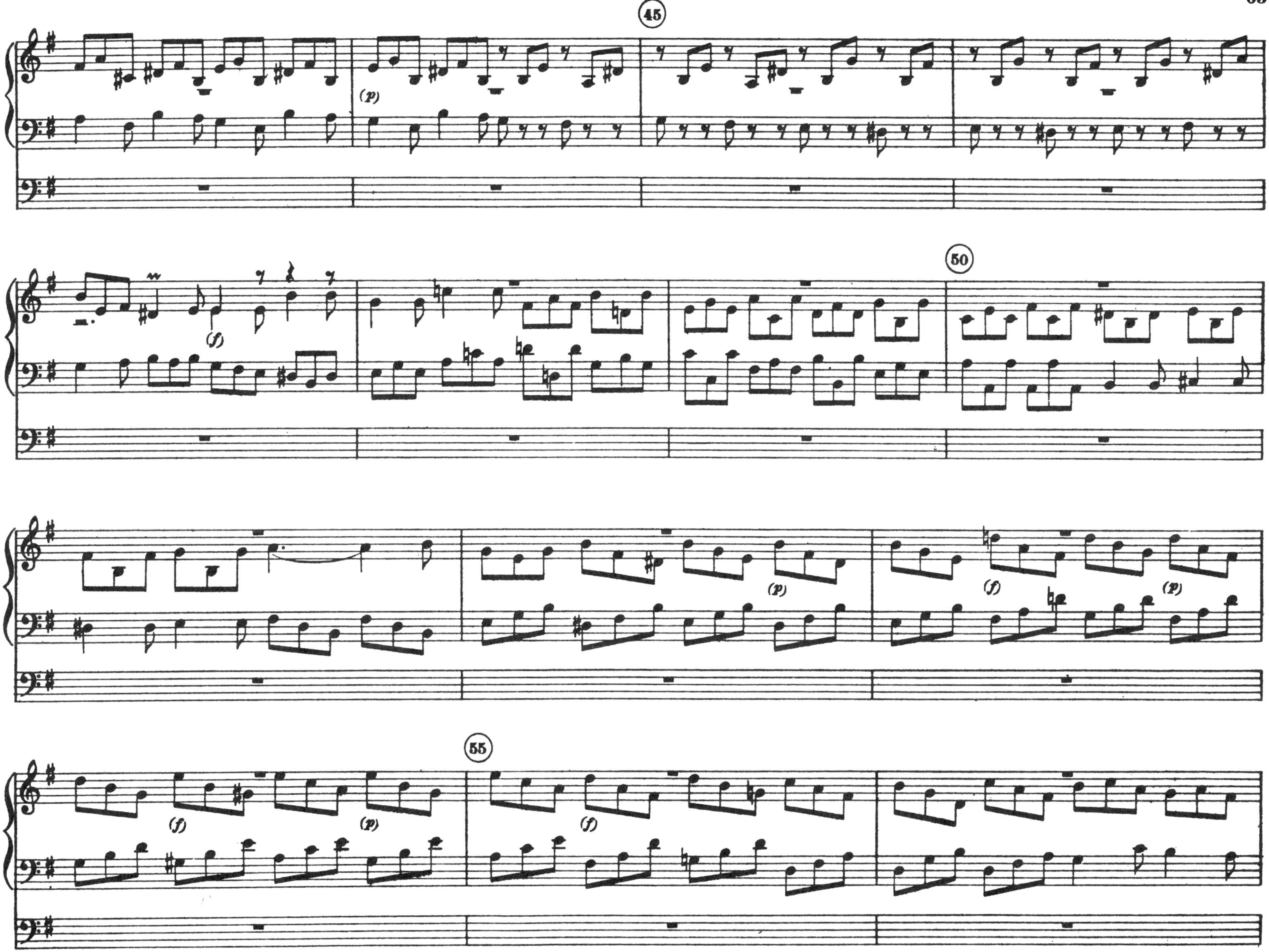
45
(p)
(f)
50
(p)
(f)
(p)
55
(f)
(p)
(f)

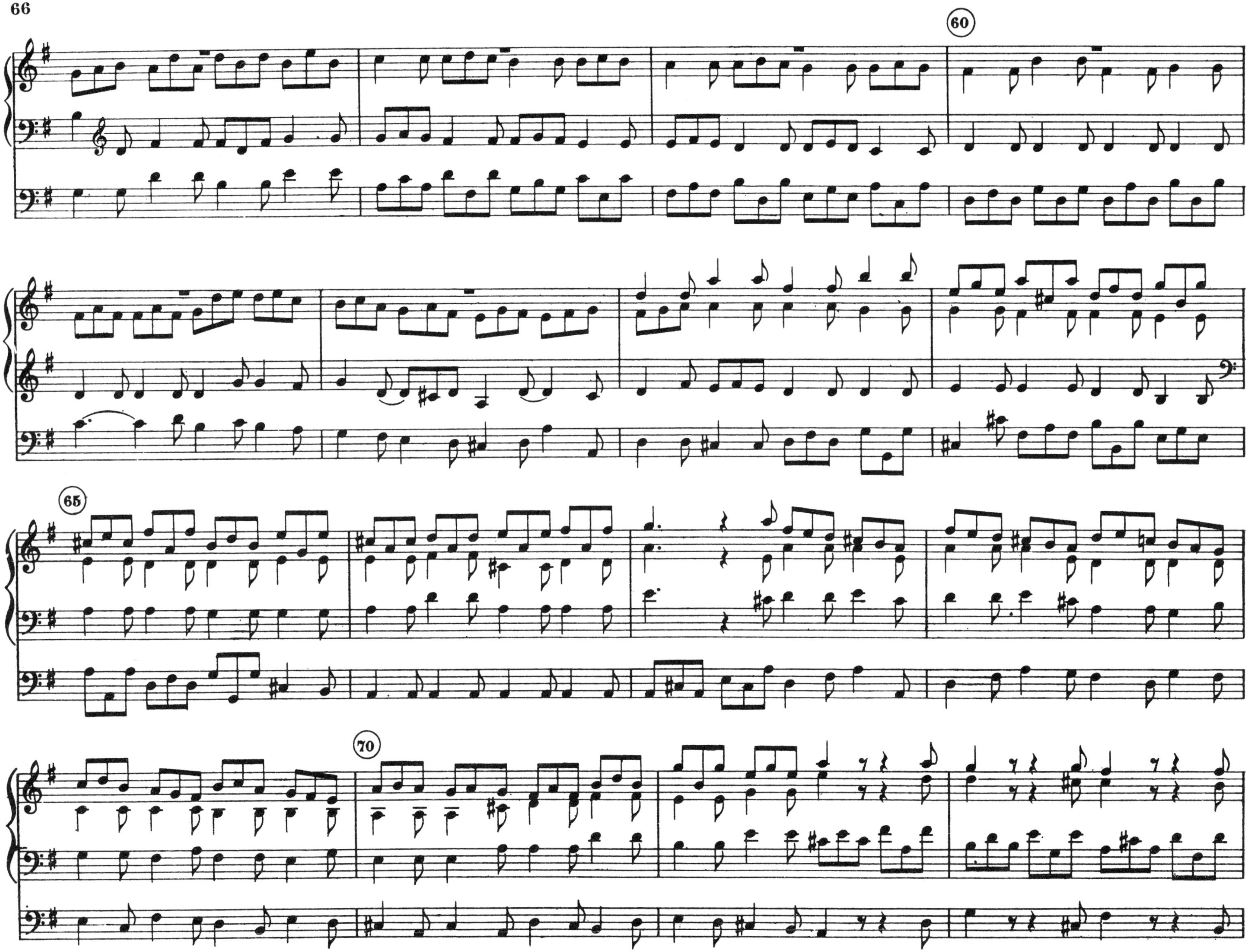
60
65
70

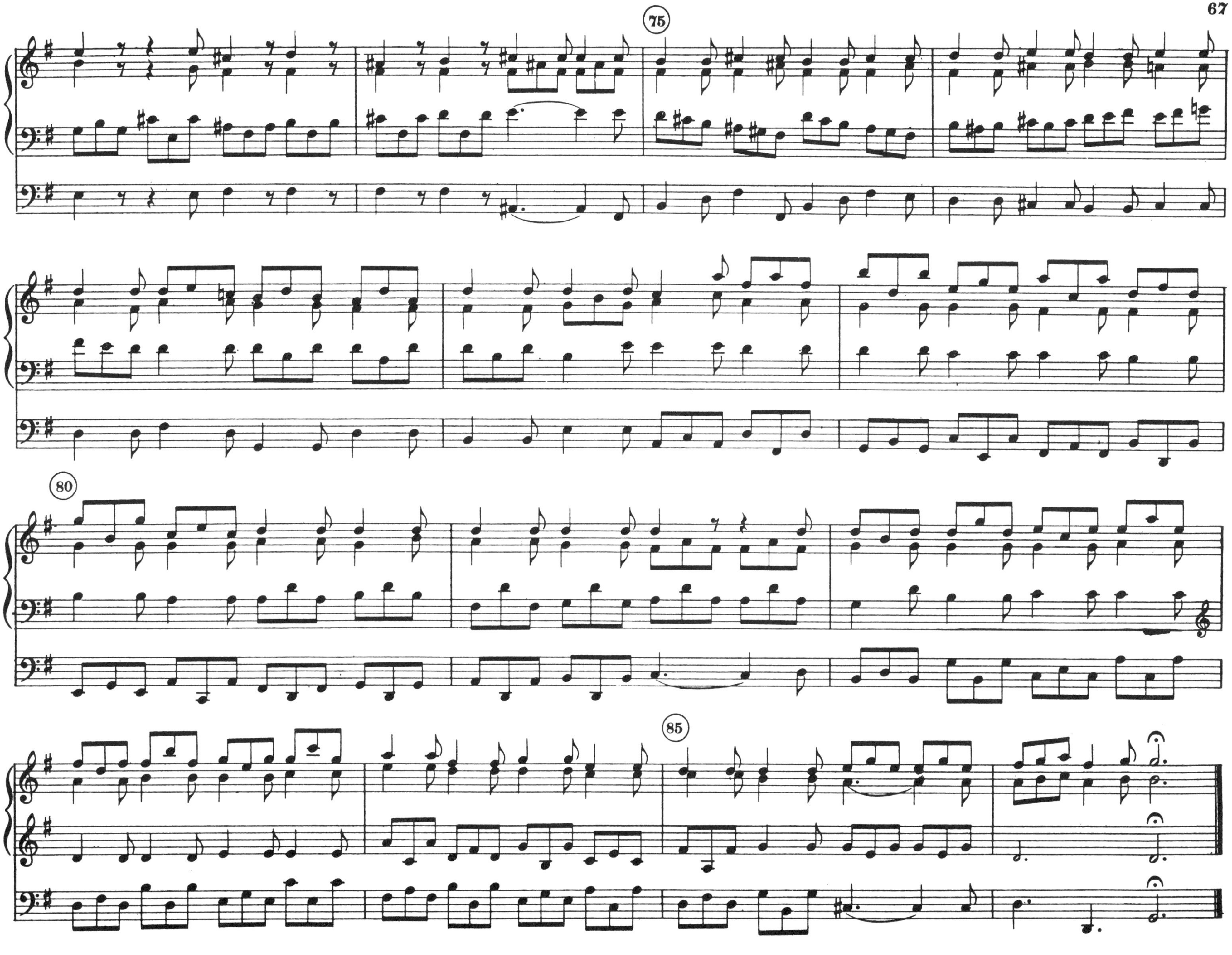
75
80
85

XI
Praeludium und Fuge in G-Dur

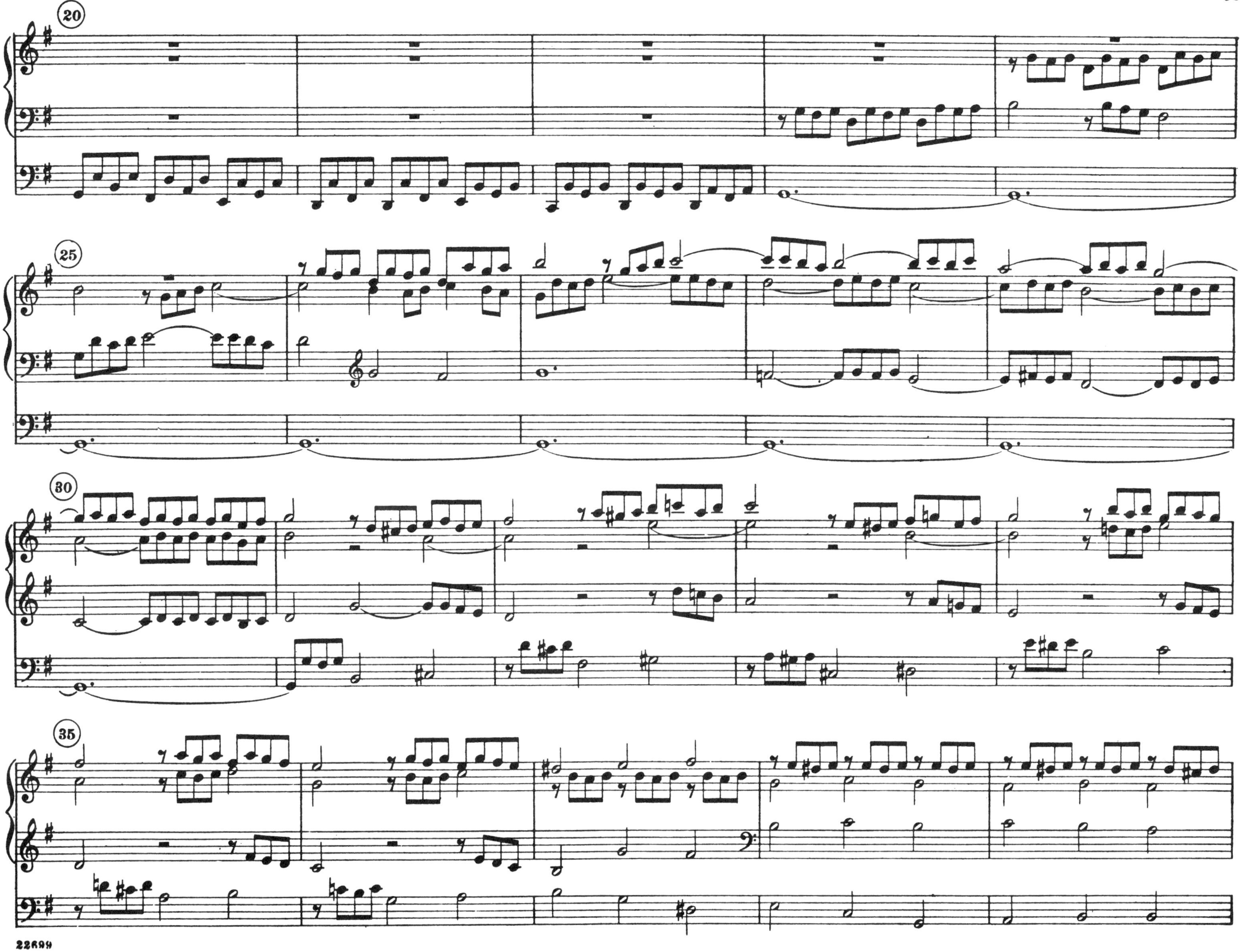
20
25
30
35

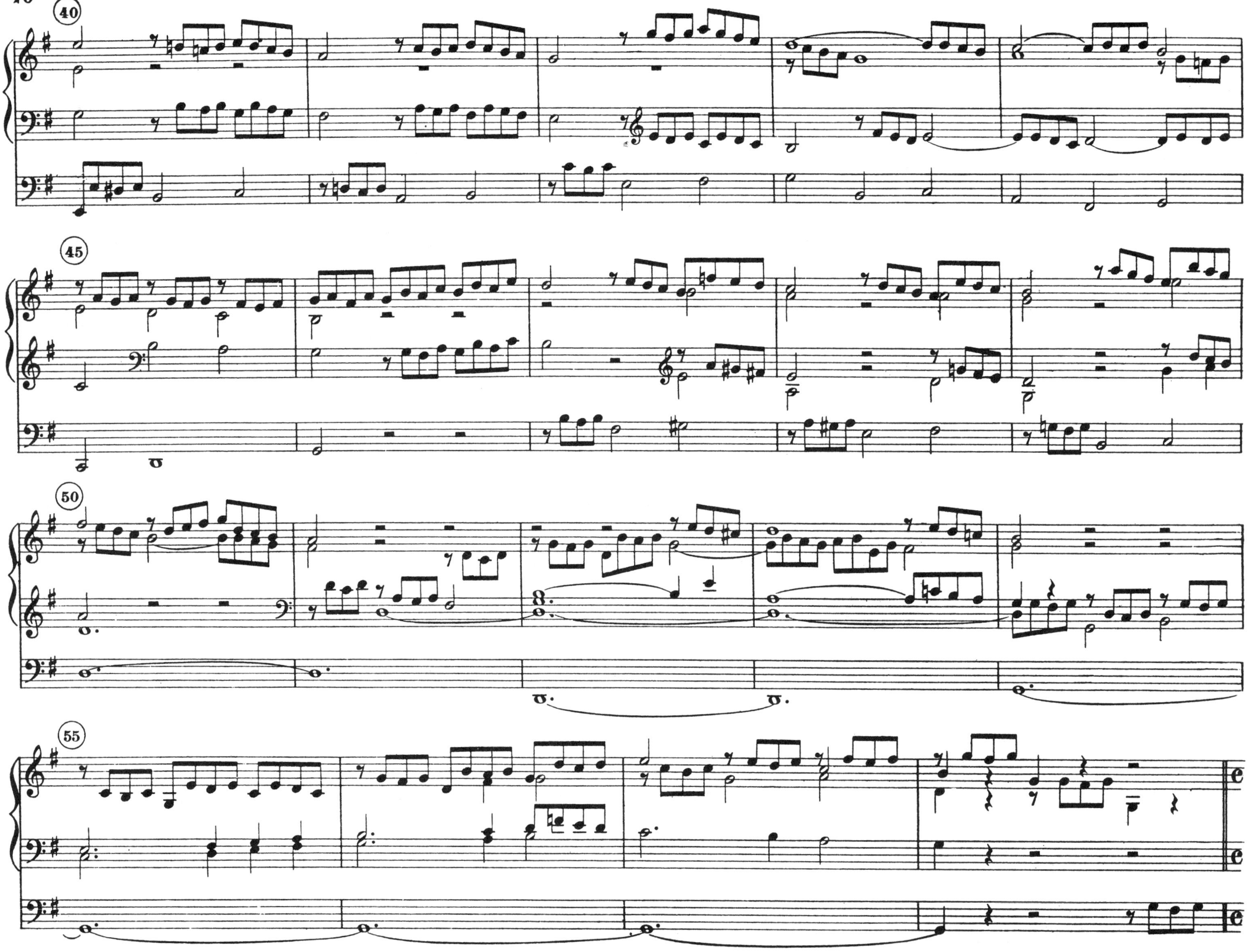
40
45
50
55

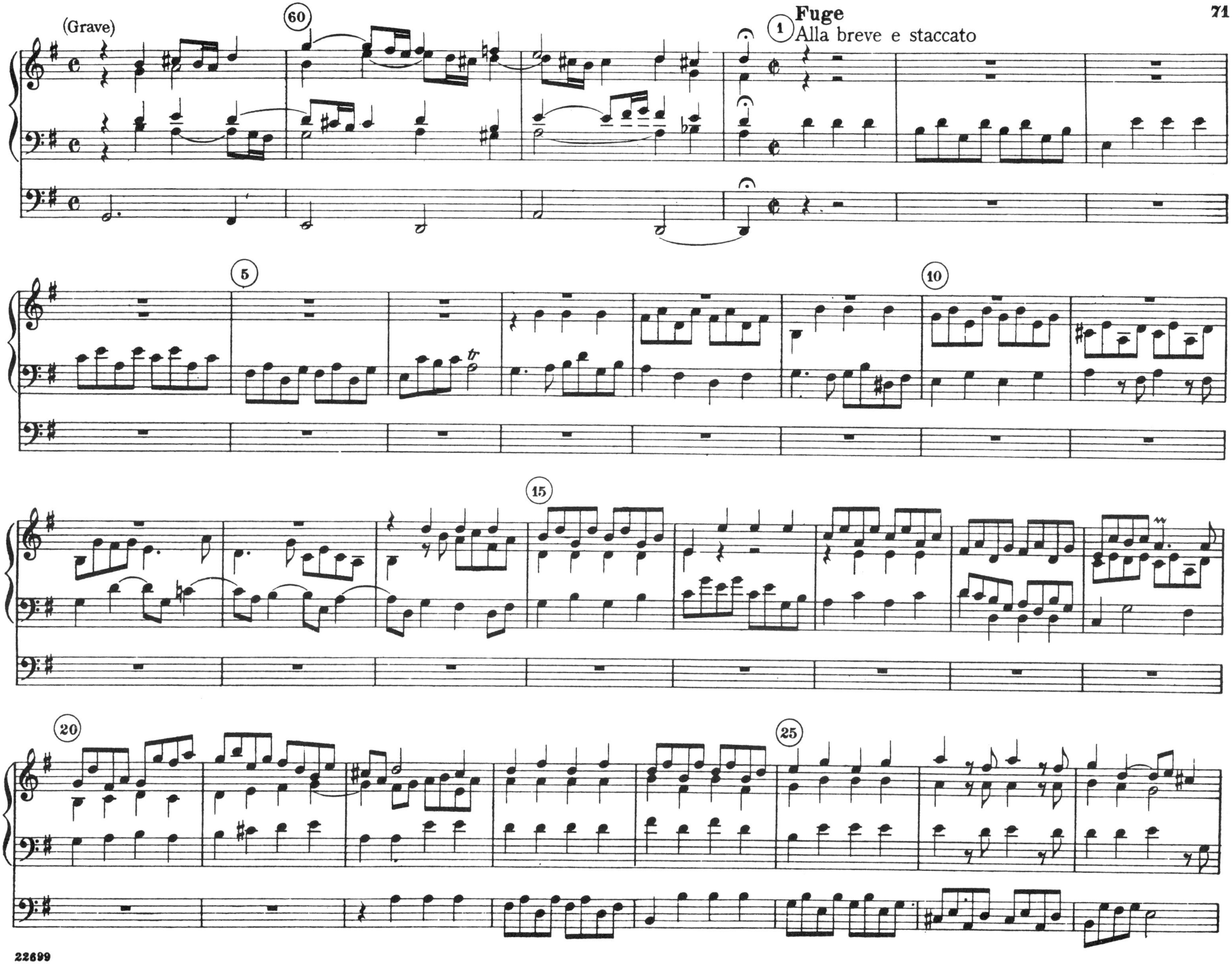
(Grave)
60
Fuge
Alla breve e staccato
1
tr
5
10
15
20
25

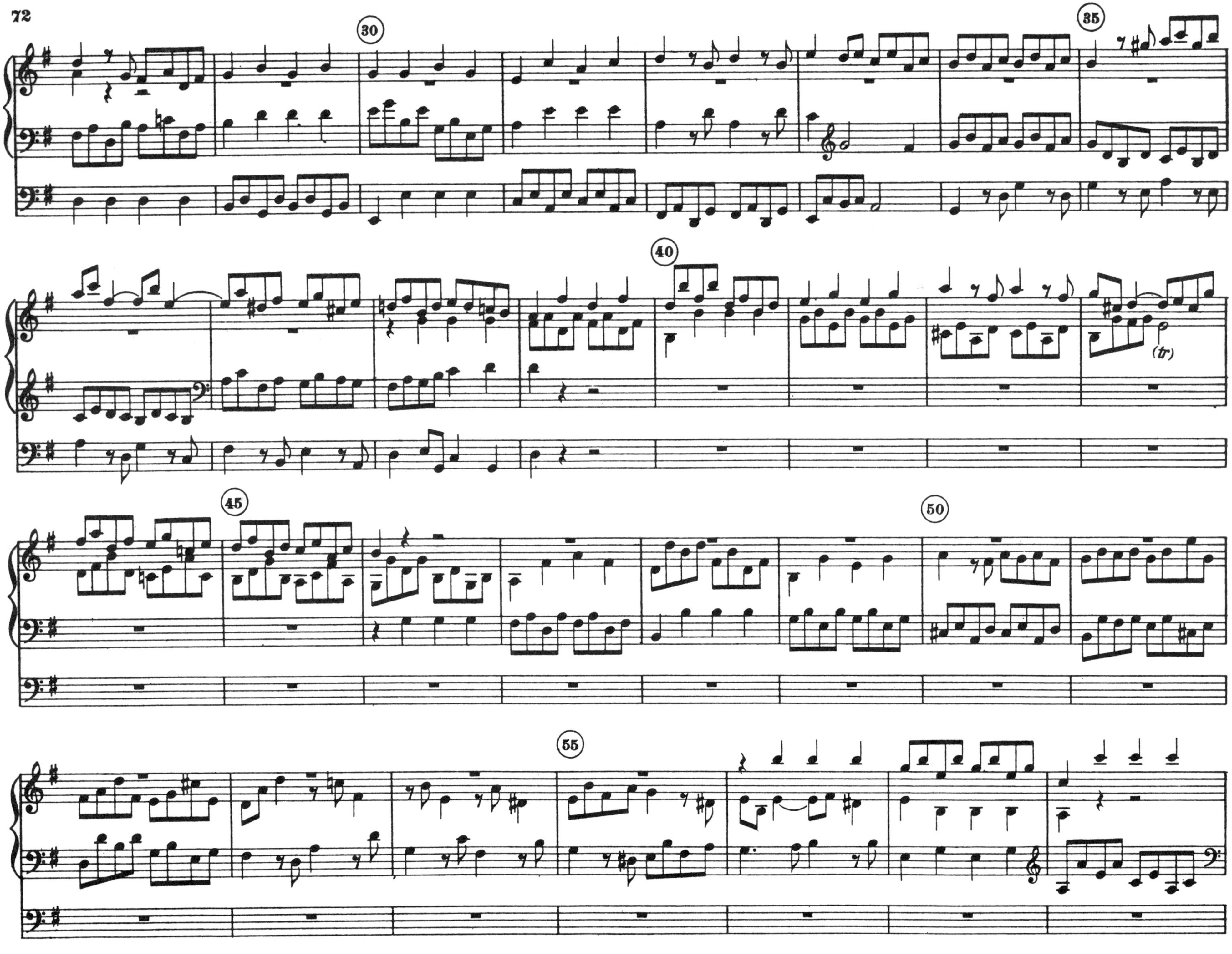
30
35
40
(tr)
45
50
55

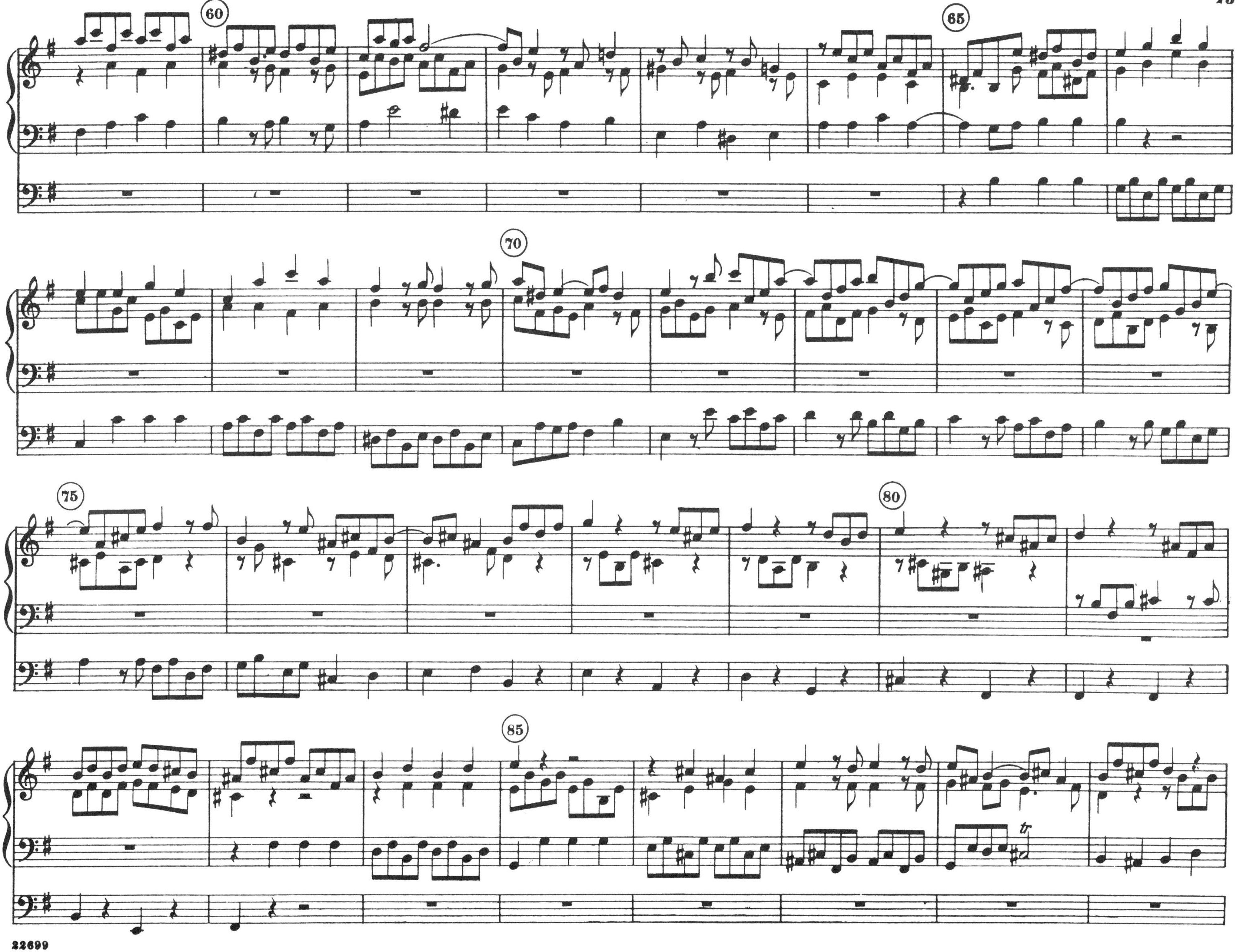
60
65
70
75
80
85
tr

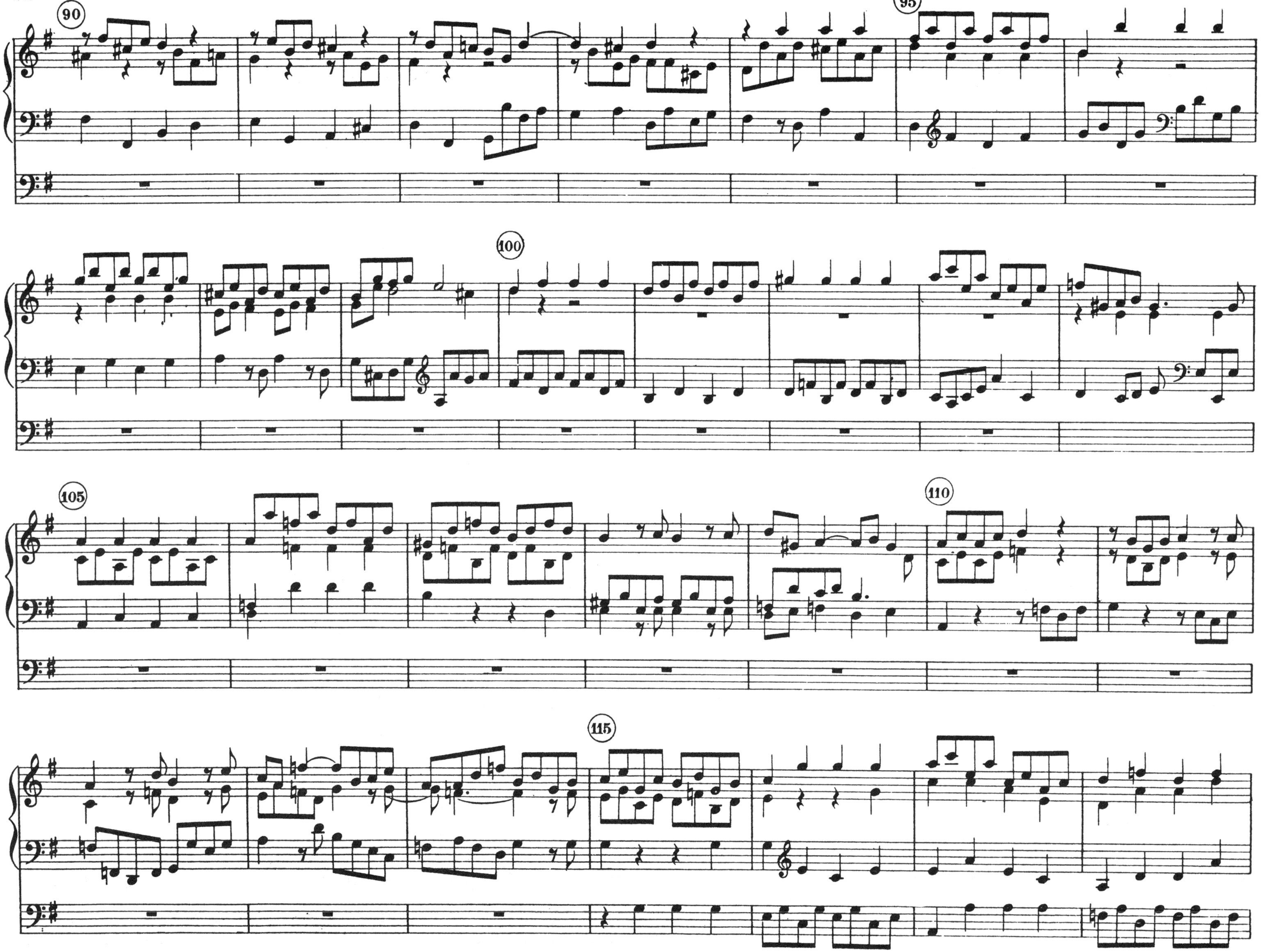

90
95
100
105
110
115

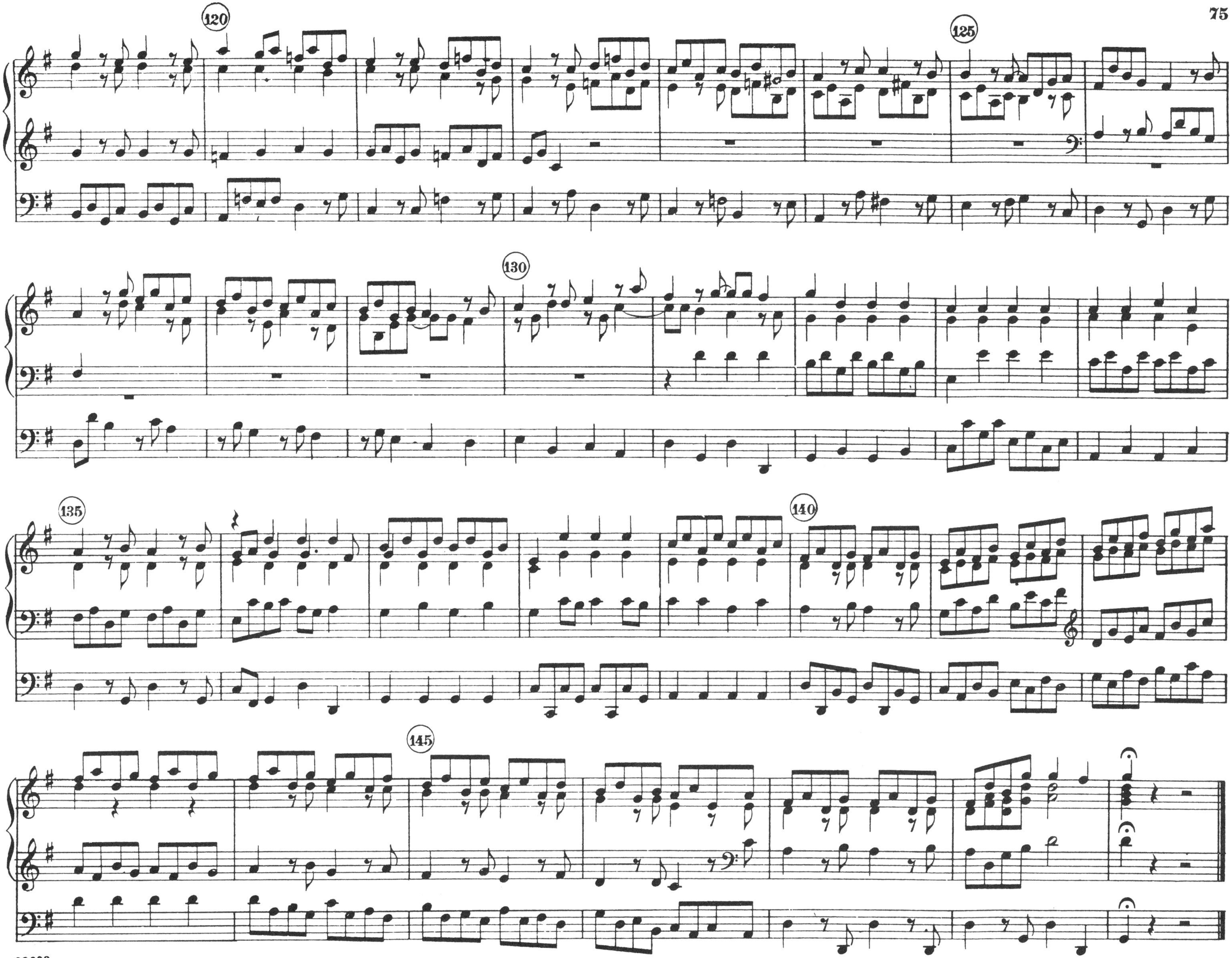

120
125
130
135
140
145

XII
Praeludium und Fuge in G-Moll

Praeludium

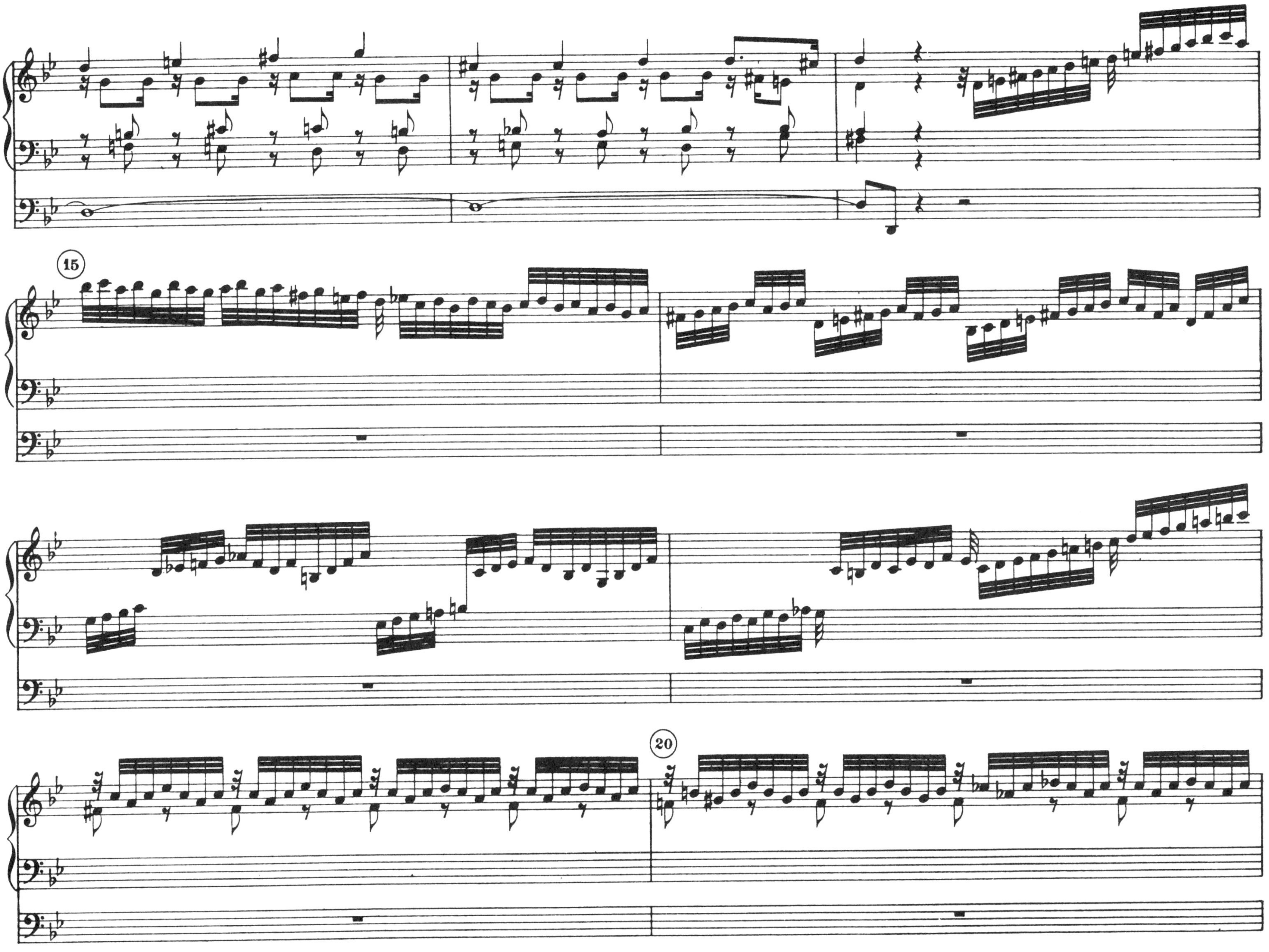
15
20

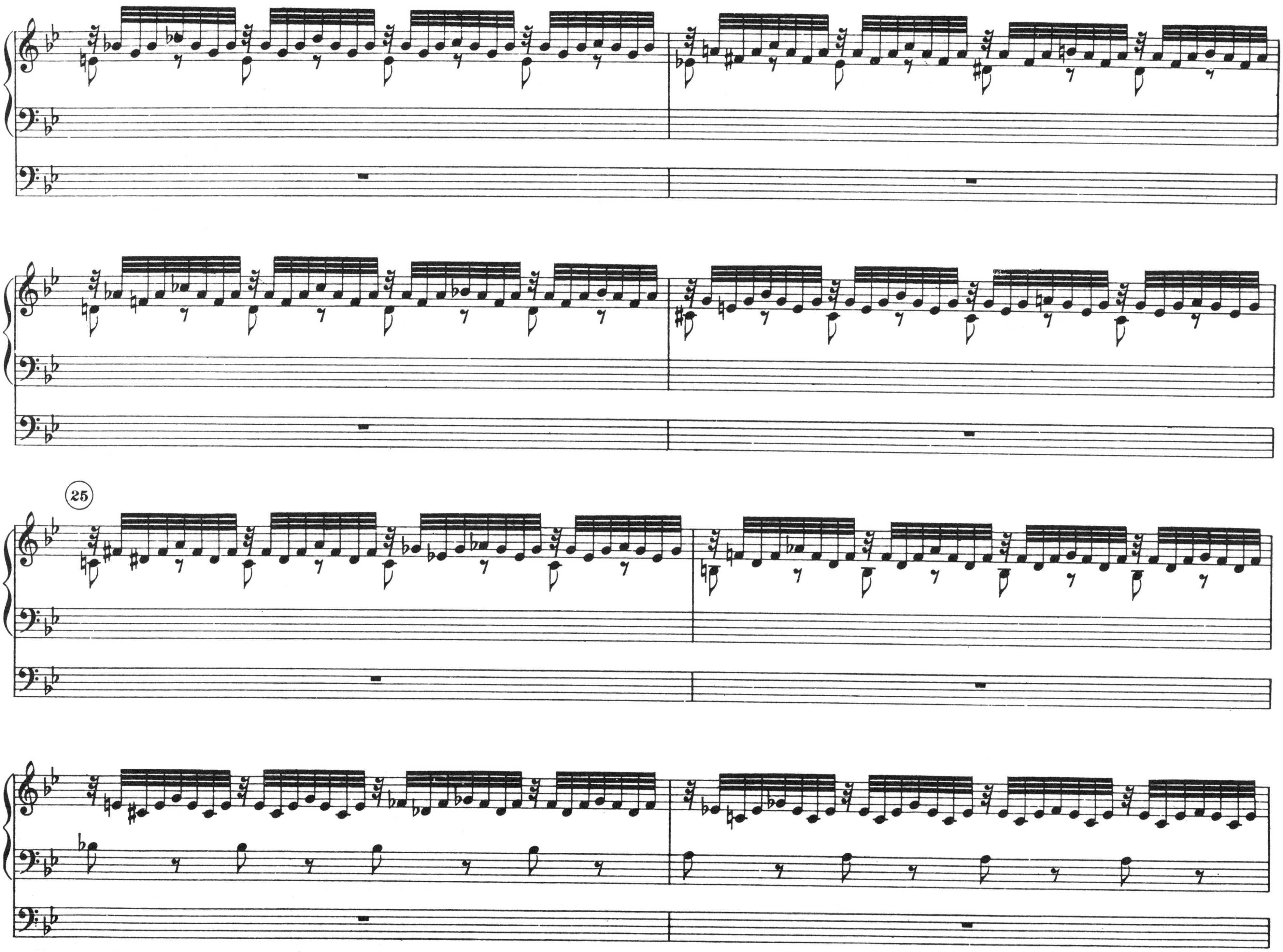
25

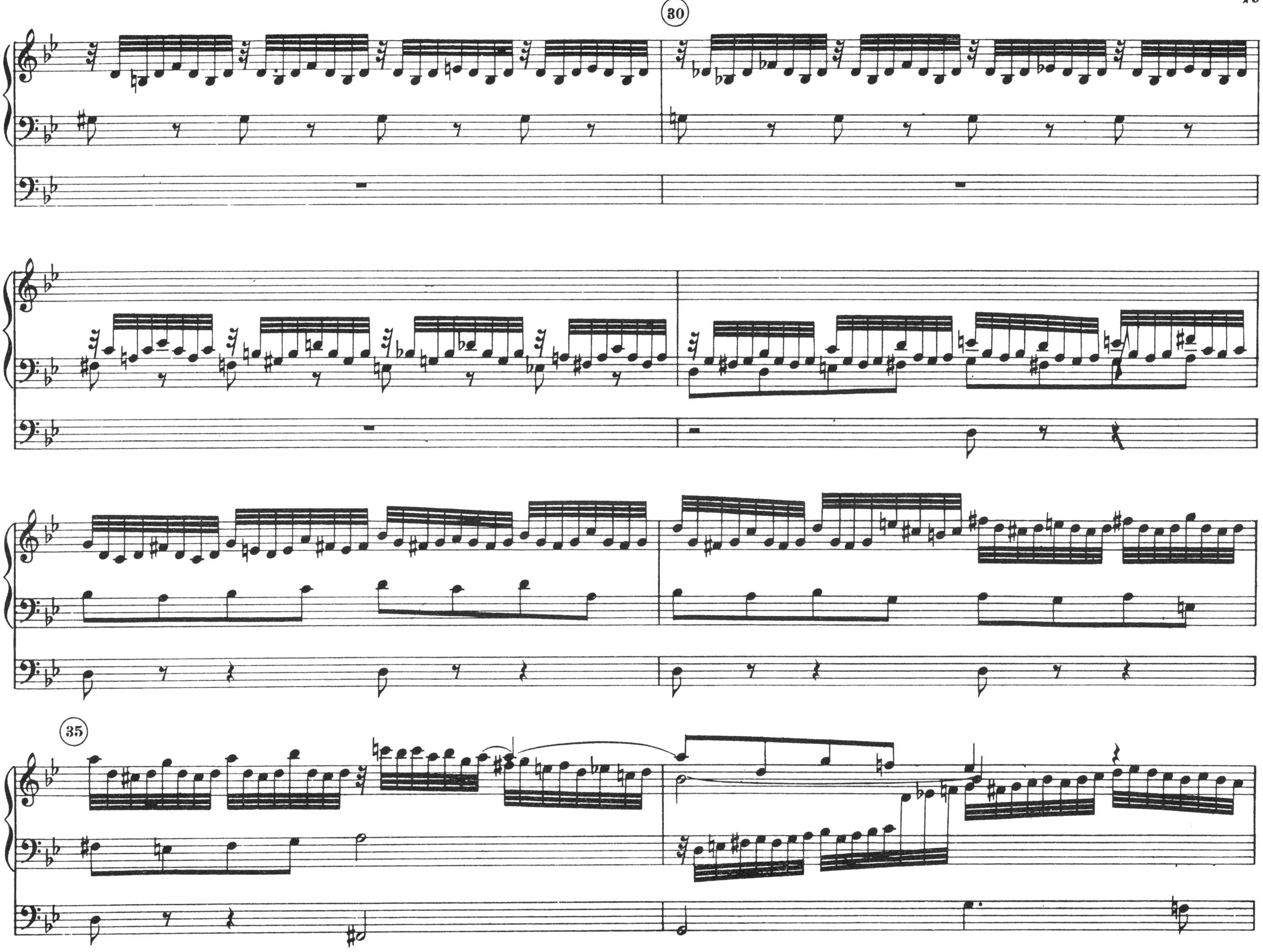
30
35

40

1 **Fuge**
Allegro

5

10

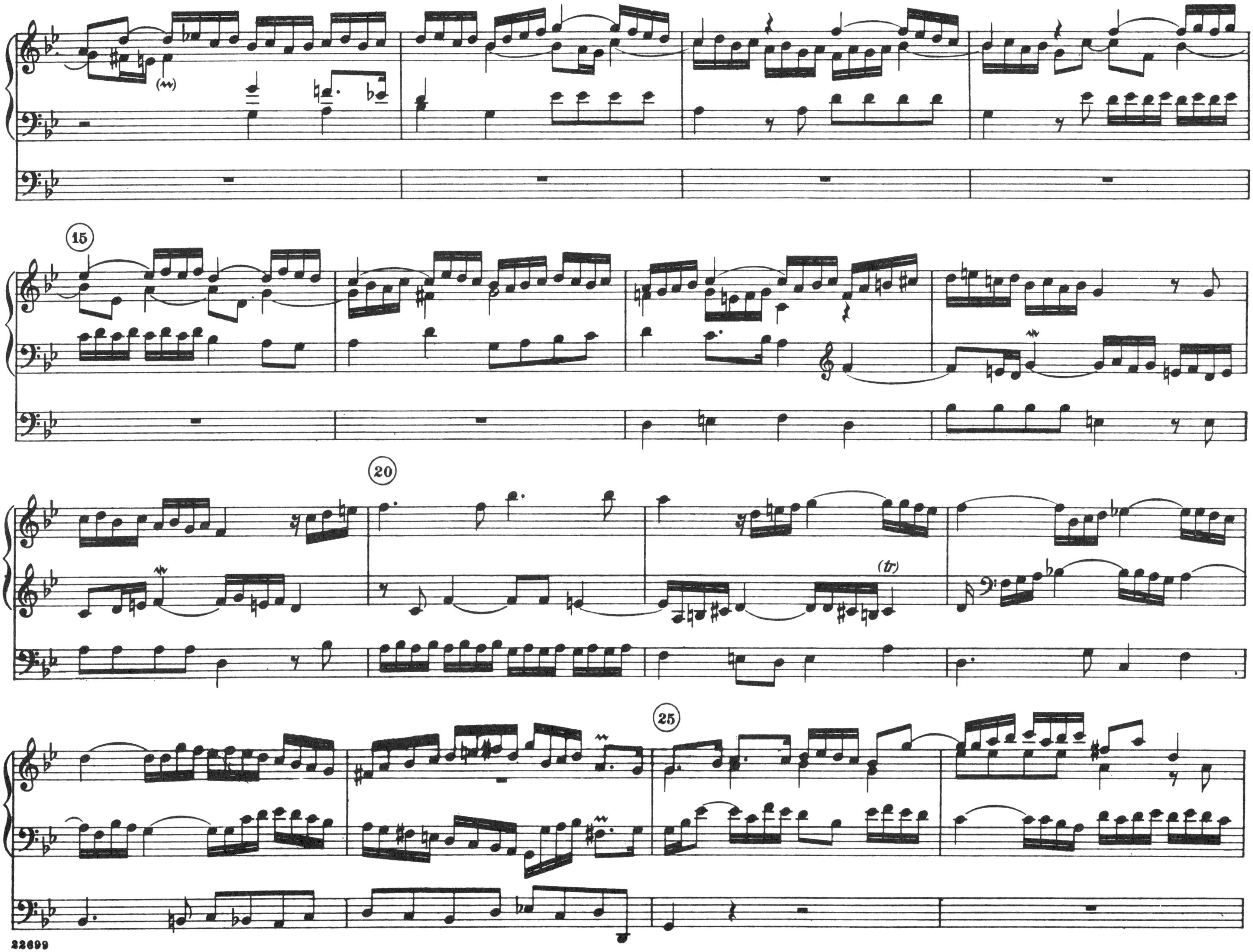
15
20
(tr)
25

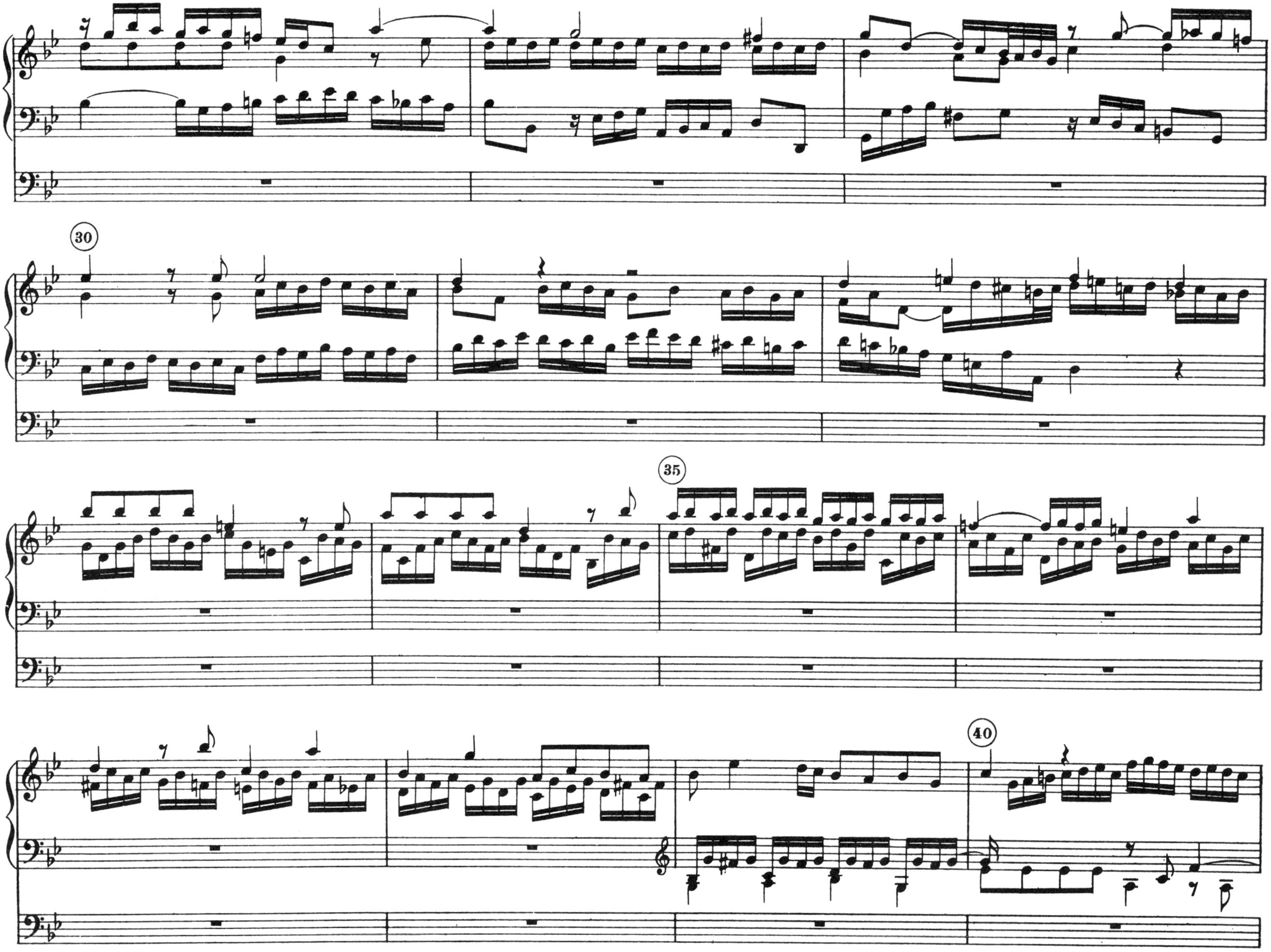
30
35
40

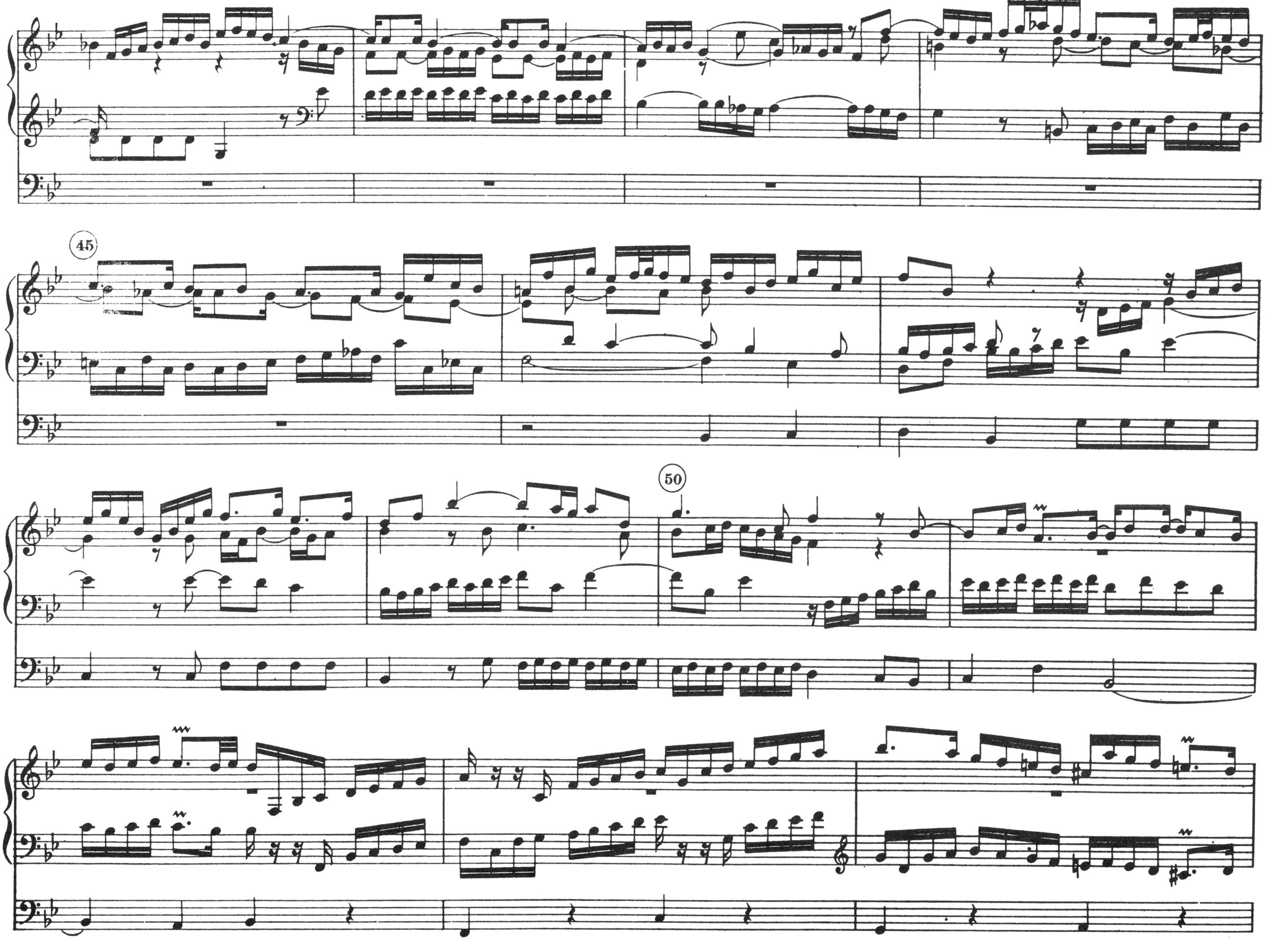
45
50

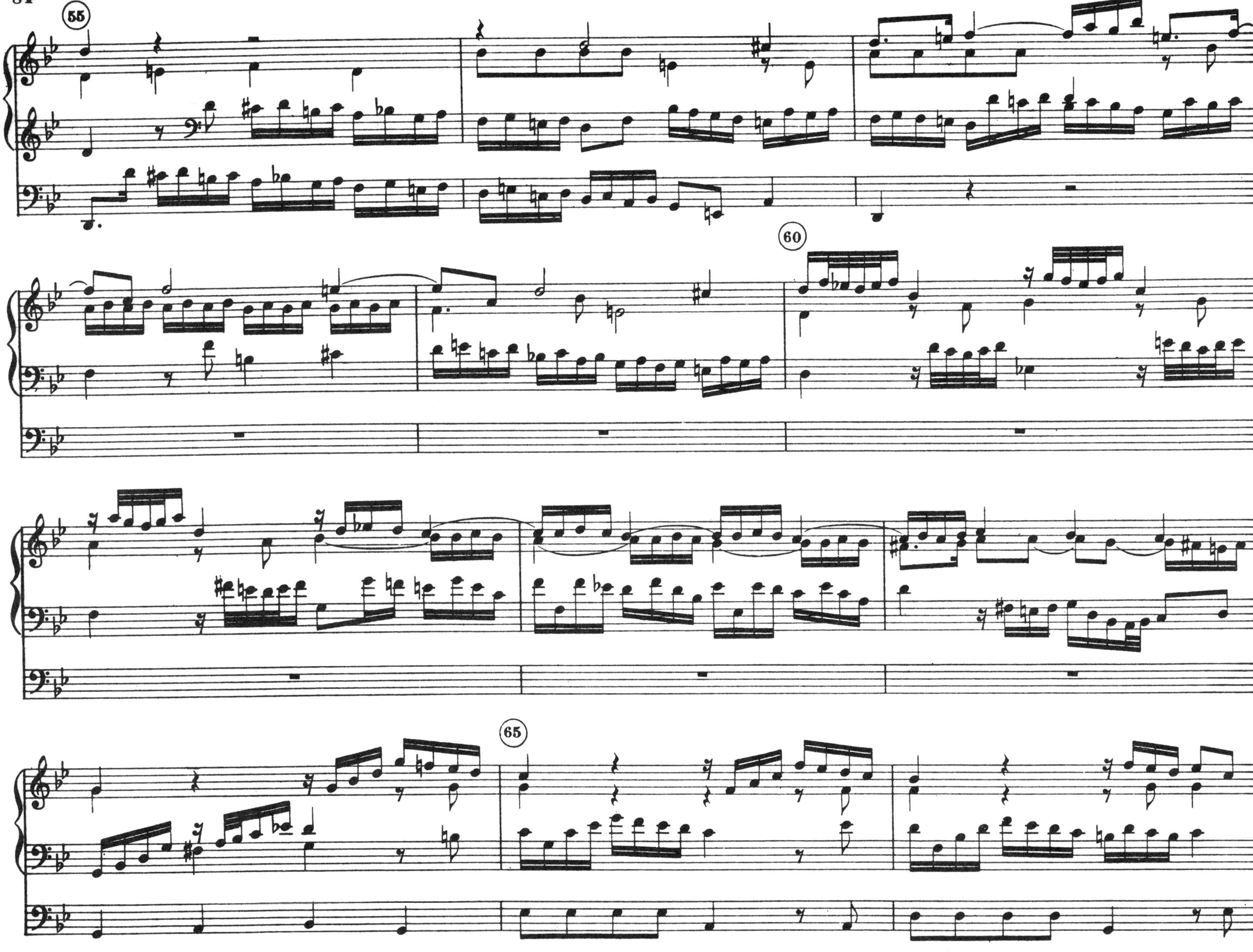
55
60
65

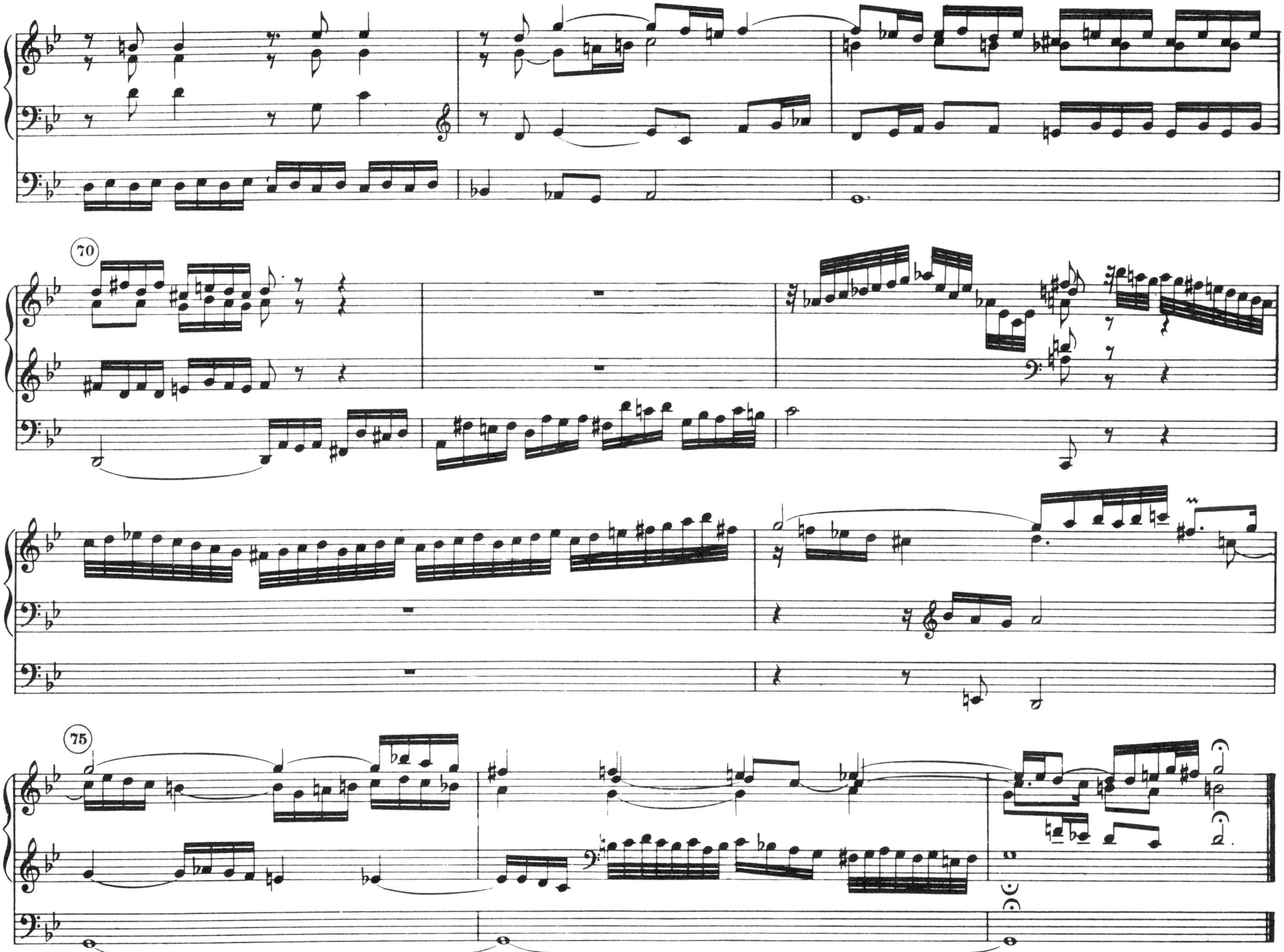
70
75

XIII
Fantasie und Fuge in A-Moll

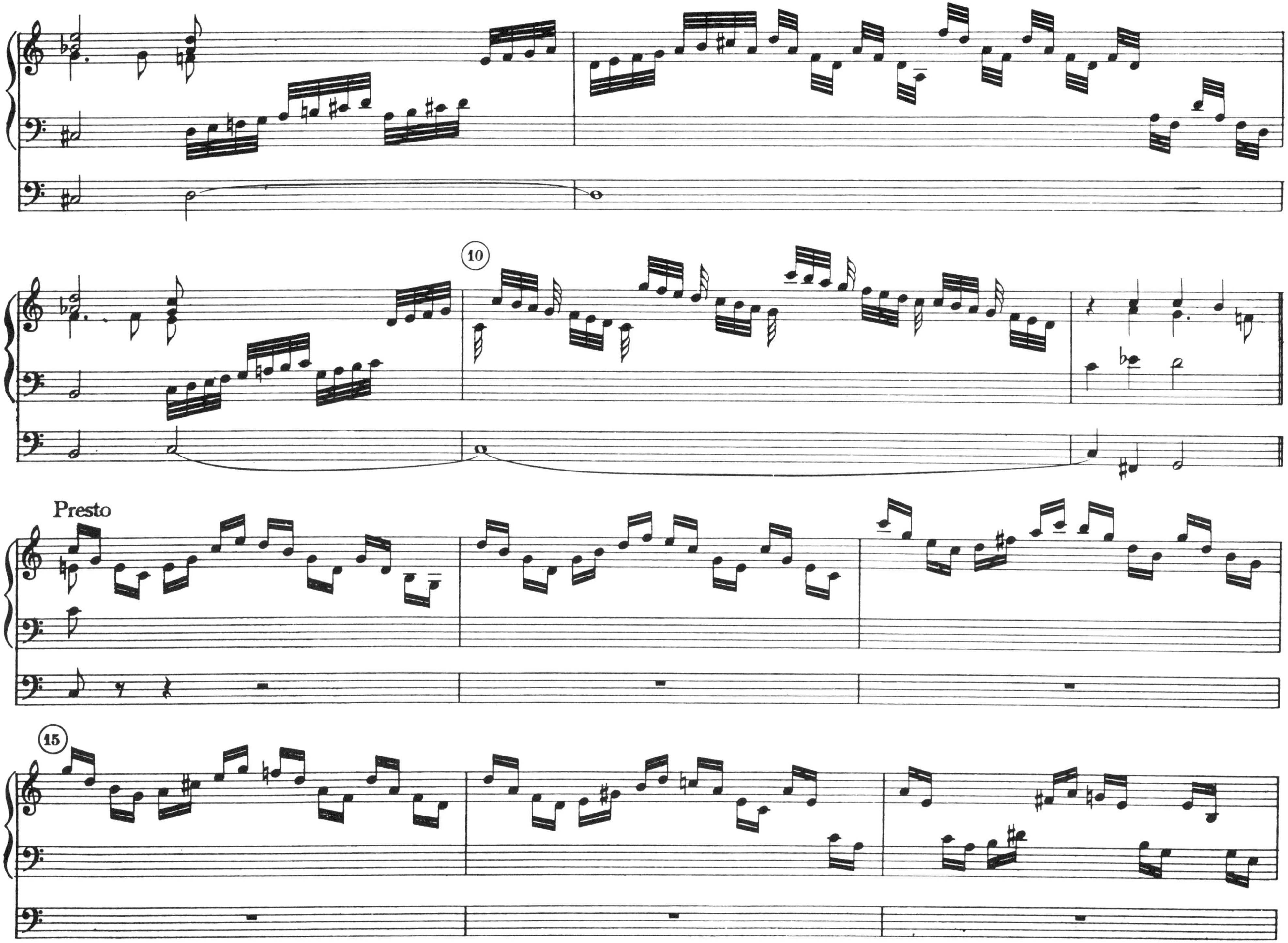

22699

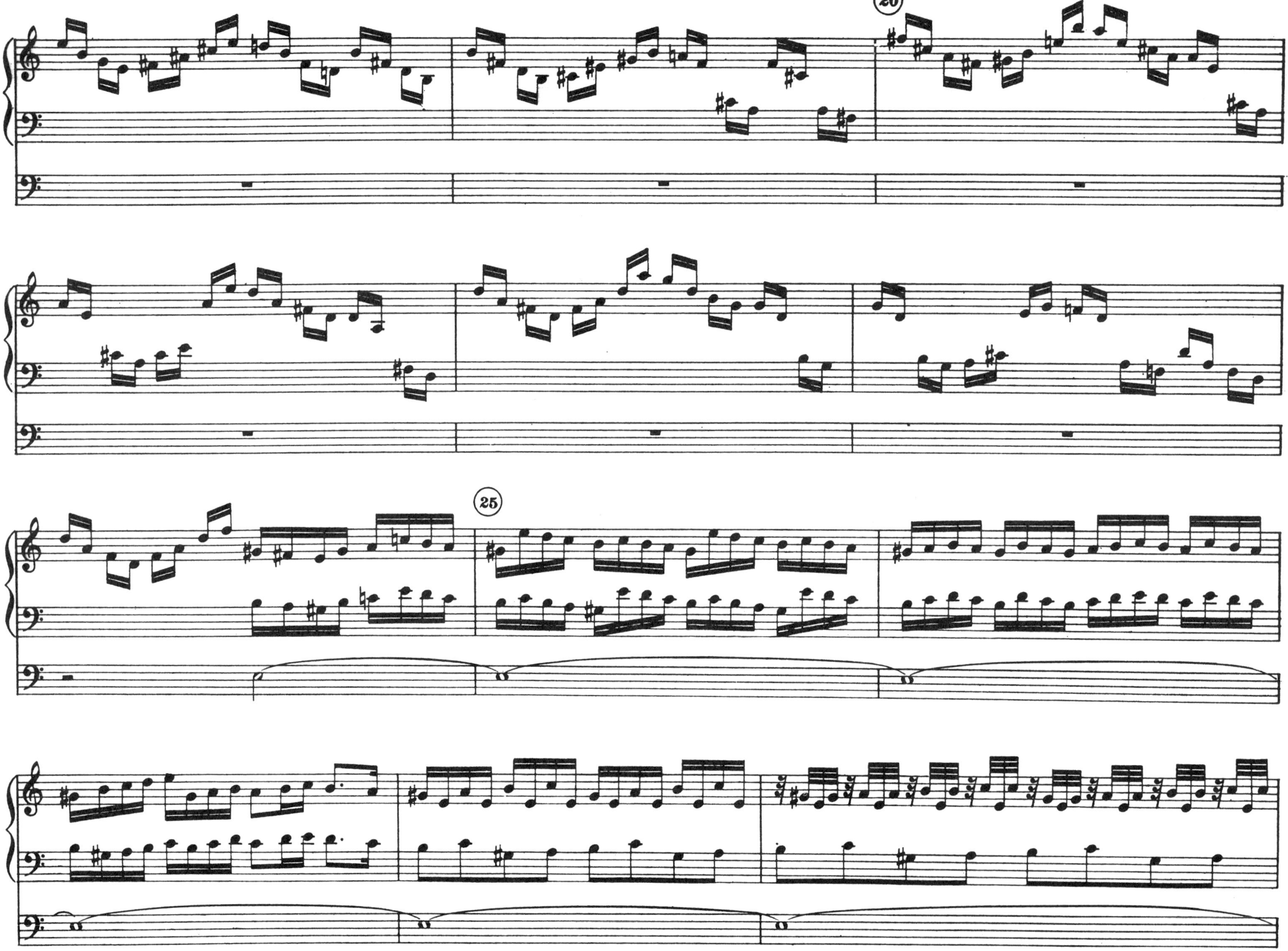
20
25

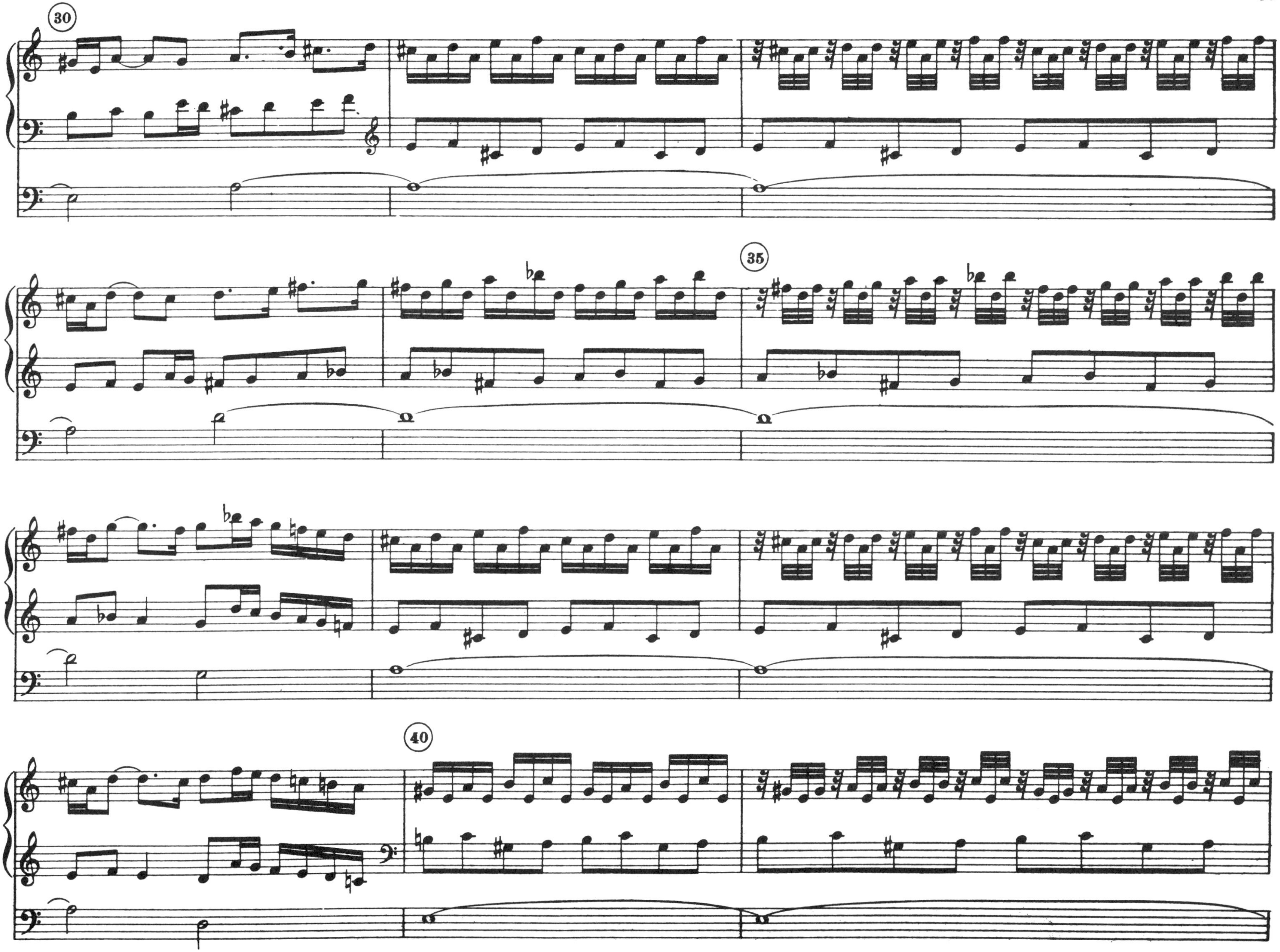
30
35
40

Fuge

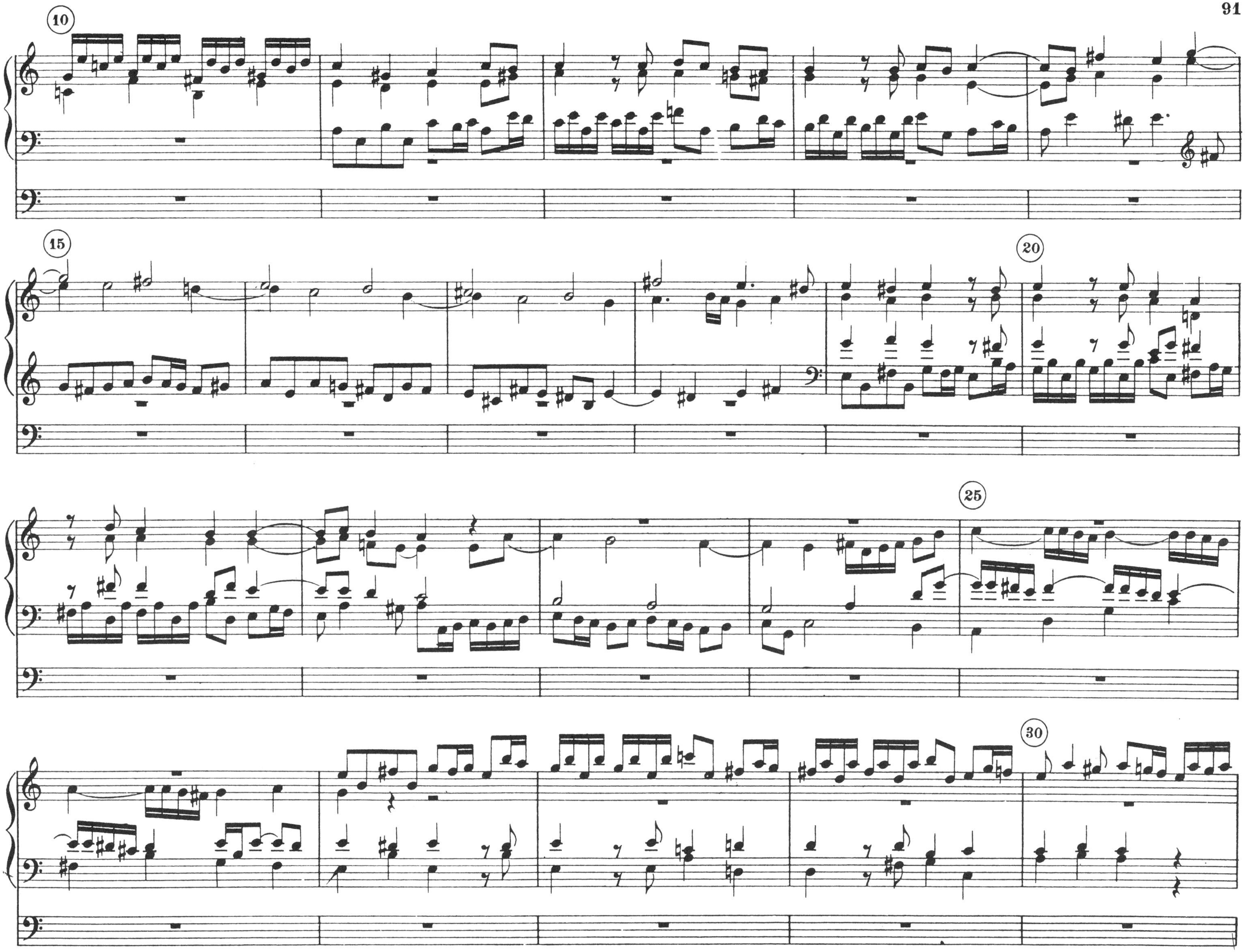
10
15
20
25
30

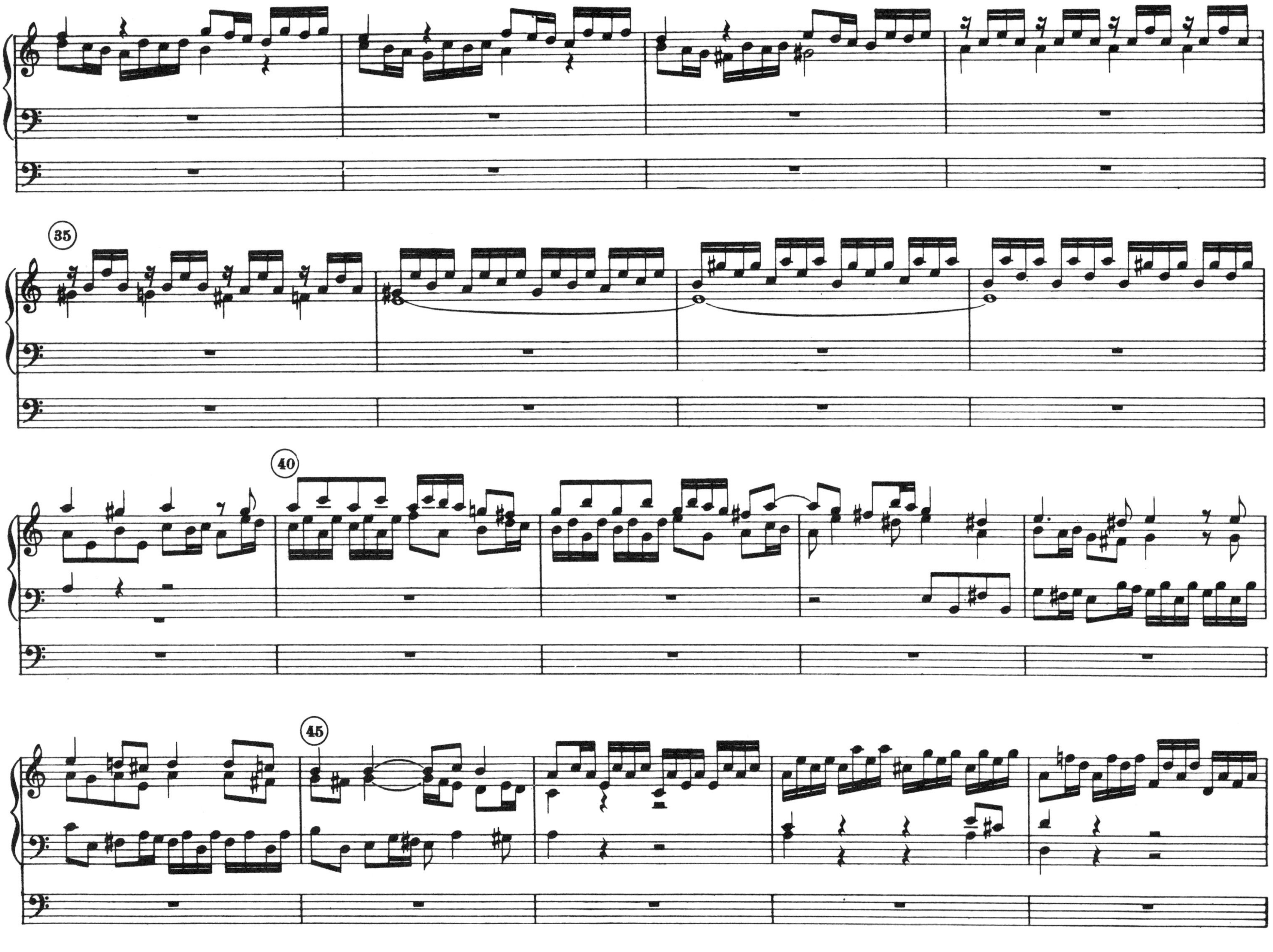

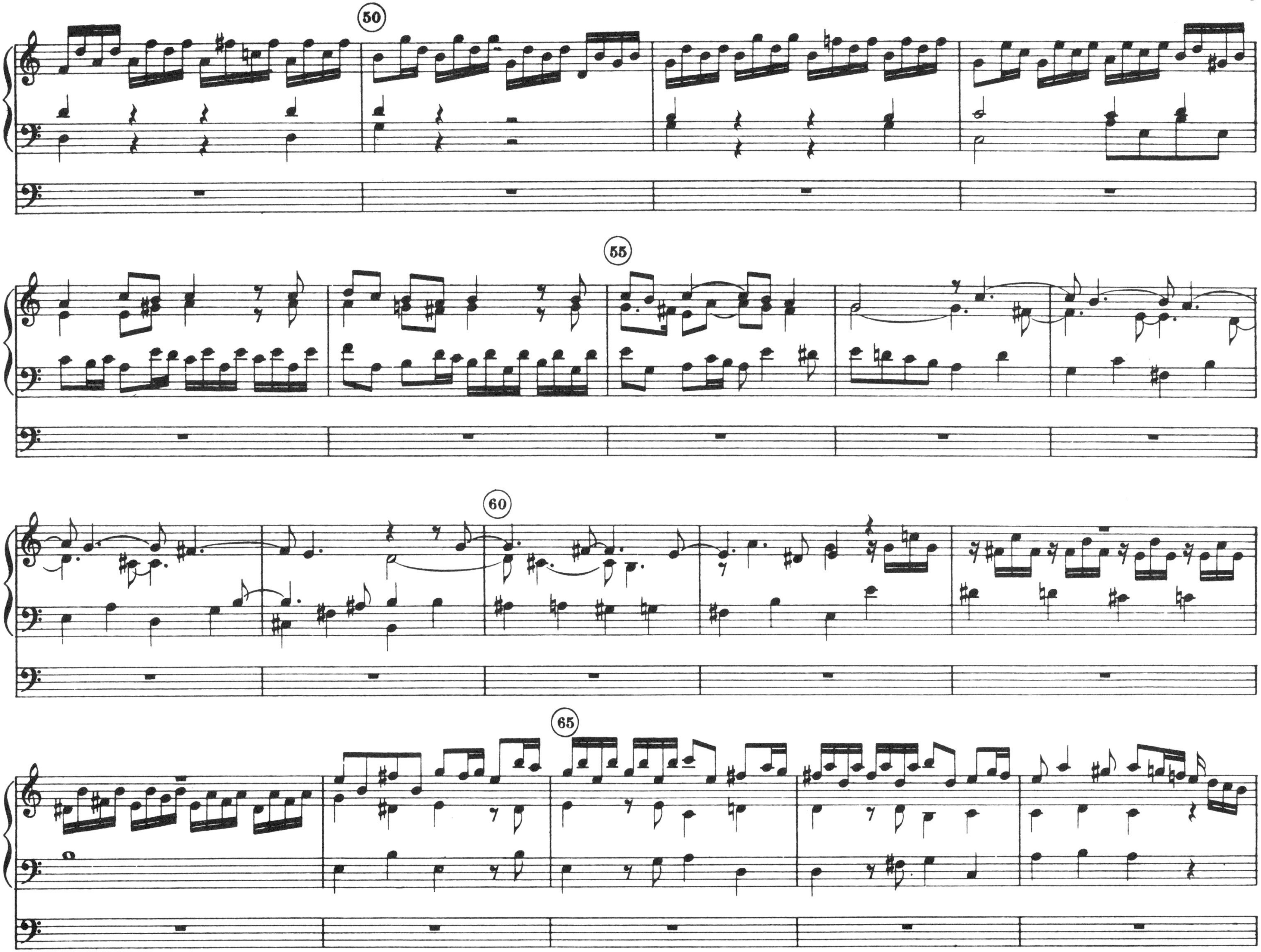
50
55
60
65

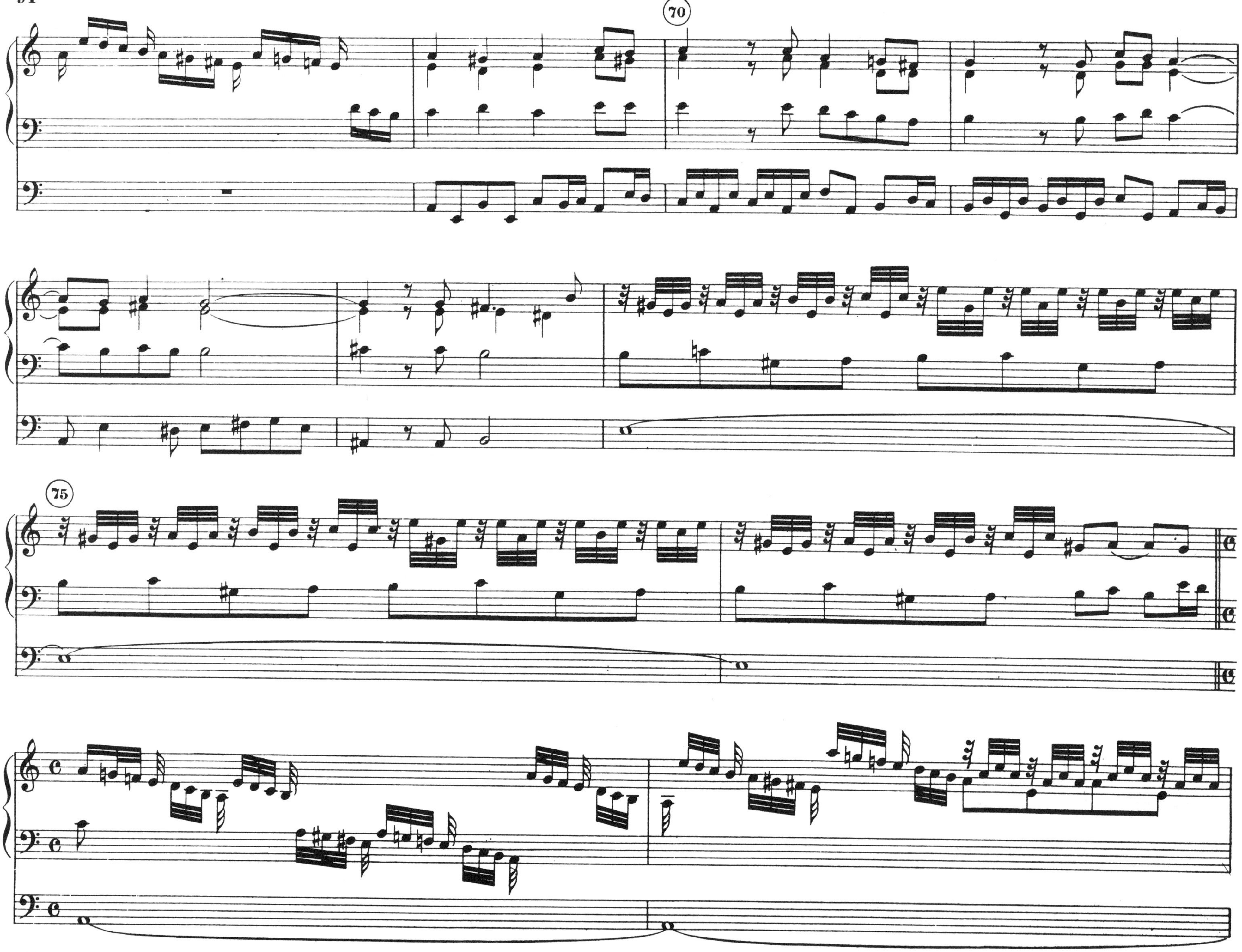
70
75

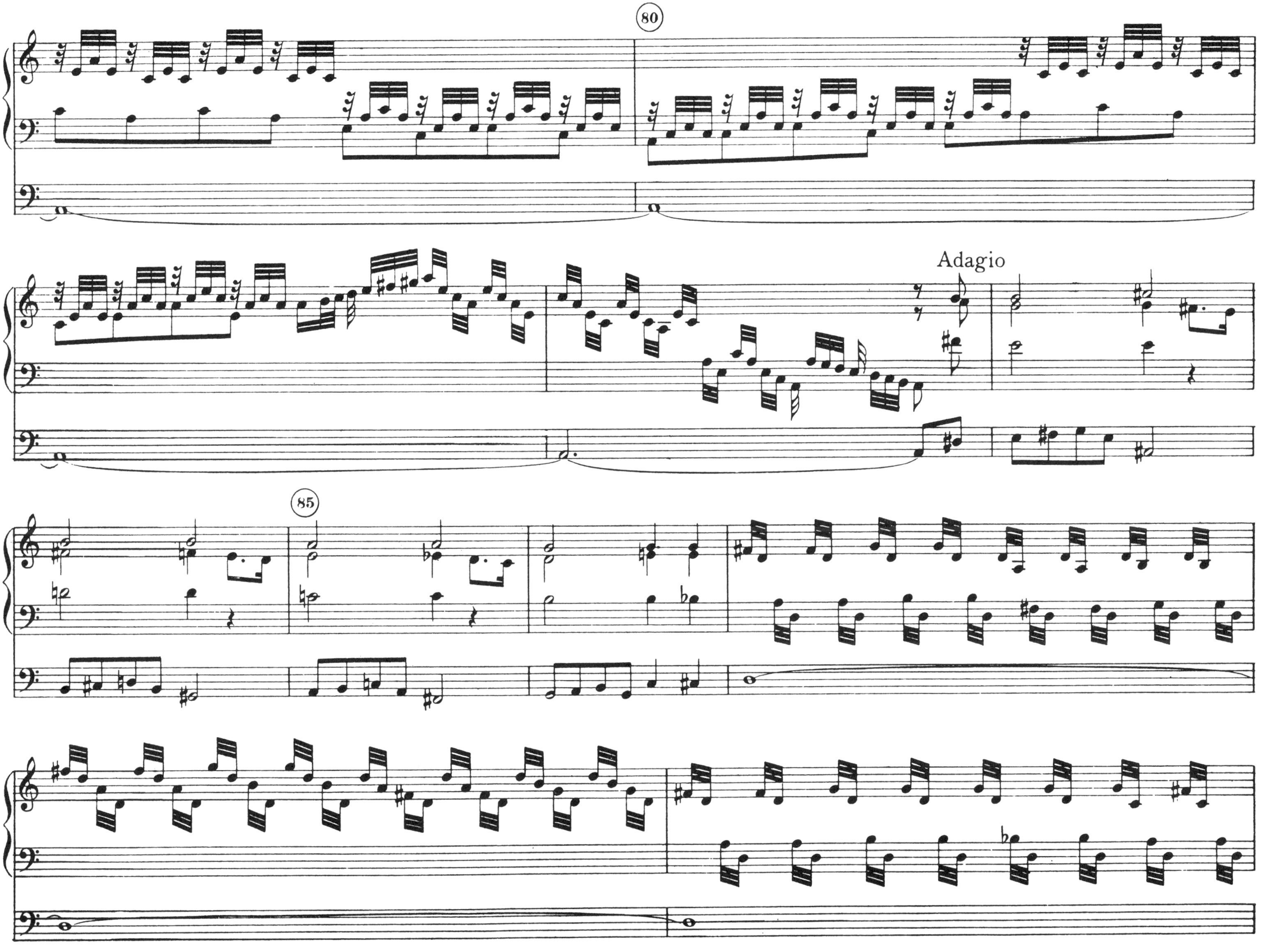
80
Adagio
85

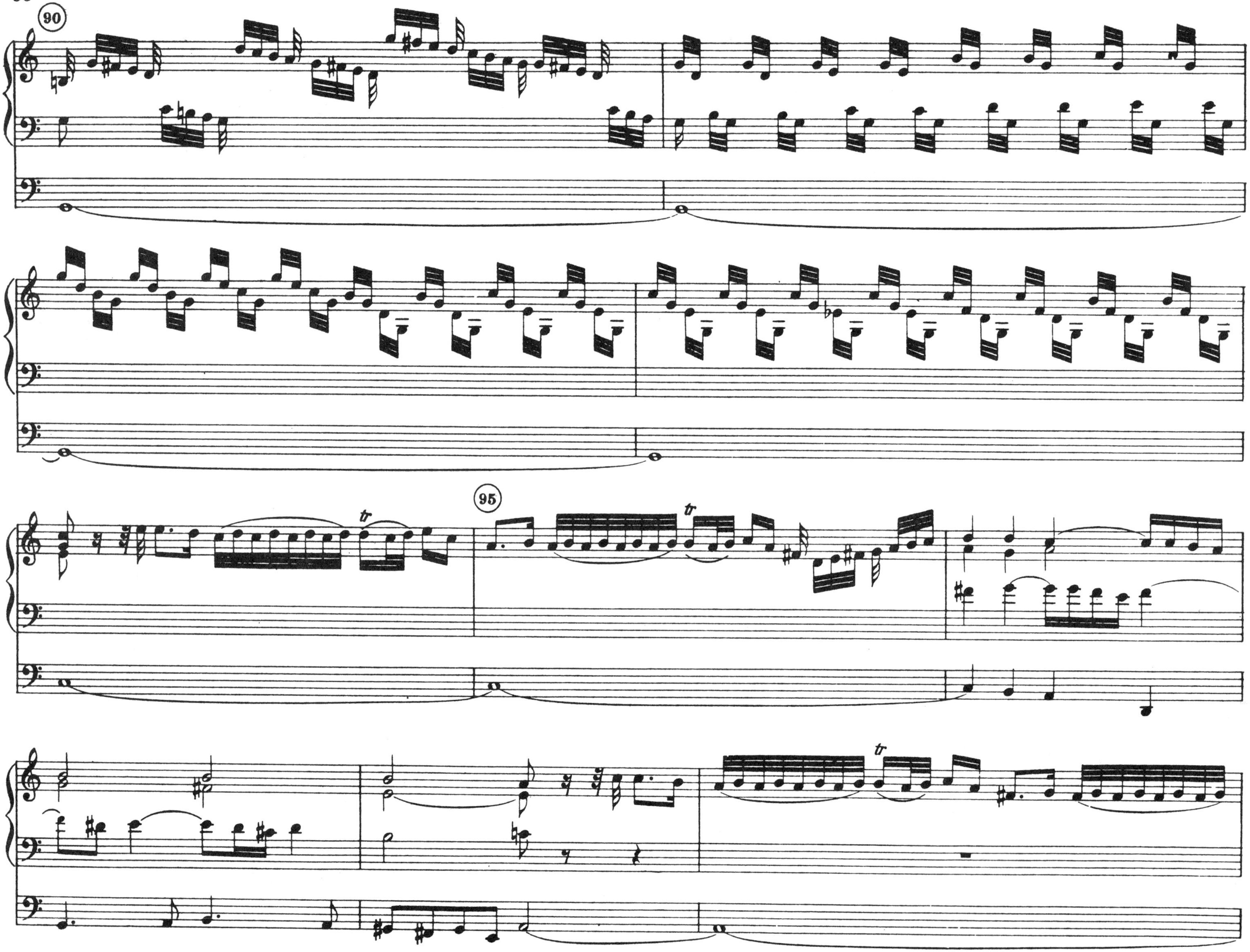
90
95
tr
tr
tr

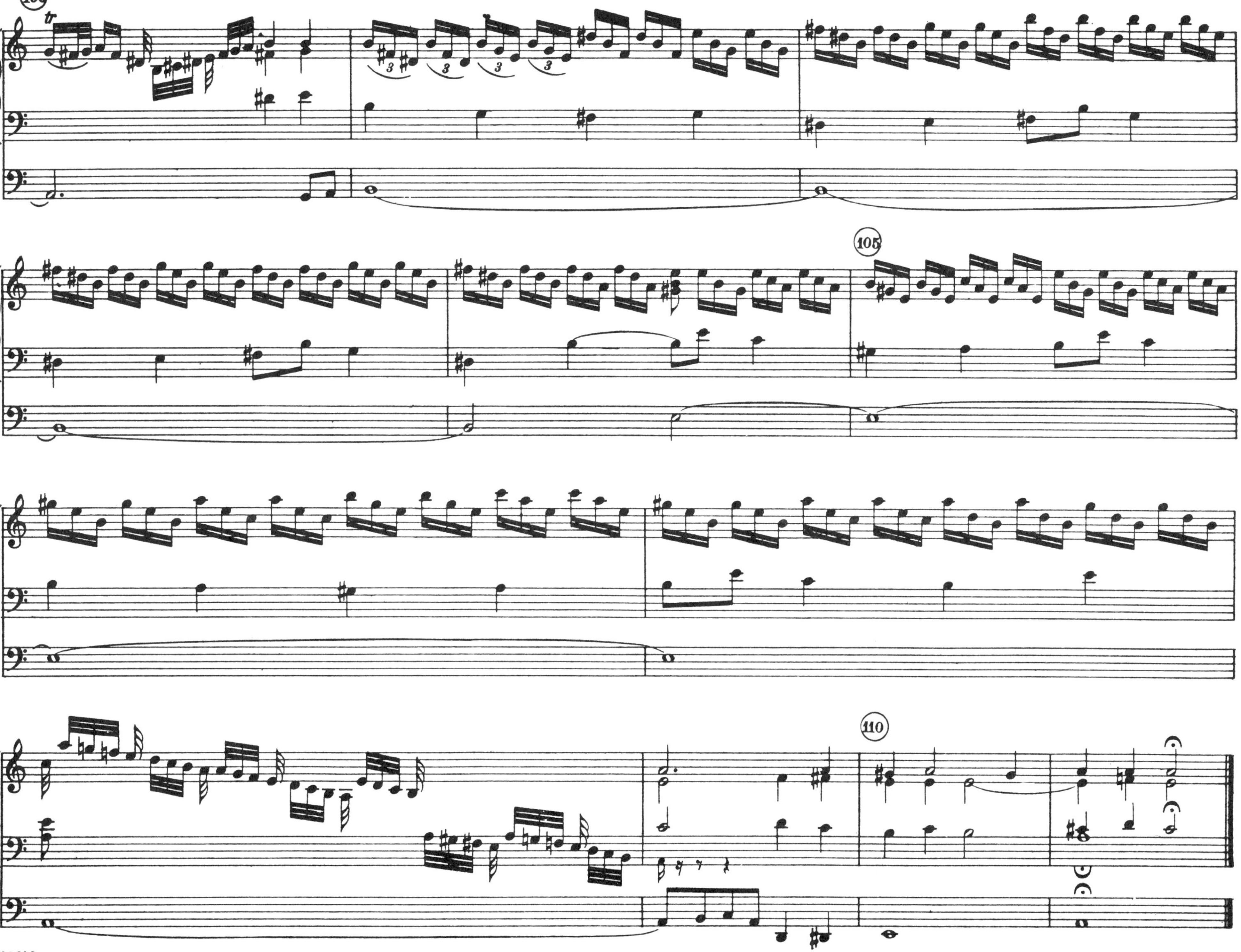
100
tr
3
105
110

XIV
Praeludium und Fuge in A-Moll

Praeludium

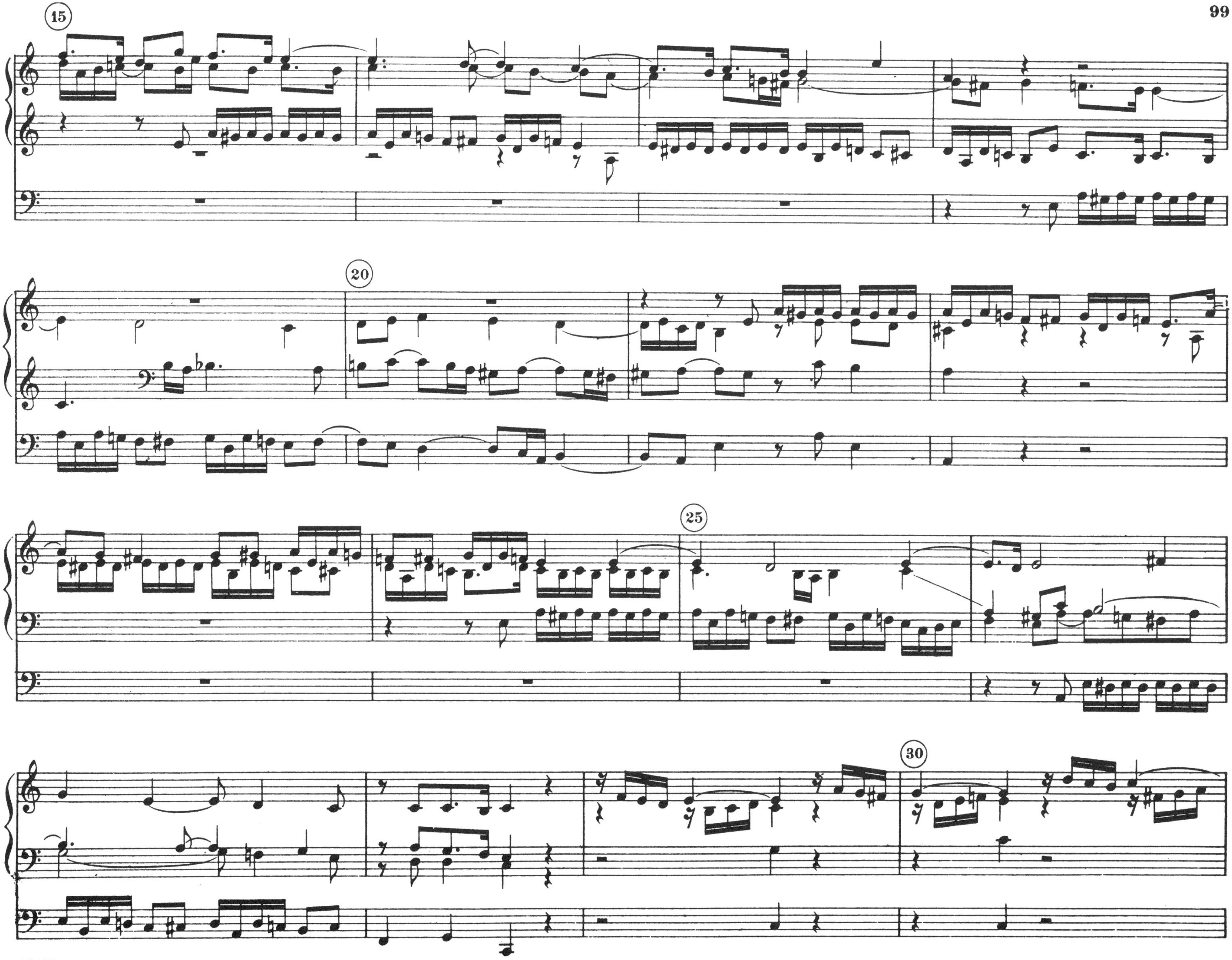
15
20
25
30

Fuge

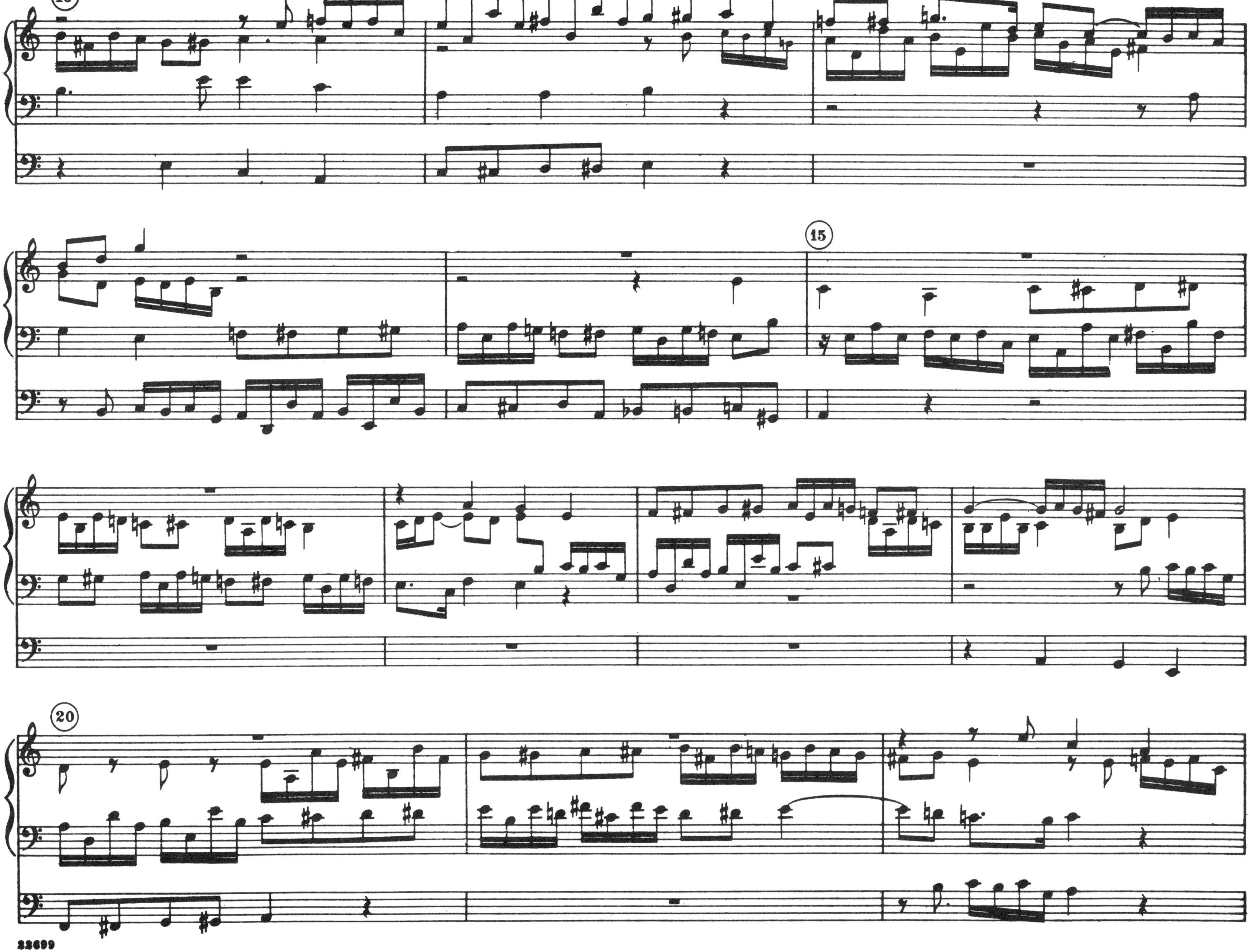
10
15
20

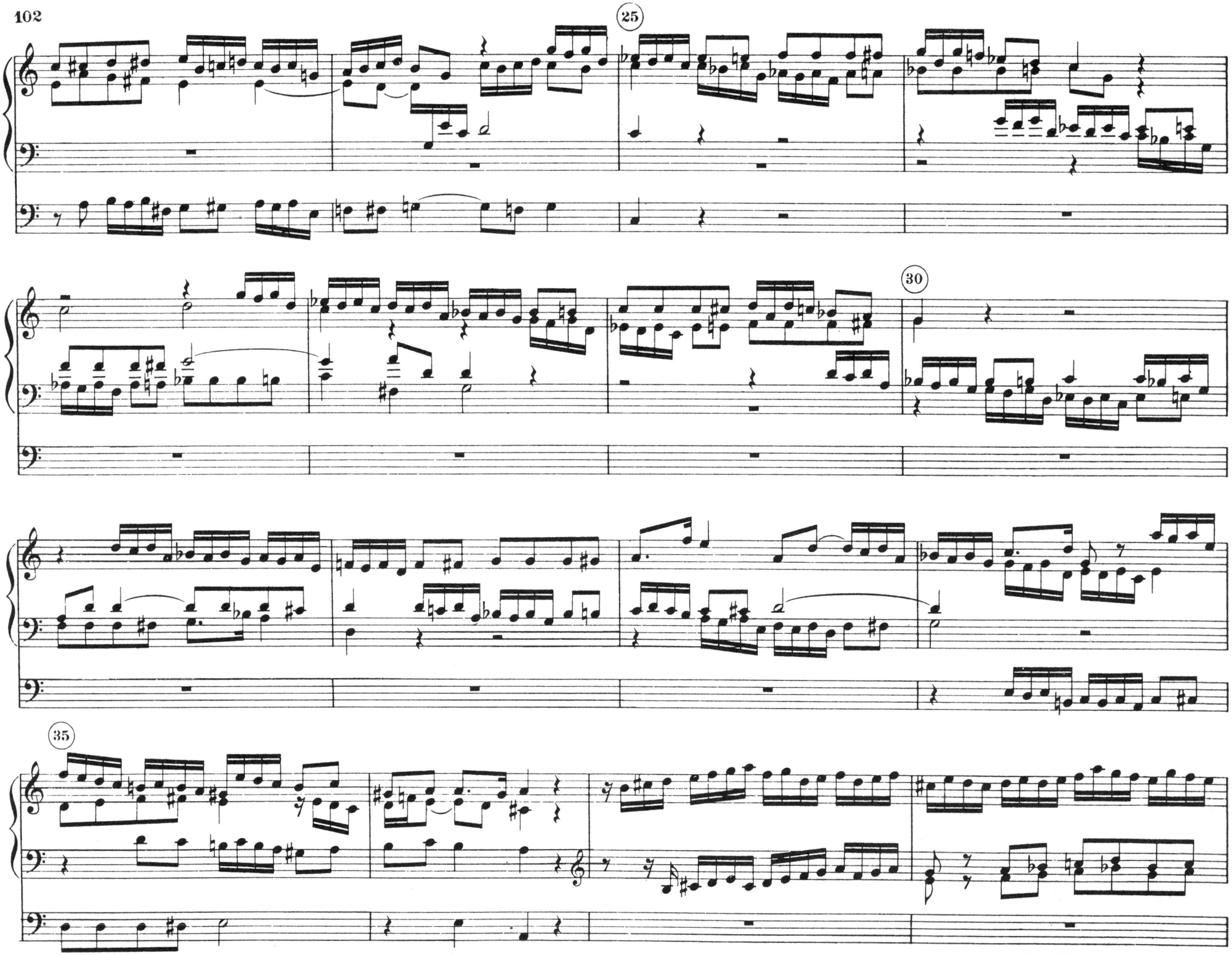
25
30
35

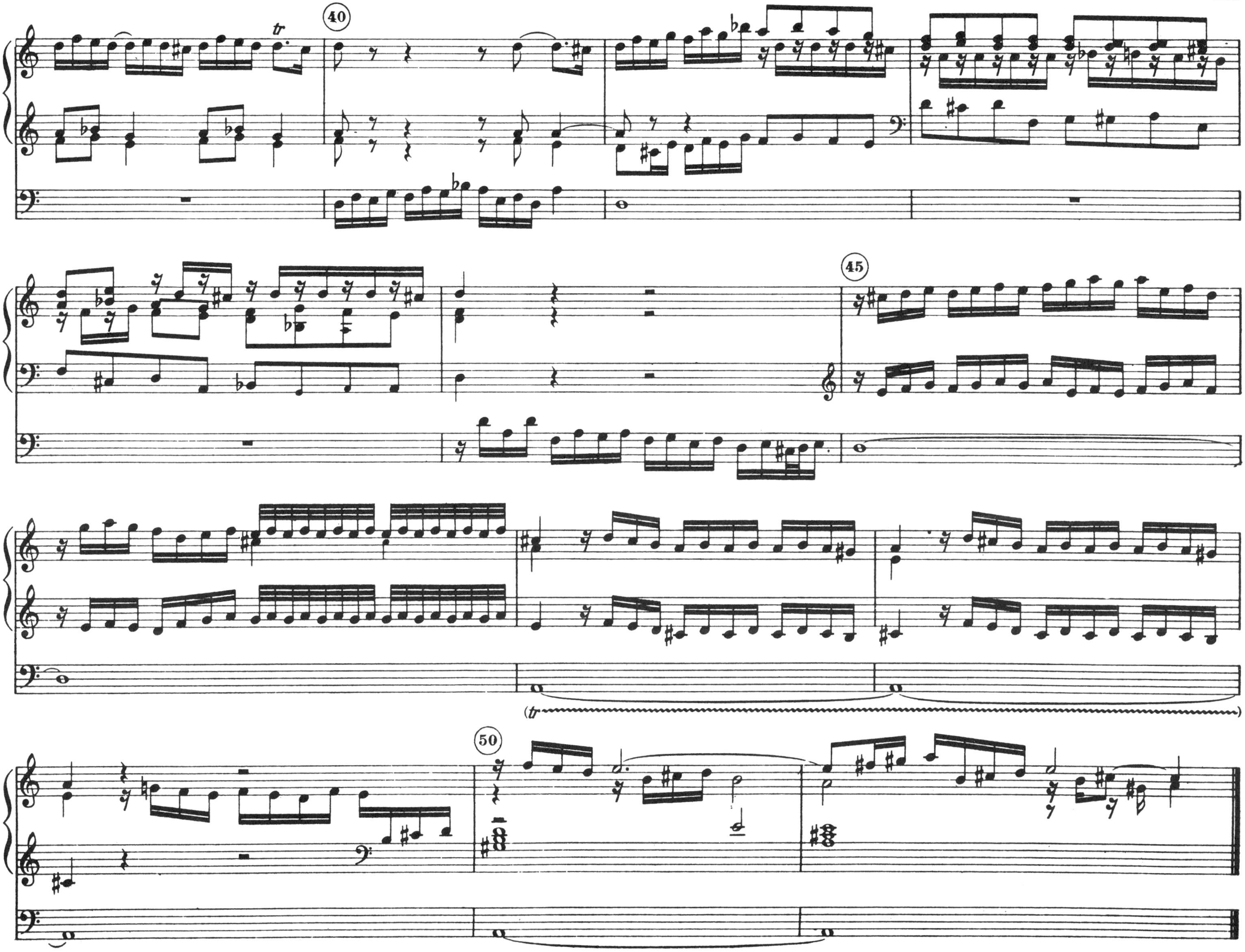
40
tr
45
(tr
50

XV
Praeludium in A-Moll

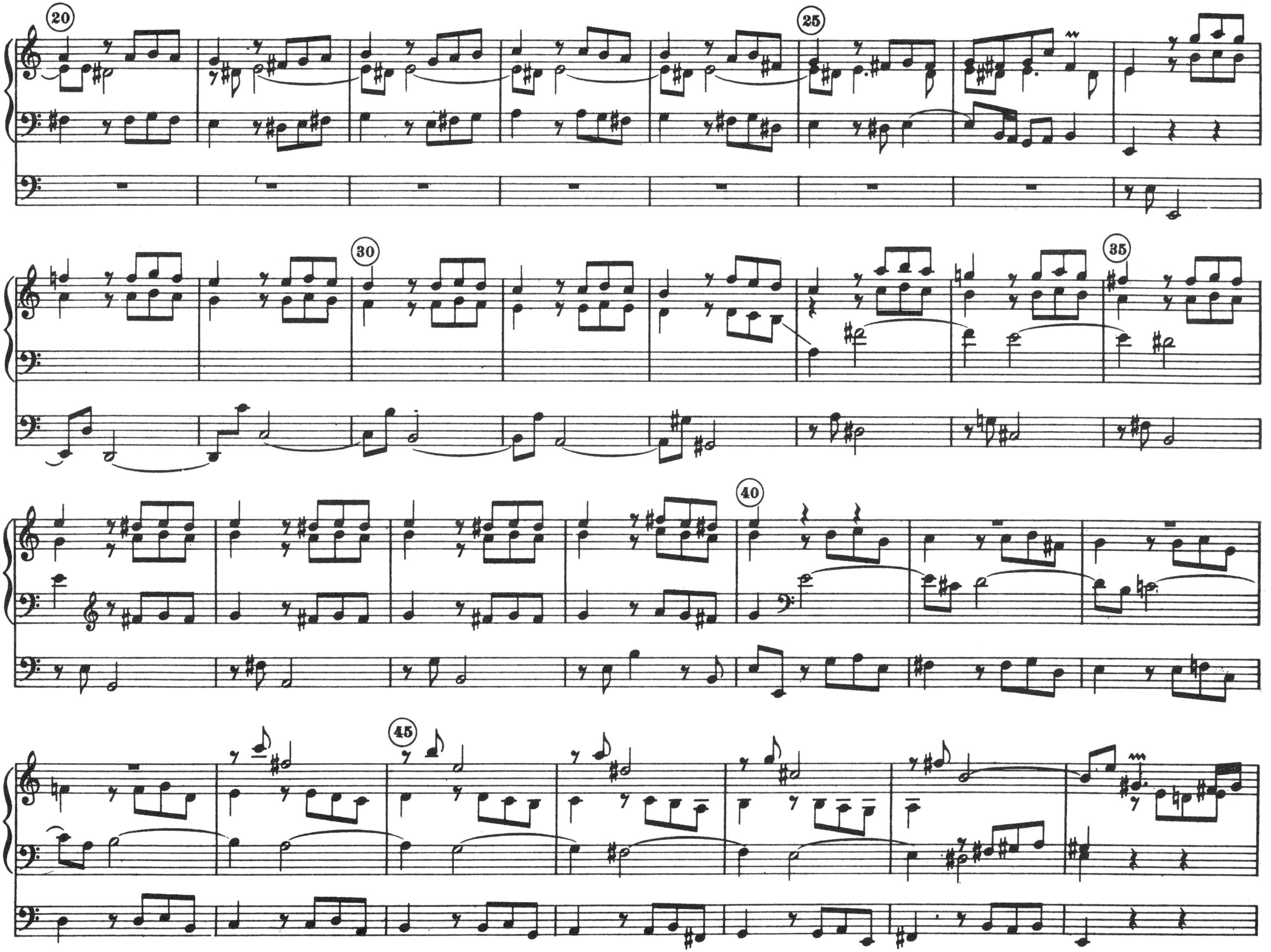
20
25
30
35
40
45

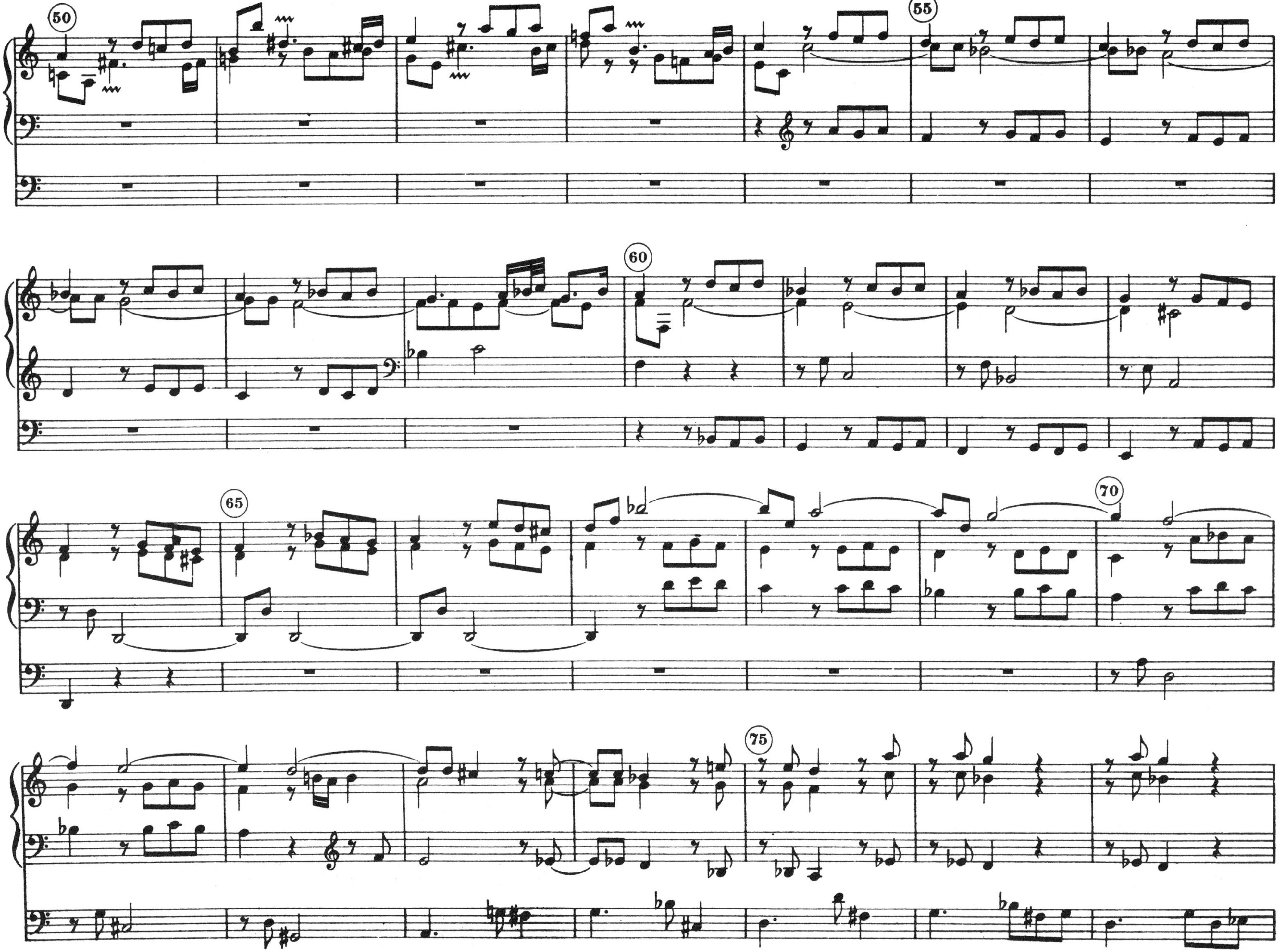
50
55
60
65
70
75

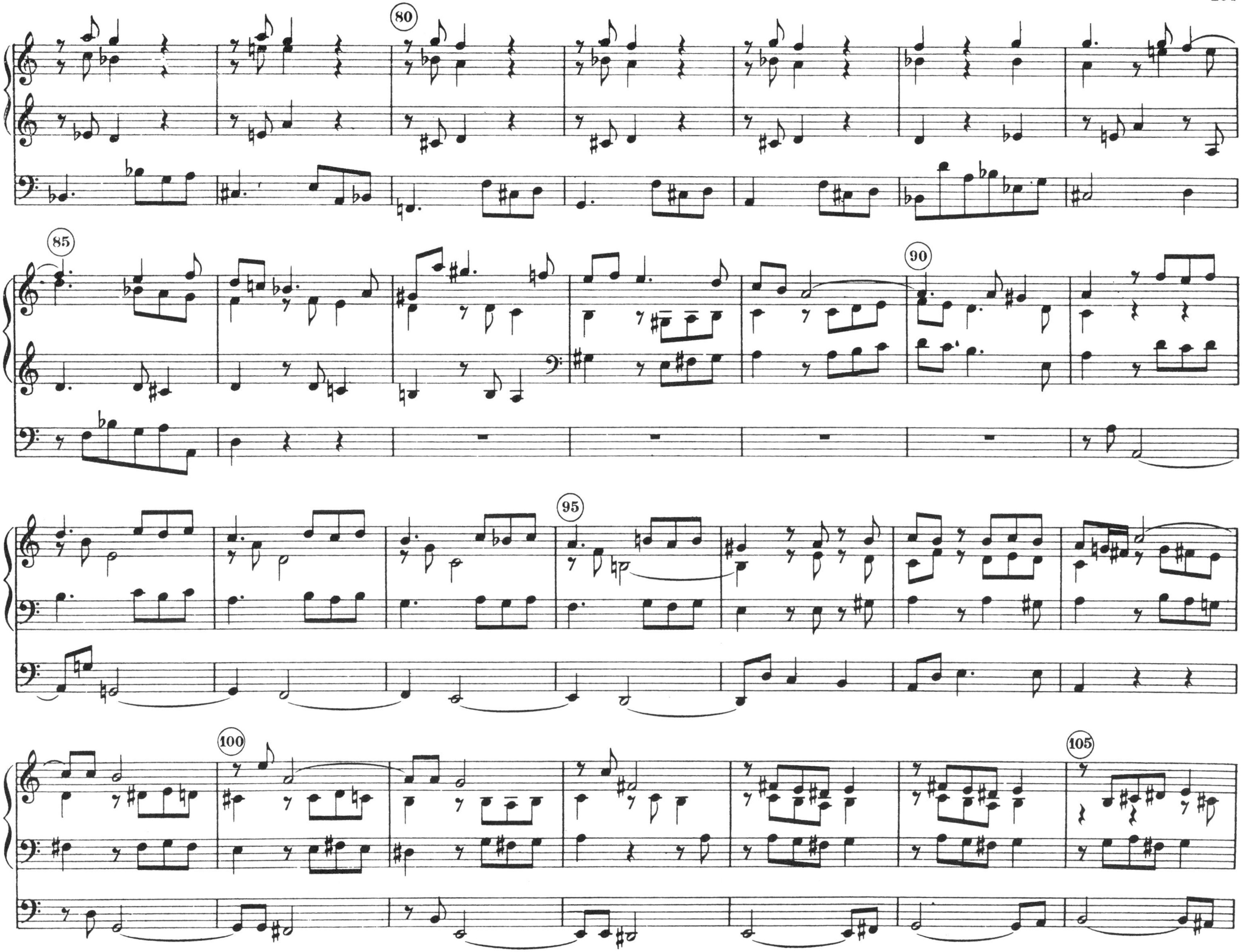
80
85
90
95
100
105

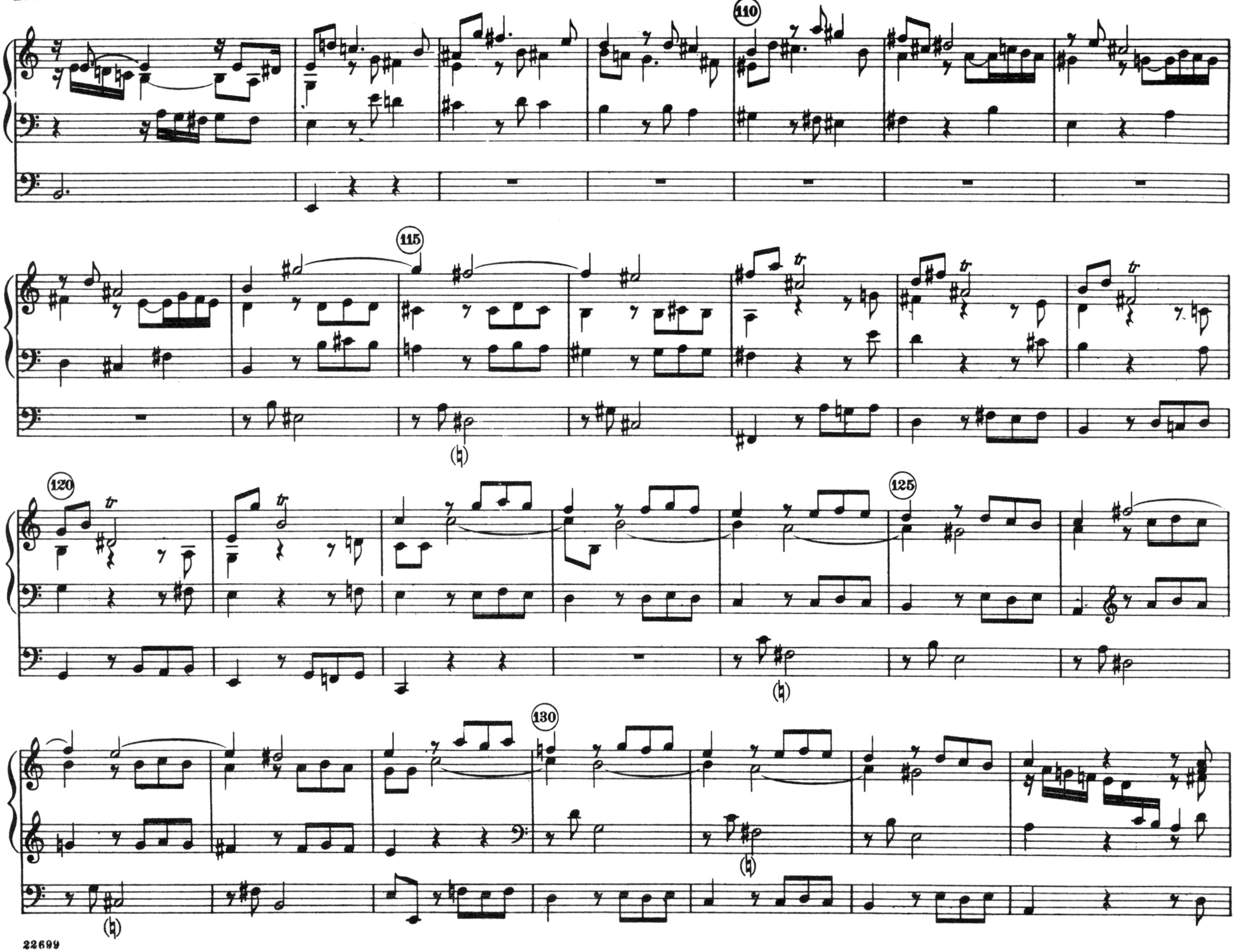
110
115
tr
120
125
130

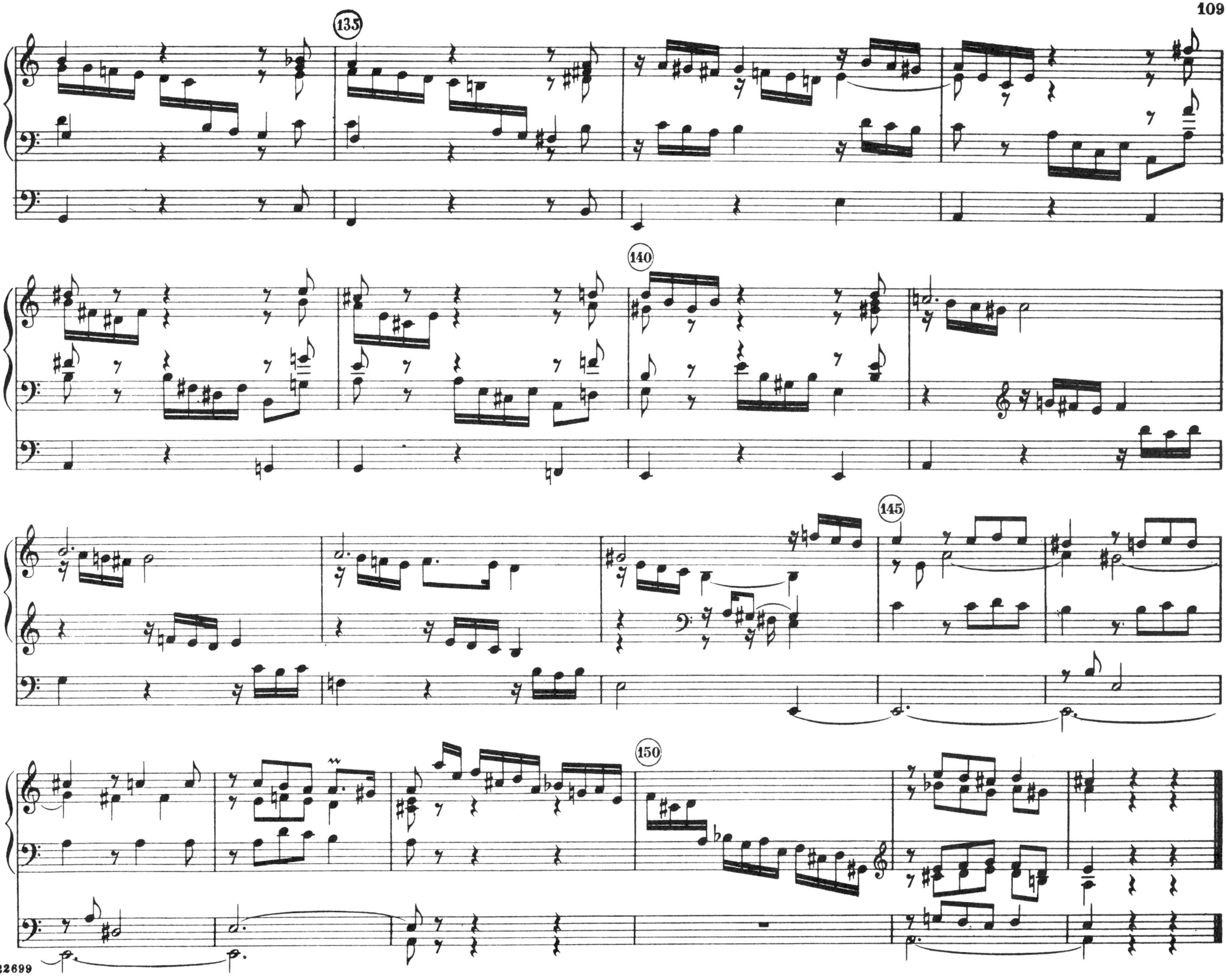
135
140
145
150

XVI
Fantasia con Imitatione in H-Moll

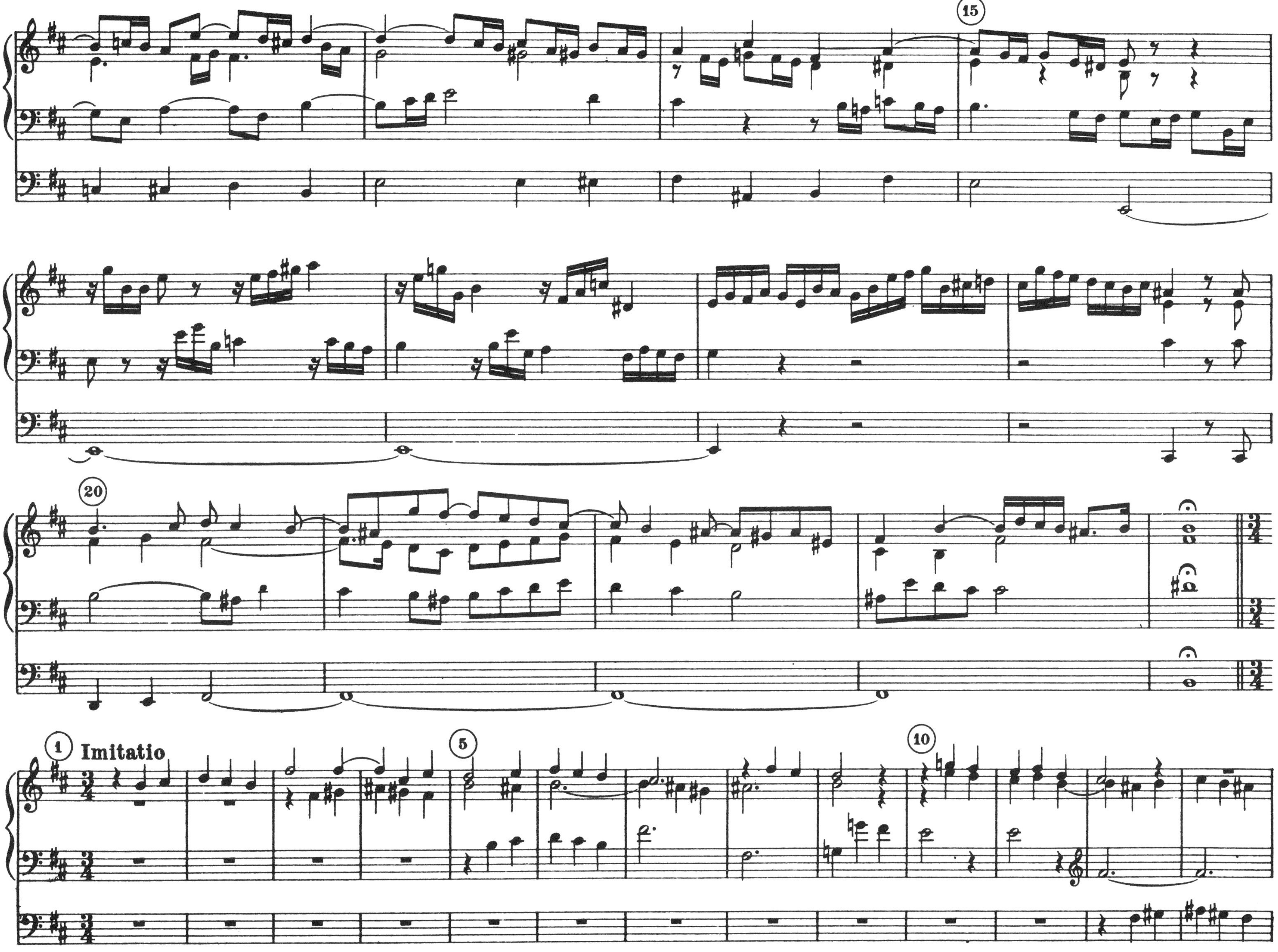
15
20
1
Imitatio
5
10

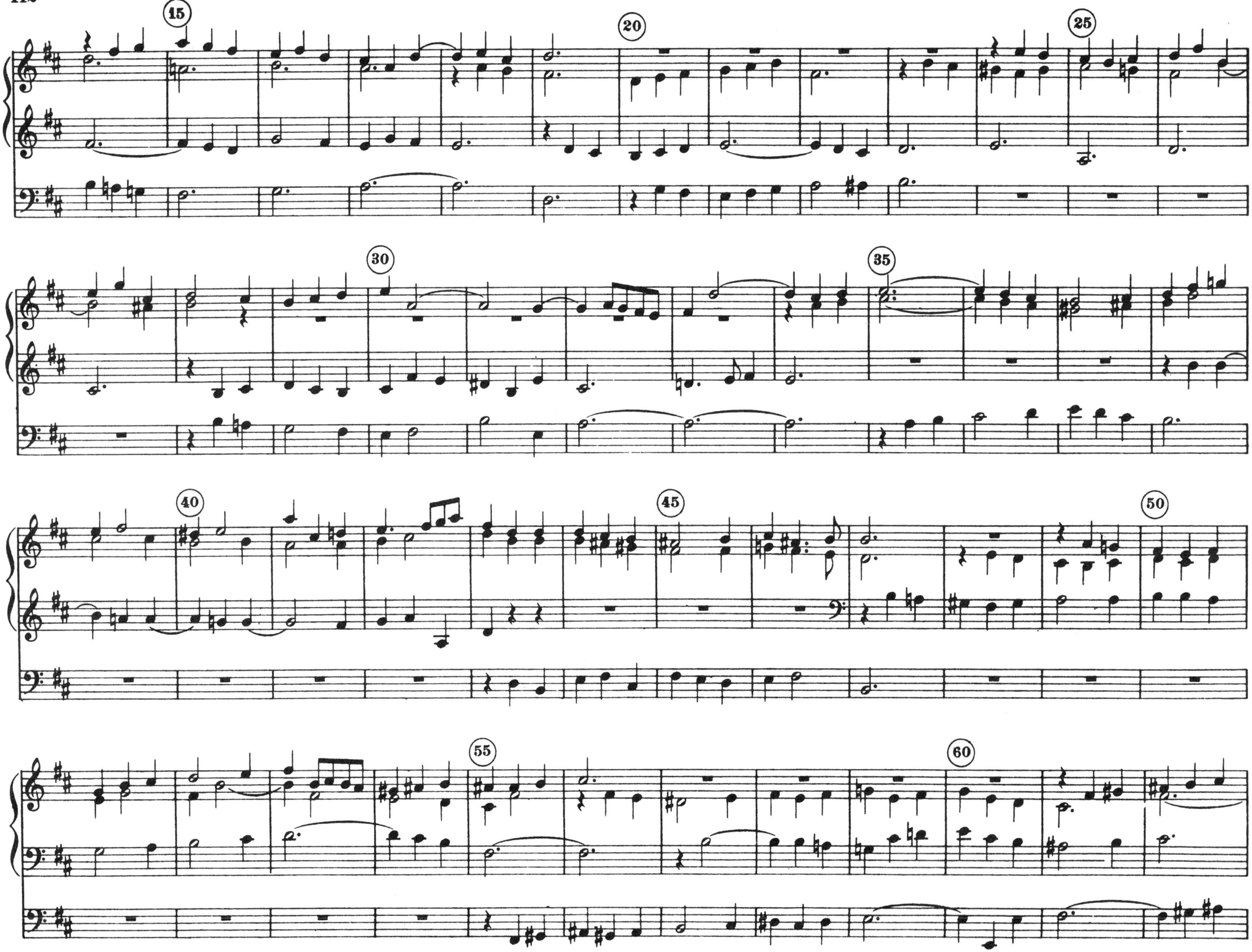
15
20
25
30
35
40
45
50
55
60

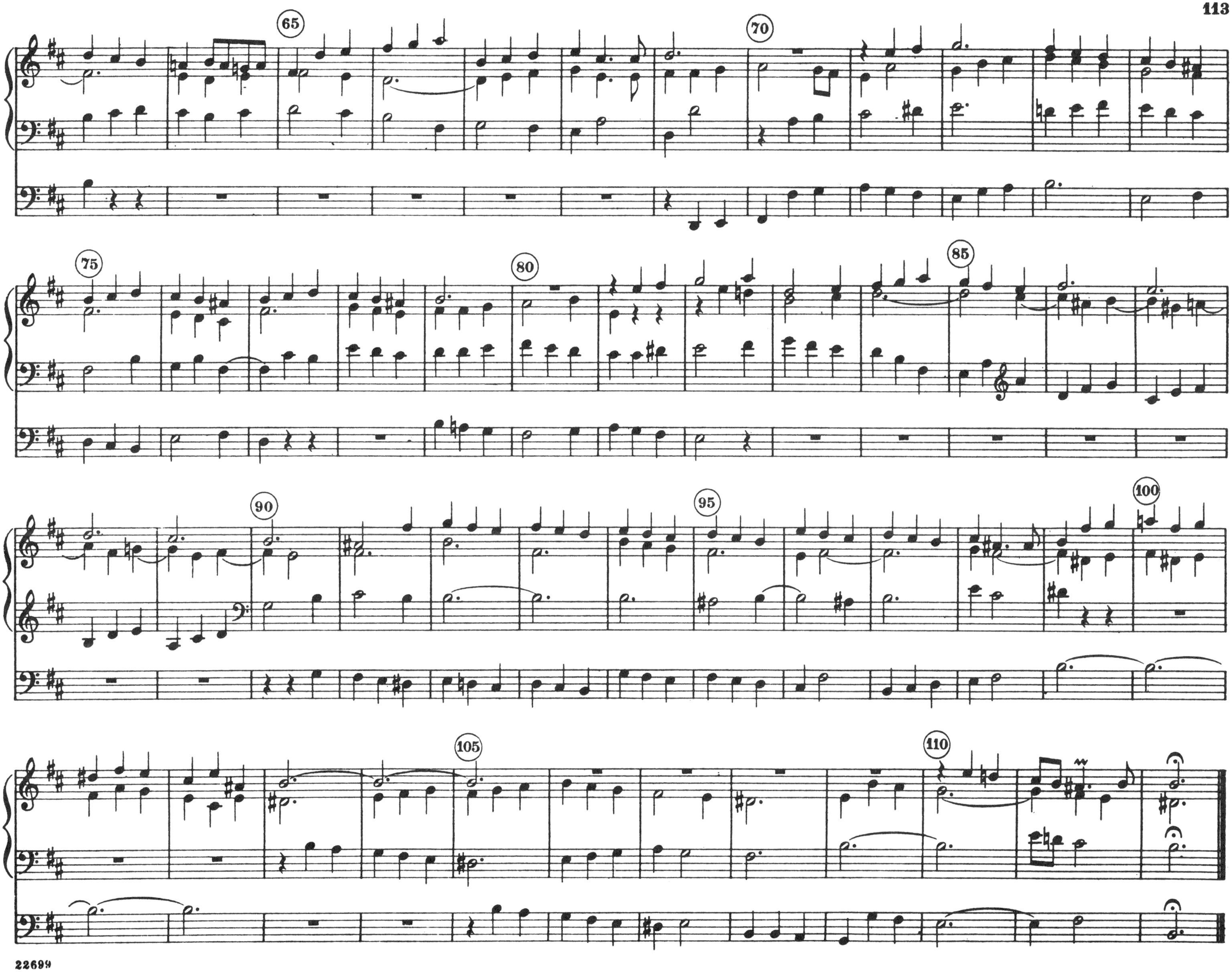
65
70
75
80
85
90
95
100
105
110

XVII
Fuge in H-Moll

Über ein Thema von Corelli (1653-1713)

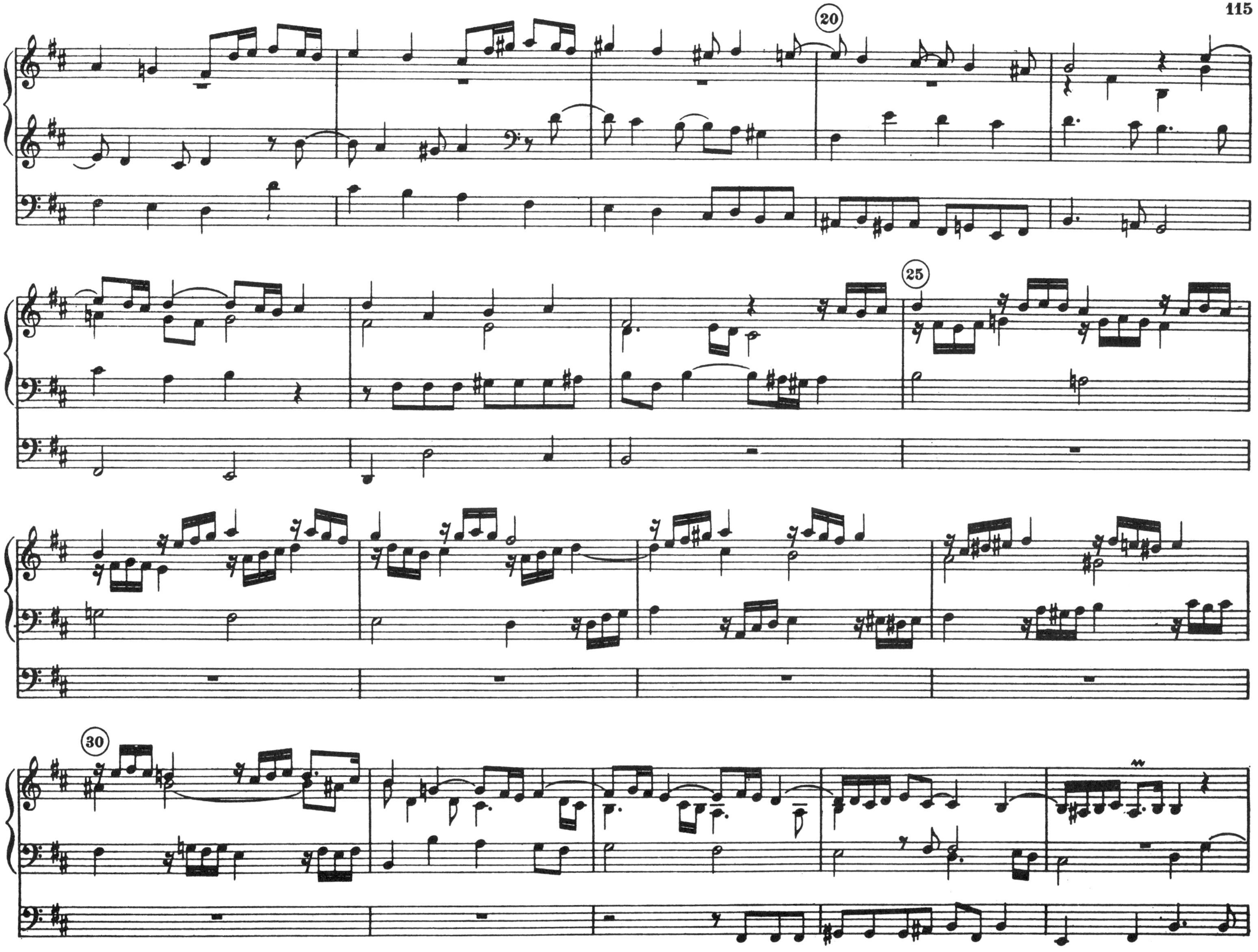
20
25
30

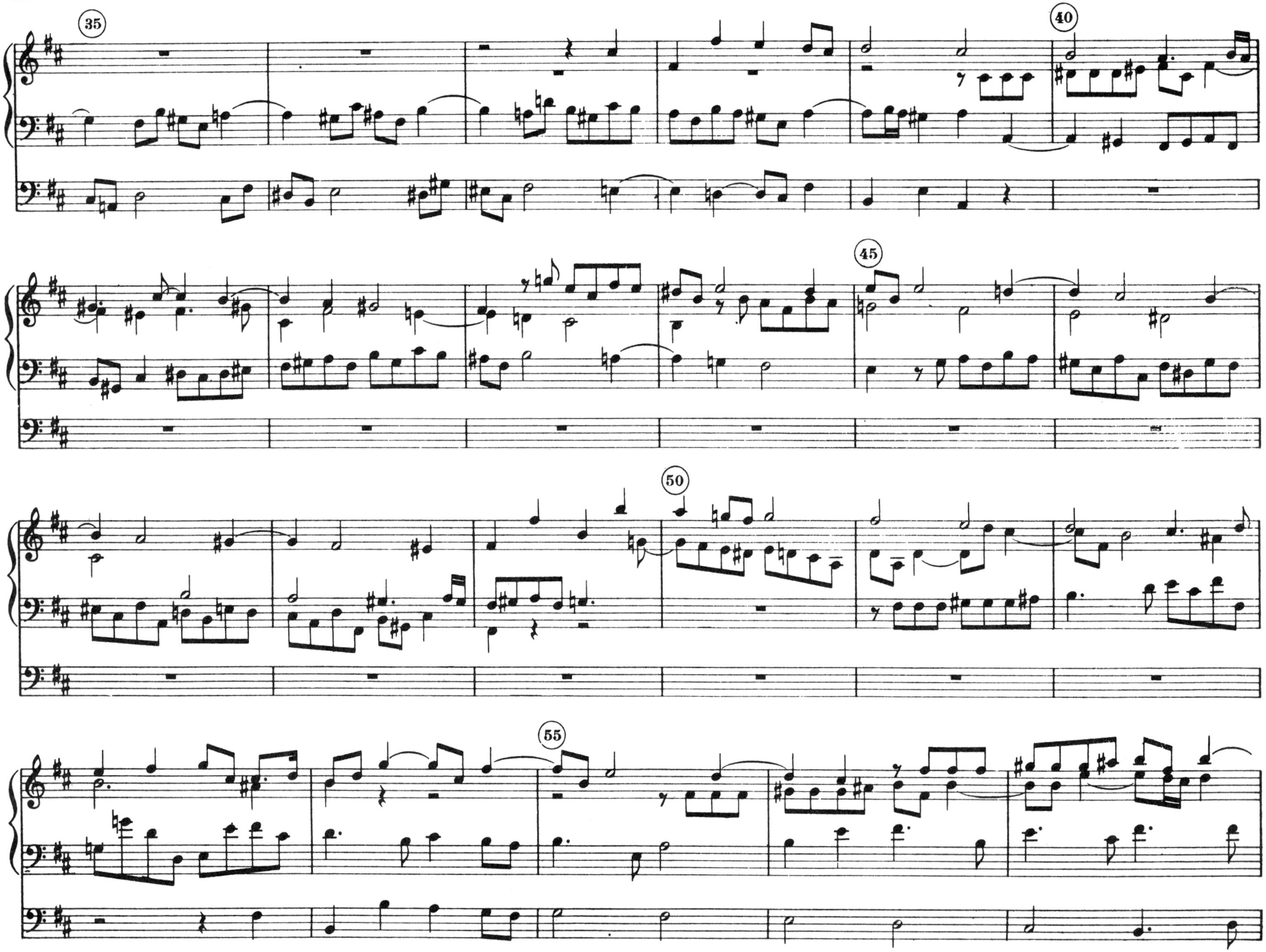
35
40
45
50
55

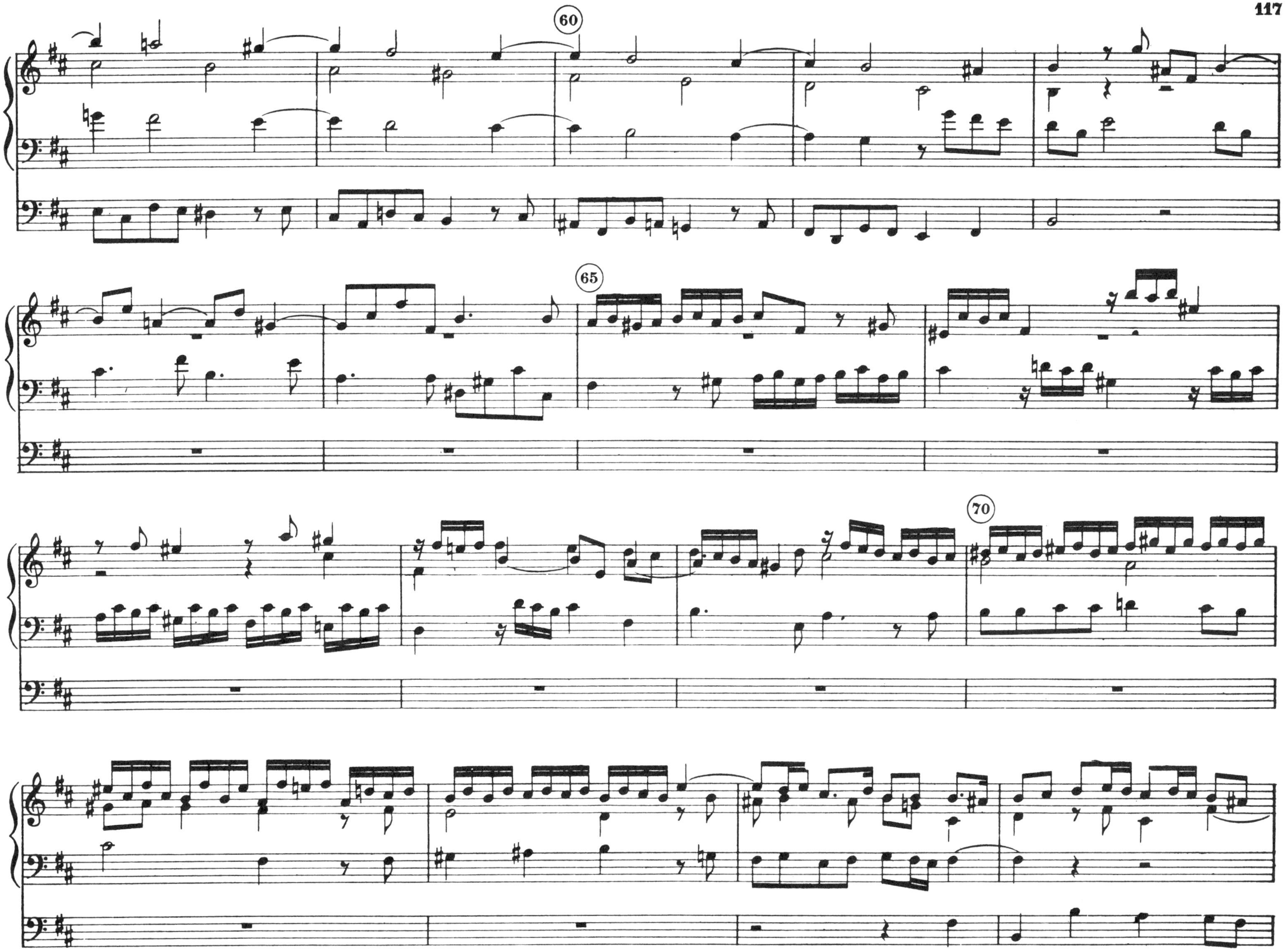
60
65
70

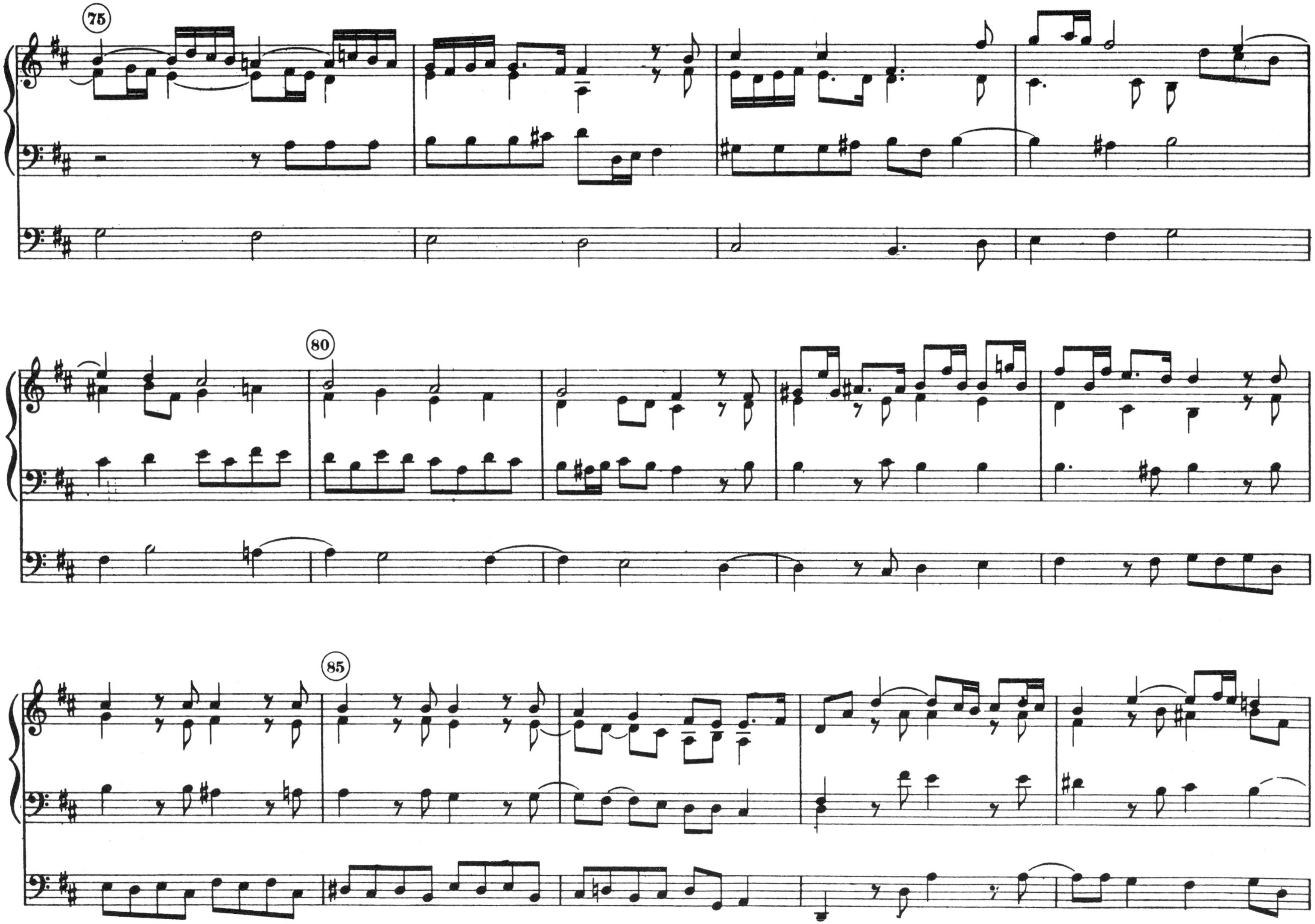
75
80
85

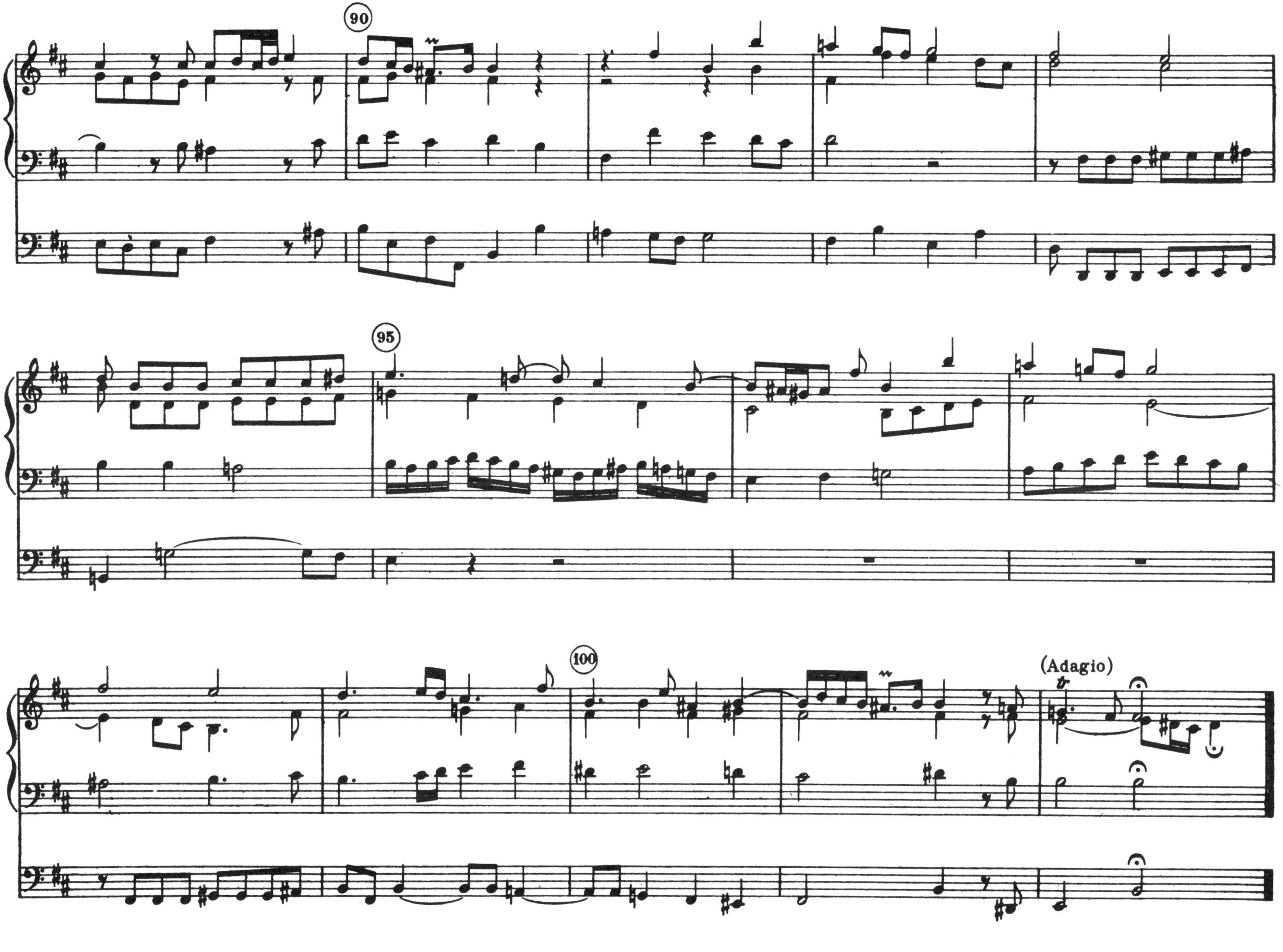
90
95
100
(Adagio)